T0360677

World Cities
Achieving Liveability and Vibrancy

World Cities

Achieving Liveability and Vibrancy

Editors

Ooi Giok Ling

Nanyang Technological University, Singapore

Belinda Yuen

National University of Singapore, Singapore

Civil Service College Singapore

iPS Institute of Policy Studies

World Scientific

Published by

World Scientific Publishing Co. Pte. Ltd.

5 Toh Tuck Link, Singapore 596224

USA office: 27 Warren Street, Suite 401-402, Hackensack, NJ 07601

UK office: 57 Shelton Street, Covent Garden, London WC2H 9HE

British Library Cataloguing-in-Publication Data
A catalogue record for this book is available from the British Library.

Individual contributors copyright © Belinda Yuen, Giok Ling Ooi, Thai Ker Liu, Peter Hall, WASTE — Advisers on Urban Environment and Development, Gouda, the Netherlands, Anne Scheinberg, Vukan R. Vuchic, Loke Ming Chou, Andrew Tan, Sock-Yong Phang, Chye Kiang Heng, Ji Zhang, Victor Savage, Ursula Schaefer-Preuss, Emiel A. Wegelin, Michael Lindfield, Euston Quah, Qiyan Ong.

WORLD CITIES
Achieving Liveability and Vibrancy

Copyright © 2010 by World Scientific Publishing Co. Pte. Ltd.

All rights reserved. This book, or parts thereof, may not be reproduced in any form or by any means, electronic or mechanical, including photocopying, recording or any information storage and retrieval system now known or to be invented, without written permission from the Publisher.

For photocopying of material in this volume, please pay a copying fee through the Copyright Clearance Center, Inc., 222 Rosewood Drive, Danvers, MA 01923, USA. In this case permission to photocopy is not required from the publisher.

ISBN-13 978-981-4280-71-6
ISBN-10 981-4280-71-2

Typeset by Stallion Press
Email: enquiries@stallionpress.com

Printed in Singapore by Mainland Press Pte Ltd.

Foreword by the Minister for National Development

Cities today confront many similar challenges arising from pressures such as urbanisation, climate change, and energy constraints. No one city has the solution to all the problems it faces. Thus, by sharing ideas and expertise, cities of the world can learn from each other as they grow and develop.

The inaugural World Cities Summit, which Singapore hosted in June 2008, aimed to provide just such a platform for sharing and learning. It attracted more than 700 distinguished participants, including mayors and governors, senior officials from governments and international organisations, academics and business leaders. With *"Liveable and Vibrant Cities"* as its theme, the conference covered extensively many of the pressing issues relating to effective public governance and the sustainable development of cities.

I am happy that the Civil Service College and Institute of Policy Studies have collaborated to capture the essence of the rich and diverse conference discourse in this book, thus extending the influence of the ideas and best practices far beyond the Summit.

MAH Bow Tan
Minister for National Development
Singapore

Contents

Chapter
1

Introduction: World Cities — Challenges of Liveability, Sustainability and Vibrancy

BELINDA YUEN and GIOK LING OOI

World cities compete in the global arena on the basis of connectivity and their contributions to the international networks and flows of goods, services and finance which constitute the world economy. More focus has been on the economic vitality of these cities rather than the impacts of rapid population growth and territorial expansion generally through sprawl and unplanned development. Increasingly, however, world cities are emphasising the importance of competing on the basis of liveability and quality of life that are on offer. This book documents the presentations and discussions that took place during the inaugural World Cities Summit held in Singapore, 23–25 June 2008. The theme of this inaugural Summit was "liveable and vibrant cities."

The World Cities Summit series was established by the Singapore Ministries of Defence, National Development, Environment and Water Resources to examine one of the growing urban issues: governance and sustainable development of cities around the world. Urban growth projections by the United Nations indicate that the world's urban population will grow from 2.86 billion in the year 2000 to 4.98 billion by 2030; two-thirds of the world's population will be living in towns and cities in the next 50 years. Asia is urbanising rapidly; 66 of the world's 100 fastest growing cities with population of more than one million are located in Asia. Its urban settlements are growing on a scale never seen before. By 2015, 12 of the world's 26 mega-cities will be in Asia. Before 2025, one of every two Asians will live in cities. Some of the important implications of this growth are its consequential impact on the availability of jobs, housing and infrastructure, and urban management.

Asia's urban challenge is enormous. Asia is home to 70 per cent of the world's absolute poor (those living on less than US$1 a day). The population in Asia's slums is growing at an estimated average rate of 110 million people per year. Developing countries in East Asia are estimated to need to spend more than US$1 trillion over the next five years on roads, water, communications, power and other infrastructure to cope with rapidly expanding cities and increasing population. The challenge for national and local governments is not only to attract business investments and global talent to maintain city competitiveness but also to address key issues of poverty reduction, infrastructure development, affordable housing, governance, environmental and ecological sustainability, social inclusiveness, and financial solvency, among others. City governments more often than not have to face fundamental development dilemmas in maintaining economic growth and ensuring sustainable communities. Meeting these challenges will require innovation in policies and institutions.

LIVEABLE AND VIBRANT CITIES

Under globalisation, cities have become more, not less, important. Cities around the world are re-examining their urban assets and remaking themselves to enhance competitiveness. Liveability and vibrancy of the built environment are discussed increasingly on a global scale. Greater attention is given to quality of life. There is a growing body of research that suggests quality of life is becoming an increasingly important factor in modern business location decisions, especially among high technology and knowledge firms (Glaser and Bardo, 1991; McNulty *et al.*, 1985). McNulty *et al.* (1985) in assessing the links between quality of life and the economic success of cities concluded that cities that are not liveable places are not likely to perform important economic functions in the future. If we agree with McNulty *et al.* (1985), enhancing liveability would then be a central objective in every city's economic transition strategy. It is no surprise that the elements of liveability are increasingly employed as economic development tools. Visions of a liveable city are growing in their relative importance. Liveability-oriented urban planning has emerged in recent decades around the world, including South Korea and Singapore.

According to *The Economist Global Liveability Index 2007*, the world's top 10 liveable cities are in Canada (Vancouver, Toronto), Australia (Melbourne, Perth, Adelaide, Sydney), and Western Europe (Vienna, Copenhagen, Geneva, Zurich). The world's 10 worst liveable cities are in Africa, Asia and Latin America — Algiers, Dhaka, Lagos, Karachi, Kathmandu, Abidjan, Dakar, Phnom Penh, Tehran, Bogota. Asia, Africa and Latin America with their fast growing population, large urban centres and hosts of urban challenges are comparatively weak in liveability. The cities that have high liveability rating are those that have reinvented themselves, and managed growth and change to provide their citizens with a vibrant and liveable environment.

What makes a liveable city? Liveability is generally defined by performance in three main areas: environmental quality, neighbourhood amenity and individual well-being (Lennard and Lennard, 1995). The key elements of a liveable city often include attractive public spaces, walkable, mixed use, higher density neighbourhoods that support a range of green infrastructure and transport, affordable housing, vibrant, exciting, sociable, human-scaled pedestrian experiences. It prioritises walking, bicycling and the use of public transport. These attributes help make places pleasant and easy to live. Liveability initiatives often meet environmental, economic and equity goals, which are also the elements for the transition to sustainability. At its most basic, the core principle of sustainable urban planning is that we should plan for a better future. In short, liveability and sustainability agendas overlap substantially. Sustainability initiatives can improve liveability.

Even though liveability is primarily a subjective experience, there is a growing consensus on the attributes of a liveable city for designing for liveability. As early as the 1960s, Jacobs (1961) has called for the sociability and liveability of dense, mixed-use urban areas. These qualities included a clear demarcation between public and private space, 'eyes on the street' of the local community, streets and sidewalks in constant use and streets with attractions on them that encourage people to linger. Lynch's (1981) good city form theory with its emphasis on qualities such as legibility, vitality, congruence, sense, access, efficiency has further influenced urban liveability planning among urban designers in the 1980s and 1990s.

Several urbanism researchers have investigated how liveable streets are created (Appleyard, 1981; Jacobs, 1993) and how to design people-friendly housing developments and public spaces (Cooper-Marcus and Sarkissian, 1986; Cooper-Marcus and Francis, 1990). In the 1990s, the new urbanism and smart growth movements in the USA have further promoted the principles for planning more liveable places. Although from different perspectives, the various research and movements contribute to an emerging synthesis of urban design knowledge of how to make cities more liveable, and how to base that design on the experience and input of the community who will use the places. Different areas will require different solutions.

Designing for liveability is not just an abstract theory. Most recently, the US Local Government Commission Centre for Liveable Communities has defined its liveability agenda as helping local communities to "increase transportation alternatives, reduce infrastructure costs, create more affordable housing, improve air quality, preserve natural resources, and restore local economic and social vitality." The desired outcomes of liveability should be measurable. In other words, there should be measurable improvements such as becoming less car-dependent with more trips taken by bicycles, public transit and walking, a better pedestrian environment, improved air quality and increased greenery. The implication is that the plan for a more liveable city while visionary will need to be realistic. While quality of life remains high on the agenda, challenges that remain include increasing population growth and its concomitant development pressures on affordable housing, infrastructure, etc.

It requires effective leadership to start and sustain a liveable city. Leadership provides impetus and direction. According to Landry (2000), successful leadership "aligns will, resourcefulness and energy with vision and an understanding of the needs of a city and its people. It has coherent ideas appropriate to local circumstances and professional traits such as charisma, spirituality . . . Leaders must develop a story of what their creative [liveable] city could be and how to get there." A combination of approaches — regulatory and incentive-based — will be necessary. Perhaps most importantly, enhancing urban liveability will also require liveability-oriented planning processes that are inclusive and participatory, which can help achieve sustained, longer term results.

What makes a vibrant city? Like liveability, the notion of vibrancy is subjective. It is dependent on the individual's past experiences, reference points and value judgements. In most cases, vibrancy of the city is enhanced through two key elements: its population and attraction. As the East Asia Liveable Cities Conference 2008 pointed out, people are the city's best potential asset. The city's population — social and cultural environment — and unique physical and favourable economic environment provide opportunity to improve its urban life and relative attractiveness. The image of the city and its local identity has become a key concern as cities attempt to raise their profile in the international marketplace. For many post-industrial cities, selling the city on the basis of image and place-marketing presents a promising future-oriented growth that facilitates economic and spatial survival.

Landscape features aside, the city's cultural content enhances identity and the value of locations. Much has been written about these 'landscapes of power' (Bianchini *et al.*, 1988; Zukin, 1991; Kearns and Philo, 1993). Entrepreneurialism has emerged as an important element in the place-marketing repertoire, leading to a change of philosophy in urban governance (Harvey, 1989). In exploring creative action for future-oriented urban economic development, a growing number of urbanists have postulated that creative cities will require creative governments (Landry, 2000; Florida, 2002). More and more, cities are recognising the importance of entrepreneurs and risk experimenting in creating vibrancy. Focus is on creating a city that is full of variety and vitality, providing a multitude of experiences.

As part of the bid to reinvent them, cities have highlighted visions of change and progress, liveability and positively valued images. Learning the approaches to creative urban development (Landry, 2000; Florida, 2002), and the successful transformation of such cities as Bilbao (Guggenheim Museum), Baltimore (urban waterfront) and Glasgow (cultural planning), many cities have started to enhance their cultural imagineering and vibrancy. The strategies include upgrading the urban environment, redeveloping redundant sites, and actively fostering the development of events and activities which focus on having significant attractions, activities and events that are a visitor attraction for both tourists and locals; cultural industries which focus on art gallery, museums, performing arts, media, etc; and the buzz quotient which focuses on enlivening the city, providing the city with more high energy places and spaces, and more options for living and recreation. Such a task is complex, and must take the full gamut of local cultural capital as its point of departure if cities are to remain distinctive and vibrant. The danger is frequently the manufacture of sameness. We have to work on it. This book though not the last word on the subject brings together considered reflection on the current state of play and critical issues in creating liveable and vibrant cities.

CHALLENGES OF LIVEABILITY, SUSTAINABILITY AND VIBRANCY

Reflecting the thematic sessions of the World Cities Summit 2008, this book covers 11 areas of concern among world cities. These range from good governance, well-being, inclusivity, waste management, sustainability, creative cities, financing to behavioural economics covered in 16 chapters. The volume of essays offers not just the highlights of the discussion during the Summit but also the learned perspective and analysis from leading experts, including academics, professionals and practitioners.

Following the introductory chapter, Theme 1 on Good Governance and Sustainable Cities is explored in the chapter by Giok Ling Ooi. The critical role of good governance in urban sustainability is discussed. Sustainable urban development has not occurred spontaneously. It will require effective leadership. Most successful cities have good governance and increased responsiveness to changing needs and circumstances. The success factors for developing cities that are liveable (i.e. good infrastructure, clean environment, good quality of life) and vibrant (i.e. economic competitiveness), the formulation of effective policies to address such key issues as water, energy and environmental sustainability are also discussed. It offers a timely reminder that good governance — the improvement of forms and modes of governance as well as the quality of the interrelationships between the parts — is critical to urban growth and development.

Well-being creates vibrant cities and further amplifies the discussion on quality of life. Thai Ker Liu revisits the Summit discussion on subjective well-being, including happiness and life satisfaction, and how this is influenced by the society and city in which a person lives among other factors. A behavioural economic model for societies is discussed to illuminate some of the key factors for a well-functioning and competitive city — law and order, food and shelter, work, economics, health, well-being, engaged citizens, brain gain, gross domestic product. Therefore, a good physical environment while providing the foundation for physical and economic vibrancy is but one development area. Developing economic and mental vibrancy is equally important. It challenges cities to think of citizens' well-being and happiness.

Using findings from a study on happiness and the provision of environmental vis-à-vis other public goods in Singapore, Euston Quah and Qiyan Ong extend the argument by including consideration on the value of public amenities and environmental goods. Most life satisfaction studies are revealing results that indicate environment and public amenities to be important dimensions in well-being. The postulation is that the city that enhances well-being creates the desirable conditions that can help cities attract successful businesses and talent.

Peter Hall discusses these conditions in his chapter on The Age of the City: The Challenges for the Creative City. Reflecting the theme of Urban Planning and Conservation: Planning for a Distinctive and Vibrant City, the discussion dwells on the urban challenges cities in history and around the world face when competing to attract and retain global investments and talents. What steps can be taken to develop the creative city, and put in place the elements that will form the foundation of the creative city in the context of new economy challenges and opportunities? Hall persuasively argues that cities function as 'incubators' of creativity and innovation. Globally, there has been extensive effort to make the city more distinctive, exciting and liveable to enhance their competitive edge and safeguard their growth and relevance in the world economy. An increasingly frequent formula is the expansion of the creative and cultural sector. Hall cautions against the creation of a city of cultural consumption. He argues that cities must promote urban innovations that will improve the quality of life in their cities, and make them models of sustainable urban living.

While solid waste collection, disposal and recycling may not be the most visible of activities in cities, they are crucial in sustaining a quality living environment. This is the thrust of concern about solid waste management: sustainable waste management choices, which is the basis of the chapter by Anne Scheinberg. Cities need to plan for the longer term to manage waste and conserve resources in order to be environmentally sustainable, socially progressive and economically competitive. The notions of integrated solid waste management and modernisation of waste management are introduced to frame the discussion. The discussion of urban specifics is carried through in the following chapter on Land Transportation.

Vukan Vuchic puts forward the case that to be liveable, cities must ensure safe, convenient and attractive areas for pedestrian movement and public transport development. Pedestrian improvement and the experience of walking are at the heart of what makes a good city. Enhancement of the local transport system is a vital part of city growth strategy. In the current context of high oil prices, it seems reasonable to focus urban effort on sustainable urban transport that will decrease automobile use. Good governance and institutional framework are fundamental to sustainable urban transport management. Long-term planning and effective implementation of sound policies, strategies and infrastructure projects are equally critical to enhancing the quality of land transport in cities and ensuring convenient in-city and city-suburban-region mobility.

The role of the different actors and sources of financing in urban development is explored in the collaboration between the public and private sectors for urban development. Sock Yong Phang in her chapter reviewed the emerging popularity of public-private partnership in urban development, the main forms of public-private partnership and evaluated its usefulness. Cities are increasingly tapping on private sector expertise and funding for infrastructure and development projects. Even though some public-private partnerships are complex and costly, much of urban development public-private partnership remains an important instrument in urban development policy.

The general conclusion is that sustainability requires governments to stay engaged, public-private partnership to be appropriately designed and regulated to benefit the community. Examples abound on how city transformation is achieved with collaboration and partnership between the government and private sector. The gap in financial resources and capability for environmental infrastructure is highlighted by Ursula

Schaefer-Preuss. Schaefer-Preuss offers a succinct review of the state of financing of environmental infrastructure, especially in terms of climate change adaptation, water supply and sanitation. Drawing on the Asian Development Bank programme experiences from various cities, new financial structuring mechanisms, approaches to capability development and coordinating structures are discussed.

The role of the city in urban sustainability is addressed in the chapter on Environmental Sustainability and Climate Change. Victor Savage details the evolution of human settlement through time and its impact on the environment. How cities can implement and balance environmental sustainability with economic development, in particular addressing the emerging challenges such as climate change is a major preoccupation of our time. Mitigating climate change for urban sustainability is urgent. Several approaches and action plans are discussed as possible ways forward in addressing climate change.

Sustainability in the built environment has become a popular discourse. More and more cities are including sustainability on their policy and development agenda. As Chye Kiang Heng and Ji Zhang review, sustainable architecture, green building and eco-urbanism have entered the urban development vocabulary. Sustainability performance indicators and benchmarking have proliferated. The challenge of sustainability in the built environment is rooted in its multiple dimensions, issues, scope and actors. To achieve sustainability in the built environment requires the cooperation of everyone, from government to developers, from consultants to users. It is no longer sufficient to develop new buildings. Sustainability necessitates redevelopment and rejuvenation. It also calls forth greater attention on urban greening. In the discussion on design and management of green spaces, some of the issues raised concern the management and design challenges in resolving competing urban land use demands in the provision of green spaces. Loke Ming Chou expounds the biodiversity in sustainable cities, arguing for its value and the need to restore and re-introduce nature. The challenge is to plan cities around nature instead of artificially forcing nature into cities.

Achieving inclusive and sustainable growth centres on how economic growth in cities could build vital social networks, and create scope for the individual and community to be involved and productive. Emiel Wegelin and Michael Lindfield address the role of the government and society in generating and sustaining growth. The main contention is that cities must plan strategically for inclusive development, and involve communities in the planning, design, finance and implementation of urban development. In their discussion, Wegelin and Lindfield also draw lessons from the key findings of the Commission on Growth and Development. The key agenda of the Commission is growth dynamics, the causes, consequences and internal dynamics of sustained high growth, especially sustained high inclusive growth.

Time and again, the critical role of city leadership in urban growth and sustainability has been underscored. As the Commission on Growth and Development pointed out, growth is the result of market forces and private sector investment operating in an environment created by effective government. Andrew Tan in the penultimate chapter highlights the key learning points, strategies and priorities from the East Asia Summit Conference on Liveable Cities that was organised in parallel with the World Cities Summit. The East Asia Summit Conference was focused on the interrelated issues of governance, urbanisation, climate change and the environment with a dedicated plenary session for mayors and governors. A final concluding chapter rethreads the various thematic discussions, emphasising the key lessons for cities in the area of governance and sustainable development.

REFERENCES

Appleyard, D (1981). *Liveable Streets*. Berkeley: University of California Press.

Bianchini, F, M Fisher, J Montgomery and K Worpole (1988). City centres, city cultures: The role of the arts. In *The Revitalization of Towns and Cities*. Manchester: Centre for Local Economic Development Strategies.

Cooper-Marcus, C and W Sarkissian (1986). *Housing as if People Mattered*. Berkeley: University of California Press.

Cooper-Marcus, C and C Francis (eds.) (1990). *People Places: Design Guidelines for Urban Open Space*. New York: Van Nostrand Reinhold.

Florida, R (2002). *The Role of the Creative Class: And How it is Transforming Work, Leisure, Community and Everyday Life*. New York: Basic Books.

Glaser, MA and JW Bardo (1991). The impact of quality of life on the recruitment and retention of key personnel. *American Review of Public Administration*, 21, 57–72.

Harvey, D (1989). From managerialism to entrepreneurialism: The transformation in urban governance in late capitalism, *Geografiska Annaler* 71B(1), 3–17.

Jacobs, A (1993). *Great Streets*. Cambridge: MIT Press.

Jacobs, J (1961). *The Death and Life of Great American Cities*. New York: Vintage.

Kerns, G and C Philo (eds.) (1993). *Selling Places: The City as Cultural Capital, Past and Present*. Oxford: Pergamon.

Landry, C (2000). *The Creative City: A Toolkit for Urban Innovators*. London: Earthscan Publications Ltd.

Lennard, SH and HL Lennard (1995). *Liveable Communities Observed*. Carmel: Gondolier Press.

Lynch, K (1981). *A Theory of Good City Form*. Cambridge: MIT Press.

McNulty, R, DR Jacobson and RL Penne (1985). *The Economics of Amenity: Community Futures and Quality of Life — A Policy Guide to Urban Economic Development*. Washington, DC: Partners for Liveable Places.

Zukin, S (1991). *The Culture of Cities*. Oxford: Blackwell.

Good Governance — Sustainability and the City

GIOK LING OOI

DEFINING GOOD GOVERNANCE AND URBAN BEST PRACTICES

Governance, economic growth, public sector management and sustainable human development are seen to be closely linked and indeed, inextricably bound (United Nations Development Programme, January 1995, p. xiii). This UNDP document goes on to list the essential components of modern conceptions of sound governance — political accountability, freedom of association and participation, reliable and equitable legal frameworks, bureaucratic transparency, availability of relevant and valid information in the public domain as well as effective and efficient public sector management. In 1993, World Bank guidelines had set down five principles for good governance — a strong participatory civil society; open, predictable policy-making; an accountable executive; a professional bureaucracy and the rule of law (Buchori, 1999, p. 29). While definitions of good governance abound, it is more evident that in practice, more examples can be found of poor or bad governance. It is therefore not surprising, that there is more consensus about what constitutes bad governance.

'Good governance' means governance which is based upon the values of merit, competence, transparency, integrity, accountability and equity. It is sad but true that good governance is in short supply in the world in which we live, to cite Professor Tommy Koh, Ambassador-at-Large with the Ministry of Foreign Affairs in Singapore. He chaired the session on Good

Governance at the World Cities Summit. It was significant that the World Cities Summit begun its discussions with the theme of good governance. Top government officials who gathered at the World Cities Summit to deliberate on good governance as well as the implications of sustainability for the city provided a large range of urban development and management issues for attention by urban leaders. The rate of urbanisation particularly in Asia was highlighted with projections showing that Asia's growth rate will be 1.23 per cent higher than the world average, according to Dr Tony Tan, Chairman of the National Research Foundation in Singapore. More than half of the population in Asia is expected to be living in towns and cities by 2030, numbering some 2.6 billion.

Such explosive urban growth is also expected to increase the demand for infrastructure and services as well as resources and environmental degradation. The latter is not inevitable as noted by the speakers in the plenary session on good governance. In his address on good governance for cities, Dr Tony Tan emphasised that "Urban sustainable development encompasses managing a whole spectrum of areas — water, waste, land use, pollution, energy and carbon emissions. To begin with, judicious urban planning establishes the framework in which cities can implement sustainable development. New technologies developed through extensive research act as powerful multipliers in the provision of sustainable development."

Air pollution has grown in most cities because of the increase in urban traffic volumes, industrialisation as well as power generation. Success stories in addressing such problems have illustrated that strong political will is needed as are clean technologies and greater private participation in financing the development of infrastructure. This applies to waste management strategies as well as the solution to water pollution problems. Water pollution and wastage because of indiscriminate and over-use have, as the speakers in the plenary session pointed out, limited supplies of fresh water for the growing urban population. Energy demands need to be met by considering and implementing technological solutions focused on cleaner and emissions-free fuels.

Singapore's initiatives in solving water supply and energy demands were shared by Dr Tan. Among the various renewable energy options, Singapore has opted for technology developments in solar energy. In Singapore, the government has committed some US$350 million for research and development, test-bedding and pilot projects in clean energy. This includes the National Research Foundation's S$170 million initiative to promote clean energy. This has become a new focus area as part of Singapore's existing environmental and water technology strategic programme. Part of this initiative is the S$50 million clean energy research programme launched in October 2008 to accelerate research and development efforts to support the growth of a clean energy industry in Singapore. At the present, solar energy costs approximately twice to thrice the price of conventional energy that is relying on fossil fuels. In the not so distant future, that is, by 2010, Mr Erik Thorsen, CEO and President of the Renewable Energy Corporation in Norway, a market leader in solar energy, predicted that parity, the point at which photo voltage electricity is equal to or cheaper than power derived from fossil fuel will be achieved in many markets. Singapore's initiative has attracted several major solar energy plants to set up their headquarters in the city-state including Oerlikon Solar, based in Switzerland and a leading supplier of equipment for making thin film solar cells.

For its initiatives concerning water supply, the Singapore National Research Foundation launched the S$500 million programme in April 2006 to finance research in the area of environmental water technologies, including developing Singapore as a global hydro hub by the year 2015. Such investments have proven to be sound by dramatically reducing the costs of recycling water from used water and desalination through the use of advanced membrane technology. In the last decade, the cost of a cubic metre of reclaimed used water and desalination fell from US$0.80 and US$1.50 to US$0.20 and US$0.50 respectively. These new technologies have broadened the possible supply sources of water-scarce cities, such as Singapore. Singapore's four NEWater plants produced some 50 million gallons per day of reclaimed waste water and a fifth plant currently being constructed will produce an additional 50 million gallons per day when it is completed in 2010.

In addition, Singapore is building a desalination plant using seawater reverse osmosis membrane technology which can supply a maximum of 30 million gallons per day of drinking water. This will bring Singapore closer to its target of eventually having non-conventional sources of water providing at least 30 per cent of Singapore's water needs. The implementation of Singapore's clean water initiative has seen extensive collaboration between the public sector, industry partners and research institutions, both local and international. Global companies set up work here like Siemens R&D centre, the Singapore-Delft water alliance, which is collaboration between Delft Hydraulics, the Public Utilities Board and the National University of Singapore as well as a new research centre by General Electric. Furthermore, there are several water treatment and membrane companies that are also carrying out a number of test-bedding projects at our water treatment plants with the aim of proving and refining on their new technologies.

Other issues facing the governance of water supply in cities, as Mr Fehied Fahad Al-Shareef, the governor and vice-chairman of the Saline Water Conversion Corporation of Saudi Arabia, reminds us, concern leakage from the water supply system and the management of water consumption. Controlling the water leakage in the network will save around 40 to 50 per cent of the water supplied. Other aspects of the water conservation effort would be to address the overuse of water in the household. While the tendency is to meet the demand for water, cities also need to work at managing water demand. Savings from these two methods in urban management should not compromise standards of living among the citizens. The government of Saudi Arabia built public awareness by working with the media to inform the people how much a drop of water costs. Then, the Ministry of Water and Electricity distributed free-of-charge water conservation devices to the households. The recovery of costs took only two weeks. Water use declined by over 30 per cent, that is, 1.8 million cubic litres a day. In Saudi Arabia, water leakage from the network is around 30 per cent which means 1.2 million cubic metres. So the total amount of water which can be saved by managing water consumption as well as leakage is three million, half of the daily production of water to meet the needs of Saudi Arabians. These easy and cheap tools for conservation, as Governor Fahied emphasised, can save cities a lot of money, time and effort.

The issues of ensuring high quality water supply for domestic and industrial uses as well as irrigation, particularly in Bahrain and generally in the Gulf region, were re-iterated by Mr Fahmi bin Ali Al-Jowder of Bahrain, the Minister of Works and the Minister-in-charge of Electricity and the Water Authority. Facing problems of deterioration in the quality of ground water because of growing salinity, the government of Bahrain has decided on recovery of waste water both to supply growing demands as well as to safeguard the natural resources of the country in the long term. In addition, efficiency has also been emphasised in managing water supply issues. In the effort on waste water recovery, Bahrain has also emphasised international cooperation through learning from the experiences of other places including Singapore.

In discussing the United Arab Emirates (UAE) solutions to water supply, the Minister of Environment and Water, Dr Rashid Ahmad bin Fahad, listed a range of activities from the building of more than 100 dams to supplement its underground water resources to conservation-friendly irrigation technologies. He, however, highlighted the success of waste water recovery for use in landscaping and irrigation with some minor use in industry for the last 30 years. Now, the country is looking towards the use of NEWater in Singapore although both local and federal governments in the UAE have decided to rely on desalinisation technologies. The challenge to which the UAE government is turning its attention has been in making the technology more environment-friendly and cost-effective.

In relation to the water needs of household, Ms Lindiwe Hendricks of South Africa, Minister for Water Affairs and Forestry, emphasised the role of women in seriously engaging with the issues of water supply, poverty and sanitation. Minister Hendricks argues that

> "Water is, after all, about the home and women are about the home. Water is about cleanliness, hygiene, it's about health, it's about food, it's about nutrition, it's about sanitation and dignity, it's also about growth and development. Tell me that women aren't critically involved in all of these issues. Again, until and unless when we speak about water we do not include women as spokespersons on the issue, we will not genuinely begin to seriously engage in a business unusual."

The appeal, therefore, was to put women at the centre of development. She pointed out that in the very poorest parts of the world, women are responsible for producing approximately 80 per cent of the food which they consume. Her question, therefore, was how such food production could be achieved without access to water, be it for the growing of their food or cooking and preparing the food?

For good governance, developing new institutions that use, manage and develop resources was the emphasis. In South Africa, effort has been made to put in place legislative as well as institutional mechanisms that are people-driven and people-centred have made considerable progress in consolidating its young democracy and governance.

The high population density in most Asian cities was highlighted and a focus of the issues in good governance discussed by the Mayor of Quezon City, the Honourable Feliciano Belmonte. Issues arising from burgeoning urban population growth in both Quezon City and the Metro Manila urban regions, of which the city is a part, include congestion, poor infrastructure and a deteriorating environment due to poor management. Emphasising the importance of political will in defining good governance, Mayor Belmonte cut the number of people on the city payroll and concentrated on funding improvements in infrastructure and social services through adjusting tax rates and boosting efficiency in the collection of taxes. Quezon City is working on the removal of urban blight, the resettlement of squatters as well as the creation of new town centres. It is also a city with the first local government in the Philippines to earn carbon credits as well as grant permits for bio-gas emission reduction projects under the Kyoto Protocol clean development mechanism.

In wrapping up the session on good governance, Mr Jim Adams, the Vice-President in-charge of East Asia and Pacific Region for the World Bank, highlighted how good governance has been key in the fight against poverty and the raising of living standards. The competitiveness of cities also depends on good governance and knowledge sharing, as evident from the greater and more vibrant successes seen among cities around the world. Two themes on urban governance have emerged from the work on urbanisation by the World Bank. "First, improving governance requires a paradigm shift in city management. This includes ensuring the professionalisation of city administrations, improving the quality of training and the education available to city officials, greater accountability both political and administrative, institutional reform and institutional strengthening," to cite Mr Adams in his address on the important aspects of the work that cities need to do. Good governance also means the creation of responsiveness to the city's own citizens with the World Bank emphasising client surveys to assess the quality of urban services. There should be participatory schemes to ensure that citizens can be involved in the decision making process and hold city officials accountable to performance. A stronger capacity to respond to environmental challenges would be an important aspect of such participation by citizens. Increasingly, both environmental issues and investments in improving environmental quality are now central to all urban agendas in the region as well as globally.

A second theme in good governance highlighted by the World Bank would be that in the running of a modern city, efficient systems in technology are necessary to deliver basic services and monitor their quality and impact. The quality of education, health and infrastructure services are key aspects to monitor. The planning of cities and efficient management of land ownership and use issues is important to initiate land reform activities as well as the strengthening of titling, mobilising resources through tariffs and property taxes. Most importantly, as highlighted by most speakers, cities have to be adequately financed in order to effectively meet the challenges they have to face. Last but not least, there needs to be a raising of civic or public awareness through better communications and continuous communications between the local state and its citizens.

INCORPORATING ENVIRONMENTAL GOVERNANCE AND SUSTAINABLE DEVELOPMENT IN CITY AGENDAS

The effort to define good governance highlights the challenge of translating such aspects of governance into sound environmental management and sustainable development in city agendas. While many leaders have focused on specific aspects of good urban governance in relation to sustainability and the management of natural resources, the concept of sustainable development calls for simultaneous and concerted efforts to deal with a slew of environmental as well as social issues (Bosselmann, Engel and Taylor, 2008). The complex issues calling for good governance includes pollution, economic development, unequal distribution of economic resources, and poverty reduction. Indeed sustainable development contends that environmental degradation cannot be addressed without confronting those human activities that give rise to it. Such activities would include urbanisation and the growth of urban populations.

To place environmental governance in government agendas and in particular city agenda, international agencies such as, the United Nations Development Programme has highlighted the need for good governance that controls the misuse of natural resources and promotes their sustainable management and use. Such an approach to governance encourages local leadership and decentralisation of power to the grassroots level and builds local capabilities. This form of good governance promotes sustainable economic development that is linked with the sustainability of the natural environment, and promoting conservation and sustainable use of natural resources to meet present needs without compromising the needs of future generations.

Observers have pointed out the challenge which remains in the integration of environmental thinking into mainstream economic and development decisions. Ministries of Environment and related agencies remain relatively weak and at the best most of them operate on the margins of significant policy decisions. In most cities and countries, traditional economic models that have yet to incorporate the costs of environmental decline continue to drive most decisions on development. Notably, the usual absence of finance ministers or trade negotiators at key environmental fora, is often cited as a major indicator of the peripheral position that has been allocated to environmental issues in development agendas of cities and countries.

More countries in the Asian region may be moving towards democratic urban governance by promoting decentralisation and local autonomy (United Nations Economic and Social Commission for Asia and the Pacific, 2005). Yet, central governments still exert considerable influence on cities and the local state at the functional, financial and administrative levels. Among the critical issues facing effective urban governance are urban economy and productivity; social issues, particularly urban poverty, lack of secure land tenure, exploitation of women and children; and environment (United Nations Economic and Social Commission for Asia and the Pacific, 2005). Cities are faced with a variety of urban environmental issues that the governments are addressing in different ways depending on the level of urban development and available sources of financing as discussed by leaders attending the Summit. Among the most important of these environmental issues are, land management; housing and urban services. The latter that have been identified by the Summit speakers include water supply, water resources, sanitation, drainage, solid and hazardous waste management and transport-related impacts; air pollution, including greenhouse gas emissions. The discussion by city leaders, however, did not include accident risk and disaster management involving natural disasters as well as others of anthropogenic origins that cities have to be prepared to face increasingly.

While it makes a lot of sense that environmental considerations should be a part of all development planning and decision-making, there are huge gaps between this sound principle and the setting of urban development agendas. There are few cases of environmental consideration being incorporated from the start of policy and program priority formulation to the implementation of project-specific activities, in the way that was emphasised by UAE Minister of Environment and Water, Dr Rashid Ahmad bin Fahad. Dr Rashid highlighted the aim of his government to consider the environmental impacts of costs of desalination technologies in the decision to focus on these to meet water demands in UAE.

Definitions of governance are applicable to both good governance and environmental governance. Governance refers to the "self organising, inter-organisational networks" that define and implement public policy (Rhodes, 1996, p. 660). Governance would then be "the processes and mechanisms through which significant and resource-full actors coordinate their actions and resources in pursuit of collectively defined objectives" (Pierre, 2005, p. 452). In brief, governance "involves government plus the looser processes of influencing and negotiating with a range of public and private sector agencies to achieve desired outcomes." (Hambleton, 2002, p. 150).

There is emphasis on good governance or environmental governance rather than government because in governance models, attention has been focused more on the need for collaboration between different stakeholders in the public, private, and non-profit sectors. Governance has been described as "... a process of multi-stakeholder involvement, of multiple interest resolution, of compromise rather than confrontation, of negotiation rather than administrative fiat" (Stewart, 2003, p. 76). Definitions of governance would mean seeing local government, in its ideal form, as the democratically accountable institution of the state enjoying specific administrative and legal powers that enable it to make collective decisions on behalf of the local urban population. In the process, governance would bring together a wider range of actors from civil society and the private sector, involving different interests, working in partnership to address shared concerns and meet common goals such as, sustainable development. Generally, environmental governance has been conceived as a system of a range of actors — both governmental and non-governmental — who cooperate and compete both vertically and horizontally in order to heighten the performance as well as benefits arising from policymaking at every level from local to national and regional. This is particularly significant when territories such as cities share natural resources with surrounding places that might include rural as well as extra-national and regional areas.

Environmental governance would also have to refer to the set of regulatory processes, mechanisms and organisations through which political actors seek to influence environmental actions and outcomes at different levels including the local and the urban. "Governance, as emphasised in much of the literature, is not the same as government. Good governance and it follows, environmental governance includes the actions of the government, that is, the state and in addition, includes actors such as communities, businesses, and NGOs. Key to different forms of environmental governance are the political economic relationships that institutions embody and how these relationships shape identities, actions, and outcomes" (Lemos and Agrawal, 2006, p. 298). There have emerged hybrid modes of governance across the state-market-community divisions. These include Co-Governance, Public-Private Partnerships and Social-Private Partnerships, some of which are themes that are discussed in this book (see Phang's Chapter on Private-Public Partnerships or PPPs). Many of these hybrid modes of governance promise solutions as well as recovery from environmental degradation and change social and natural systems.

Economists such as Levy and Newell (2000) use the term "environmental governance" to signify the broad range of political, economic, and social structures and processes that shape and constrain actors' behaviour towards the environment. These economists see environmental governance as referring to the multiple channels through which human impacts on the natural environment are ordered and regulated. Hence, environmental governance implies rule creation, institution-building, and monitoring as well as policy and programme enforcement. By this definition, environmental governance would also imply what Levy and Newell label as a soft infrastructure of norms, expectations, and social understanding of acceptable behaviour towards the environment, in processes that engage the participation of a broad range of stakeholders.

A major reason behind the current debate on re-thinking the implications of environmental governance has been the gap between the historical development of environmental institutions and the new institutional requirements posed by the sustainable development initiative of the United Nations Conference on Environment and Development (UNCED) of 1992. Hence, sustainable development has significantly broadened the environmental agenda by stressing that the issues of development and the environment need to be simultaneously addressed in order for policies to concentrate on the impacts of their interaction. The core of the sustainable development agenda reflects new thinking among the environmental and the developmental communities about the linkages between key issues on the international agenda (Pronk and Ul Haq, 1992; Holmberg, 1992; Nelson and Eglinton, 1995). The main criticism has fallen on the all encompassing nature of new agenda as threatening to dilute the environmental agenda as well as divert attention from the long-standing developmental goals of fighting poverty, reducing military expenditure, increasing respect for human rights, and promoting democracy. Applied to cities in particular, the concept of sustainable development would imply the inherently unsustainable nature of urbanisation and urban growth. Cities depend on territories well beyond their boundaries to provide food, water, energy and other natural resources for their development.

Yet, the new agenda for sustainable development provides opportunities to engage more substantively with environmental governance. There would be the need for an integrative approach to economic development that includes environmental protection along with other goals of growth, social equity, and, according to the leaders speaking at the World Cities Summit, democratisation of development agendas. Sustainable development would have to pay attention to the participation of citizens in policy decision making. Sustainable development and the United Nations' Agenda 21 highlight the need for broader participation in policy decision making. Indeed, Agenda 21 emphasises multiple stakeholder participation, or "major groups," at multiple levels of discussions, including NGOs, scientists, business as well as industry, farmers, workers and trade unions, local authorities, together with groups that might have been neglected before like indigenous people, women, youth and children.

Furthermore, governance for sustainability is premised on the awareness that citizenship comes with the recognition of rights and responsibilities towards the community and public interests shared by the citizenry. These are the rights that are important for the protection of individual freedom as well as wider societal, political or economic interests. The rights of citizenship include the fundamental right to participate in public decision making at all levels from the local to the national. Citizens too, have to recognise that responsibilities are key to protecting and safeguarding the proper functioning and well-being of the community. Such responsibilities would have to include the protection of ecological boundaries. Few communities can be considered to have sustainable futures without recognising such a fundamental responsibility.

Hence, the idea of governance for sustainability differs from conventional theories of governance (Bosselmann, Engel and Taylor, 2008). The concept of good governance emphasises transparency, accountability, and participation, as has been discussed above. Governance for sustainability would require more than these aspects of governance. For a start, good governance and good citizenship are seen to be interdependent. Governance for sustainability seeks a definition of the sense of citizenship. It calls for citizenship to be defined in terms of rights as well as responsibilities. Ecological citizenship would best describe this sense of citizenship and the subscription of citizens to sustainable communities. Governance for sustainability would then be a set of written and unwritten rules that link ecological citizenship with institutions and norms of governance. The emphasis is on 'link' since no form of governance can succeed if there is no common bond between those who govern and those who are being governed (Bosselmann, Engel and Taylor, 2008, p. xiv).

European cities are considered to be well ahead of those in other continents in terms of the planning that has been implemented to protect the environment. In the comparative analysis of city planning, the observation is that "Europe displays an environmental priority through policy at the European scale and in the enthusiastic take-up of environmental planning in most cities" (Newman and Thornley, 2005, p. 271).

Liveable cities, as the essays in this book will emphasise, require strong as well as sound approaches to city planning and urban design with sufficient bottom-up processes to ensure comprehensive representation of citizens' needs. The discussion among urban leaders have emphasised that rapid urbanisation has created most of the challenges faced by many cities and while hotly debated still, there are arguments that dense urban living if properly planned and designed for, can reduce the ecological footprint of people on the planet's resources and capacity (Mau, 2004). Among the positive outcomes would be that higher density living in cities requires less investment in transportation, fewer sewer and power lines, roads and cars, again if designed properly, be more energy efficient. Thus, urbanisation need not and indeed, should not create an unsustainable environment that would make living conditions untenable in the medium as well as long term (Boone and Modarres, 2006).

GOVERNANCE FOR SUSTAINABLE URBAN DEVELOPMENT — CHALLENGES OF ASIAN CITIES

Good governance, therefore, concerns issues that go beyond those highlighted in the presentations of the national as well as city government leaders who spoke at the World Cities Summit. Indeed, Asian cities face major challenges in positioning themselves to govern for far greater sustainability than seen before. If more cities have been placing sustainable development in their agendas, there are equally as many cities in Asia which do not appear to have gone beyond the rhetoric of becoming environmentally more sustainable. While many city governments have given priority to water and energy management issues for both economic as well as ecological reasons, air and water pollution issues remain largely unaddressed in Asian cities. Added to these more basic issues, as the urban and national leaders have stressed, are those concerning poverty, poor infrastructure, financing and climate change.

The governments of many Asian cities unlike their European counterparts have remained ambivalent about sustainable solutions to urban traffic congestion with relatively tepid approaches towards the development of public transport infrastructure (Ooi, 2008). To a large extent, the models of urban governance in the Asian region imply tensions that constrain many city governments from effectively placing sustainable development in their agendas. These tensions see differences between central and city governments in policy directions as well as intervention by the former in financial and related matters that determine the ability of city governments to act in response to urban developmental issues and problems. The tensions are examples of the issues that Asian cities and their national governments need to rise up to in order to face the challenges posed by sustainable urban development.

REFERENCES

Boone, CG and A Modarres (2006). *City and Environment*. Philadelphia: Temple University Press.

Bosselmann, K, R Engel and P Taylor (2008). Governance for sustainability: Issues, challenges, successes. *International Union for Conservation of Nature and Natural Resources IUCN Environmental Policy and Law Paper No. 70*.

Buchori, M (1999). Assuring good governance: A discussion. In Print, J Ellickson-Brown and A Razak Baginda (eds.), *Civic Education for Civil Society*. London: Asean Academic Press, 29–32.

Hambleton, R (2002). The new city management. In Hambleton, R, HV Savitch and M Stewart (eds.), *Globalism and Local Democracy. Challenge and Change in Europe and North America*. London and New York: Palgrave.

Holmberg, J (ed.) (1992). *Making Development Sustainable*. Washington DC: Island Press.

Lemos, MC and A Agrawal (2006). Environmental governance. *Annual Review of Environment and Resources*, 31, 297–325.

Levy, DL and P Newell (2000). Oceans apart? Business responses to the environment in Europe and North America. *Environment*, 42(9), 8–20.

Mau, B (2004). *Massive Change*. London: Phaidon Press Ltd.

Nelson, J and SJ Eglinton (1995). Global goals, contentious means. *Policy Essay* No. 10, Washington, DC: Overseas Development Council.

Newman, P and A Thornley (2005). *Planning World Cities. Globalisation and Urban Politics*. Busingstoke: Palgrave.

Ooi, GL (2008). Cities and sustainability — Southeast Asian and European perspectives. *Asia-Europe Journal*, 6(2), 193–204.

Pierre, J (2005). Comparative urban governance: Uncovering complex causalities. *Urban Affairs Review*, 40(4), 446–62.

Pronk, J and M Ul Haq (1992). *Sustainable Development: From Concept to Action*. The Ministry of Development Cooperation (Netherlands), UNDP and UNCED.

Rhodes, RAW (1996). The new governance: Governing without government. *Political Studies*, 44(4), 652–67.

United Nations Development Programme (UNDP) (1995). Public sector management, governance and sustainable human development: A discussion paper. New York: United Nations Development Programme, January.

United Nations Development Programme (UNDP) (1997). *Human Development Report: South Asia*. Chapter-IV. http://hdr.undp.org/reports/detail_reports.cfm?view=100

United Nations Economic and Social Commission for Asia and the Pacific (UN-ESCAP) (2005). *Urban Environmental Governance. For Sustainable Development in Asia and the Pacific: A Regional Overview*. United Nations ESCAP.

Chapter

3 Well-being Creates Vibrant Cities

THAI KER LIU

INTRODUCTION

This chapter is centred on the connection between well-being and cities. It draws on the dialogue session that took place during the World Cities Summit 2008 on the topic "Well-being Creates Vibrant Cities".

Throughout the Summit, we heard from speakers from all over the world on topics such as good governance, urban planning, land transportation, public-private sector collaboration and environmental sustainability. Well-being is a less tangible product, but no less important to people. What is the relationship between happy citizens and vibrant cities? Is happiness an accident of individual attributes and attitudes, or can it be influenced by the conditions in which people live? Should governments care only about what we could call objective conditions of well-being, or should they pay attention to subjective well-being too?

I will start by outlining the key points of our two speakers and then give a few comments on the theme of this session. The first speaker, Mr Jim Clifton, Chairman and Chief Executive Officer (CEO) of Gallup Organisation, USA, explained the significance of brain gain for economic growth, and introduced the Gallup behavioural model for societies, which traces the upward path of societies from basic, material needs (law and order, food and shelter) to intangible, post-material needs (well-being and citizen engagement), talent attraction and retention, and ultimately economic growth. Professor Ed Diener, the Joseph R Smiley Distinguished

Professor of Psychology at the University of Illinois at Urbana-Champaign, USA, elaborated on the concept and sources of well-being, explaining that subjective well-being depends not just on individual character but on the conditions we live and work in. We can think of it as a positive feedback loop: vibrant cities can help create the conditions for happiness, and happy citizens contribute to vibrancy in cities.

A BEHAVIOURAL ECONOMIC MODEL
FOR SOCIETIES

Brain Gain

Mr Jim Clifton started the session with a provocative thought: a handful of people can change the world, or at least the economy.

He told us that some 30 years ago, he watched a group of economists on television predict the gross domestic product (GDP) of the United States, Japan and Germany in 30 years. According to their projections, Japan would end up at about US$5 trillion, Germany at about US$4 trillion, and the United States would come in third at about US$3.5 to US$3.8 trillion.

Today, we can see that their predictions were quite close for Japan and Germany — Japan's economy was around US$4.5 trillion in 2007, and Germany's economy was over US$3 trillion. The United States' economy, on the other hand, was around US$14 trillion in 2007 — roughly three times the size, or US$10 trillion more, than it had been projected to be.

The Gallup Organisation was intrigued by the large difference between the experts' predictions and the actual GDP of the United States, and so sat down one day to count all the people who had contributed the additional US$10 trillion to the United States' economy over the last quarter of a century. To their surprise, they counted only a thousand people. And of that thousand, only four hundred were born in America; the other six hundred were foreign-born.

That was what the economists had missed 30 years ago — the importance of *brain gain* to economic growth. Brain gain is defined by Gallup as a city or country's attraction of talented people whose exceptional gifts and knowledge can create new businesses and jobs, and henceforth increase that city's or country's economy. The economists had underestimated the value of innovation and entrepreneurship that led to the technology revolution in the United States. The next predictor of economic growth would not be land or natural resources, or a good port or airport, but global migration patterns — the 600 immigrants that had contributed part of the unexpected US$10 trillion. Mr Clifton's prediction was that economic growth would follow talent; the next economic powerhouse would rise wherever they were.

What the World Wants

But where do talented people want to go? To put it another way, what affects global migration patterns?

Mr Clifton had a two-part answer for us: people go where they can find good jobs, and where they can have a high level of well-being.

The Gallup World Poll, initiated in 2005, is a collection of behavioural economic indicators across citizens in more than 140 countries. It asks respondents 100 questions across seven critical conditions — law and order, food and shelter, work, economics, health, well-being and citizen engagement.

What the world wanted, according to the World Poll, was a good job. The Great American Dream used to be to have a family, to have peace, to own your own home but not any more. Now, it was to have a good job. At the most fundamental level, all across the world, people went where the jobs were. If they are spoilt for choice, as talented people often were, they could go to cities where they could enjoy a higher level of well-being.

The Gallup Behavioural Economic Model for Societies

Gallup built on the insights of the World Poll to draw up a map of a society's economic development, showing the conditions that needed to be in place to create brain gain and ultimately higher GDP. GDP here serves much the same purpose as a company's stock price, as the single most useful indicator that a country is running well. Brain gain was picked as the single most important predictor of GDP, at least in the next 20 to 30 years or so. The Gallup model, as shown in Figure 1, can be seen as Maslow's hierarchy of needs writ large, and updated for the twenty-first century.

The most fundamental condition is *law and order*. Any society that lacks law and order has to make their restoration its first priority.

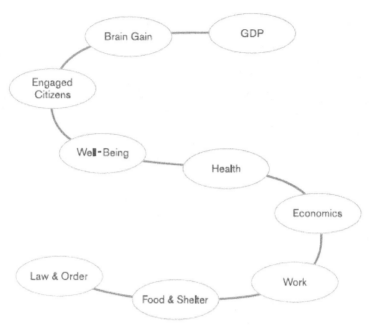

Fig. 1   Gallup's behavioural economic model for societies

Source: Gallup, Inc

The next condition is *food and shelter*. These are highly correlated with life expectancy in lower-income countries. Food and shelter are basic material needs, but come in second because they depend at least in part on law and order in the society.

Next is *work*. The most important discovery of the World Poll, as Mr Clifton introduced to us, is that everyone in the world wants "a good job". Work is related to net migration in higher-income countries and GDP growth in lower-income countries. We can think of law and order, and food and shelter, as basic needs, associated with self-preservation. Work is where our social nature begins to show itself — where the positive emotions that lead to creativity and openness are developed.

The fourth condition is *economics*, meaning people's perceptions of the economy and in particular their confidence in the economy. If confidence is generally high, or if innovators and entrepreneurs think that the economic climate is good, they are more likely to try and implement their ideas in that country, to start a business, to put down roots in the community.

The fifth condition is *health*, referring to both physical and mental health. Good health is correlated to well-being in low and middle-income countries. Having healthy people creates more vibrant communities and more productive work places.

If a society can get the first five conditions right — if it can establish law and order, ensure that its people have food and shelter, a good job, a stable economy, an environment conducive to business, and good health — then that society already has a huge productivity advantage over other societies.

The final two conditions are more difficult to bring about. Subjective *well-being* comes next, meaning, according to Gallup, the presence of suffering or thriving, misery or inspiration, feeling controlled or feeling independent. Well-being affects people's ability to innovate, improve and invent. Well-being is still felt on the individual level, like the first five conditions. We will discuss the impact of well-being on our ability to be good workers and good citizens in the next section.

The next bubble in the behavioural economic model is *engaged citizens* — opportunity and willingness to participate in and engage with the community, to build relations between different individuals and groups in the community. This enhances trust and cooperation within the community, and helps boost productivity. It also creates a positive environment that is welcoming to others, and can attract talented people to work and live in that community. That brings us back to *brain gain* and higher *GDP*, completing the model.

It seems to me that most governments understand the importance of the first five elements. Governments today seek to reduce crime, to raise families above the poverty line, to provide adequate housing for all who need it, to create jobs, to ensure macroeconomic stability and a competitive environment for business, to provide good health care. But what can governments do for well-being? This was the subject of the next speaker, Professor Ed Diener.

WELL-BEING CREATES VIBRANT AND ATTRACTIVE CITIES

Professor Diener spoke on the subject of well-being, and why governments should pay attention to the well-being of their people.

What is Happiness?

What do we mean by "happiness"? Professor Diener started with what happiness was *not*. Happiness is not smiling and laughing all the time. It is not a perpetual state of ecstasy or euphoria.

There are many definitions of happiness, or more accurately of subjective well-being. Broadly, individuals have a high level of subjective well-being when they think and feel that their lives are going well. This includes feeling positive emotions, such as calmness, contentment, enjoyment, gratitude and love. It includes cognitive judgements that their life is worthwhile and all the ways in which individuals evaluate their life in positive ways. It does not mean that they are never sad or worried or angry, but that they do not experience *chronic* levels of unhappiness or stress or anxiety or other negative emotions.

Why Should We Look Beyond the Individual?

The science of happiness tends to focus on individual sources of happiness, such as an individual's character and attitude to life, and the choices that he or she makes. While this is important, it is not the whole story. Global surveys of well-being like the Gallup World Poll have revealed large differences between levels of subjective well-being in different countries, larger than we would expect if happiness depended only on the individual. Professor Diener's thesis is that the conditions for happiness go beyond the individual to the community they live in. Conditions in an urban environment or organisations can influence individual happiness.

The Gallup World Poll includes a set of questions of life satisfaction. Respondents are asked to put their lives on a ladder from zero to ten, where zero represents the worst possible life they can imagine for themselves and ten the best possible life. The higher the rung on which they place themselves, the more satisfied they are with their lives.

It turns out that one of the happiest countries in the world is Denmark. Most of the Danish respondents put their life satisfaction at eight on the ladder. Denmark has all the fundamentals which characterise other happy countries, namely economic prosperity, low corruption, low conflict, good health outcomes and high social capital. One of the unhappiest countries, on the other hand, is Togo. Most of the respondents from Togo placed

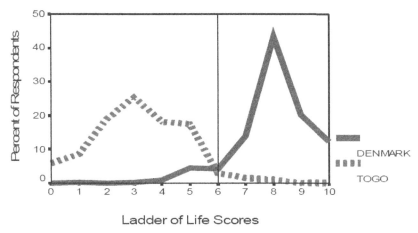

Ladder of Life Scores

Fig. 2   Well-being scores for Denmark and Togo

Source: Professor Ed Diener's presentation at the World Cities Summit

themselves on the second to fourth rung of the life satisfaction ladder. Togo is one of the poorest countries in the world, and has been driven by political tension and violence over the last few fears. Please refer to Figure 2 for well-being scores for Denmark and Togo.

Professor Diener clarified that surveys of well-being with contrary findings, such as the result that the happiest countries in the world were the poorest and most messed-up countries, tended to have methodological flaws and were not reliable. Studies with robust data generally found a positive correlation between GDP and life satisfaction.

We can find similar characteristics in happy cities. Professor Diener compared Detroit, a city on the decline, to Myrtle Beach, South Carolina. Happy cities like Myrtle Beach tend to be characterised by safety, job opportunities, short commuting times, good schools and a high degree of multicultural integration.

The same ideas hold for companies too — happy companies are more productive. Take, for example, a company in which only 40 per cent of the workers are engaged and satisfied with their work, and 60 per cent were disengaged. It is still possible to improve productivity, but the management would have to spend time and resources watching their workers, offering incentives, and punishing laziness and shoddy work. Even the 40 per cent who enjoyed their jobs and wanted to do well would probably be affected by the 60 per cent who did not. Conversely, a company in which 80 per cent of the workers are engaged is likely to be more productive and profitable.

Is Happiness Desirable?

Gustave Flaubert said, "To be stupid, selfish and have good health are three requirements for happiness, though if stupidity is lacking, all is lost." Even if we accept that happiness depends not just on the individual's emotions and attitude towards life but also on the society he lives in, does it follow that happiness is desirable?

Professor Diener begged to differ. First, happiness is desired by individuals. According to data from the Gallup World Poll, happiness is an important goal for young people the world over, after good health and so forth. Second, happiness is also desirable for organisations and communities. Research has found that happier people are healthier and live longer, are better workers and colleagues, and are better citizens and community members. We will take each of these points in turn.

Happy people tend to live longer. One study in the United States found that pleasant emotions expressed at age 22 in women who entered a Catholic convent predicted longevity after age 75 — nuns with high levels of pleasant emotions as young women lived on average for nine years longer than nuns with low levels of pleasant emotions. Another study, done on psychologists, also found a connection between well-being and longevity. The happy psychologists in this study lived five years longer than the unhappy psychologists.

It seems odd that happiness would have an effect on longevity, until we think about the connection between happiness and health. Happy people tend to have better health. They have a stronger immune system, because stress weakens the immune system and renders people more vulnerable to infections. They have a stronger cardiac system; negative emotions like anger can increase the likelihood of a heart attack. People who have had heart attacks are less likely to have another heart attack if they were happy after the first attack than if they were depressed. Happy people also tend to have better health behaviour — for example, they are less likely to smoke, less likely to become alcoholic, more likely to do things like wearing seatbelts.

Well-being has an impact on behaviour in the work place as well. Happy people are more likely to be good organisational citizens — they are more likely to be willing to help their colleagues even when it lies outside their job scope. They are less likely to steal from the work place, more likely to promote their company, and less likely to take unnecessary sick days. A few years ago, Professor Diener and other researchers studied the link between cheerfulness and future income by measuring the level of cheerfulness of college students in their first year of college against their income nineteen years later, when the students were in their late thirties and now part of the work force. The study found that higher cheerfulness in the first year of college correlated with higher income in their late thirties, even after controlling for factors like the students' majors and their parents' income.

Happy people are also better citizens in general. They tend to be more cooperative, more willing to trust other people, more pro-peace and less aggressive, and more willing to volunteer to help members of their community and stick with volunteering once they do volunteer. Research has found that happy people have better social relationships — men and women with more friends, for example, have lower levels of distress than those with fewer friends. One study of older people found that their participation in community service and other social activities was associated with greater life satisfaction, after statistically controlling for social support, individual personality differences, health and their levels of life satisfaction prior to the study.

In other words, happiness is good for the individual *and* for the company, city or country — not just in terms of attracting talented people to the community or brain gain, as Mr Clifton told us, but also because happiness is related to good health, good work behaviour and good citizenship. Table 1, taken from one of Professor Diener's academic papers, offers a summary of some likely advantages accruing to individuals with high well-being.

What Produces Happiness?

If happiness is a desirable outcome, then what sort of city can people be happy in? What conditions should cities have in order to be conducive to happiness?

Table 1   Likely advantages accruing to individuals with high well-being

Domain	Advantages
Society	Well-being of the populace might facilitate democratic governance.
Income	Happy people later earn higher incomes than unhappy people.
Work	Satisfied and happy workers are better organisational citizens than unhappy workers.
	Work units with high satisfaction have more satisfied customers than units with low satisfaction.
	Satisfaction of work units may correlate with productivity and profitability.
Physical Health	High well-being may correlate with longevity.
	Individuals low in well-being have compromised immune systems and are more likely to have certain diseases compared with individuals high in well-being.
Mental Disorders	The happiest individuals score low in psychopathology.
Social relationships	High well-being is associated with increased probability of marrying and staying happily married. It is also associated with increased numbers of friends and social support.

Source: Diener, E. and Selignman, M.E.P. (2004). Beyond money: toward an economy of well-being. *Psychological Science in the Public Interest*, 5(1).

The Gallup World Poll contains a set of questions on positive emotions. Income does predict positive emotions, but only up to a certain level of income. Beyond that, it has at most a modest effect on happiness. However, the following factors were strong predictors of positive emotions:

- I learn new things every day.
- I have control and autonomy over how I use my day.
- I am able to use my abilities and my talent every day in the work I do.

That is to say, after their basic, material needs have been met, people look for conditions that would allow them to fulfil less tangible, post-material desires and give them positive experiences: happiness, self-development, and challenging and interesting work.

Professor Diener shared an anecdotal example that illustrated what potential immigrants looked for in their host country. Four of his PhD students and two other colleagues from the University of Illinois in Urbana-Champaign were moving to Singapore this year to work. Only one of the six was Singaporean. When asked what attracted them to Singapore, they told him that they were drawn by the intellectual opportunities here, our multicultural diversity and harmony, and good food. No one spoke about income or material needs (other than good food!).

Through his research, Professor Diener found that cities with high average levels of happiness tend to share certain characteristics. First, as discussed earlier, basic conditions have to be in place and material needs have to be met, i.e. the city has to have low corruption, safety and jobs. Once these conditions are well established, post-material factors become more important in predicting life satisfaction. For example, research has found that air pollution tends to decrease life satisfaction. In Germany, life satisfaction increased after measures were taken to lower air pollution levels. Another factor is commuting time; it was found that in the United States, people who had to commute an hour each way to work and back had lower levels of life satisfaction than those with shorter commuting times. A good deal of research has been done on the link between green space and happiness: green space has been found to help people relax, to reduce stress levels, and to help people concentrate better. Low noise is important, because people generally have higher life satisfaction when they can concentrate and work in peace. People also tend to look for cities with good jobs and a stimulating intellectual climate. Last but not least is social capital; where social capital is high, i.e. people trust each other, can work with each other despite coming from different cultures, are willing to volunteer and help their fellow members of their community, and are engaged in and care for the community, life satisfaction tends to be higher. Professor Diener ended with a challenge for governments — to produce cities that create happy, engaged citizens.

REFLECTIONS AND COMMENTS

We have just been taken through two very enlightening lectures about the growth path of a society and how happiness and jobs play very important parts in it. Let us revisit some of the key points.

The Gallup behavioural economic model offers societies a map of this journey, from basic, material needs (including jobs) through to post-material desires like well-being and engaged citizenship. We can see part of the

Singapore story through this model — we have probably moved up to the circle labelled *health*, but we have some way to go in the areas of *well-being*, *engaged citizenship* and *brain gain*.

From Professor Diener, we learnt that the conditions for happiness go beyond the individual. Happy people function better. They are in better health and take better care of themselves; they are more productive and effective at work; they are more engaged in their community and more willing to help others. (They also earn more money and they live longer.) We can bring the Gallup model down to the level of the individual: once basic needs are met, what predicts life satisfaction is not income but post-material conditions: low pollution, low noise, short commuting times, a stimulating intellectual environment, green spaces, high social capital. What predicts positive emotions is our ability to learn new things every day, to be in control of our time, to be able to bring our abilities and our talents to bear on our work. Money clearly is not everything.

The conditions described by Professor Diener fit what we have heard about the Gallup behavioural economic model that cities should start by meeting the basic needs of their citizens and then move up the value chain to fulfil post-material needs like well-being and community engagement. Well-being is important because it is not just an individual good, but also a social good: happy citizens tend to be good citizens, good workers; they tend to be creative, energetic, engaged; they help attract others to come to live and work in their community.

Mr Clifton, on the other hand, showed us how a small number of people could make a difference to a country. The future of a country can be read not in the natural resources or physical capital that it controls, but in its brain gain — its ability to attract and retain the next generation of innovators and entrepreneurs. What drives global migration patterns turns out to be universal across all countries: a good job and a high level of happiness. The next wave of talented workers will go where they can exercise their talents and enjoy a high level of well-being.

Let me attempt now to relate the theoretical framework by both Mr Clifton and Professor Diener to the reality of Singapore, and for that matter, the majority of cities around the world.

There are three issues. The first is the relation of the key tenets of the two speakers to the physical environment of a city. The second is the importance of creativity to Singapore. The third and last is the relation of the theoretical framework with the vibrancy of our own as well as other cities.

The Physical Environment

If you consider their main points carefully, you will find that many of the sources of well-being described are embedded in a good physical environment. After all, a city, at its most basic, is the spatial organisation of people and places. Good governance is required to create the physical environment which provides the foundation for a well-functioning city.

In Mr Clifton's economic model, food and shelter, work, economics and health all need to reside in the physical environment. Similarly, Professor Diener described for us the characteristics of cities, such as high personal safety, low corruption, low conflict, low air pollution, low noise, short commuting times, green spaces, good jobs, a stimulating intellectual climate, and high social capital. These urban attributes also need to find expression through the physical environment.

To underscore the point — for shelter, we need attractive residential estates which offer a high quality of living; for work and economics, centres for business and economic activities, complemented by a good transportation system, that can draw workers and customers without creating negative amenities like congestion; for health, a clean and green environment; with public parks and spaces, and recreational and community places. None of these conditions would be possible without a good physical environment.

In Singapore, we have done well in shaping our physical environment. We have a high level of home ownership, clean air, blue skies, a green environment, flowing traffic, well-functioning infrastructure. Singapore does well in the *health* category. The 2008 Mercer Quality of Living survey, for example, puts us at 32nd place worldwide and top within Asia. The question is, what comes next? How do we move up the Gallup model to reach *brain gain*? How do we take up Professor Diener's challenge of creating a city that can nurture happier and engaged citizens?

A Creative Society for Singapore

If the first part of the answer to Professor Diener's challenge is a good physical environment, then the second part has to be creativity.

In his book, *The Rise of the Creative Class*, Richard Florida argued that the creative economy requires creativity across different dimensions: "technological creativity, which is innovation, new products and ideas and technologies; economic creativity, which includes entrepreneurship turning those things into new businesses and new industries; and cultural and artistic creativity, the ability to invent new ways of thinking about things, new art forms, new designs, new photos, new concepts. Those three things have to come together to spur economic growth."[1] In Singapore, we are often reminded of the need for the first two kinds of creativity, to spur innovation and entrepreneurship. Happily, we have begun to pay greater attention to cultural and artistic creativity. For example, we have seen the Esplanade, the Singapore Tyler Print Institute and the Arts House at the Old Parliament open their doors. In January 2008, the School of the Arts took in its first batch of students. This is the beginning of an essential and exciting journey for us.

Culture and the arts are important not just for their own sake, but for the possibilities they offer us. We cannot run away from our first and foremost constraint: Singapore is small. It is small in terms of land size and natural resources. Small land size limits the diversity of experience and exposure. Singapore is also young, with limited claim to great historical stories. If the identity of a nation can be profiled by joining the dots of legacies left behind by our historical heroes and cultural giants, then our national profile requires much work. But, on the other hand, we must believe in our own potential greatness.

We need time to build up a sense of identity and community that can anchor Singaporeans to our shores and attract other talents to live and work here. While we continue to improve on what we have already accomplished, we should also find ways to overcome our constraints and shortcomings. Culture and the arts are the key to make this next leap forward. Just as travel enlarges our physical world, art expands our mental space. The study of the arts nurtures passion, instils discipline, and, most importantly, fosters imagination. As Sir Ken Robinson, a retired professor of arts education, puts it, "everything achieved in human endeavour begins with 'what if?'"[2] Without the imagination there can be no invention or

---

[1] Interview with Richard Florida on salon.com — Dreher, C (2002). Be creative later or die. Salon.com, 6 June Accessed 26 September 2006.

[2] Speech delivered at the World Summit on Arts and Culture, which was held in Newcastle, Gateshead, England, from 14 to 18 June 2006.

creativity of any kind. Culture and the arts are important not so much to nurture the next generation of poets and painters, but the next generation of creative, innovative, entrepreneurial workers.

To look at the matter in another way — the 2008 Global Competitiveness Report by the World Economic Forum outlined three stages of development. The first stage is driven by factors of production, the second stage by efficiency, and the third stage by innovation. In my view, Singapore's economic development can be seen in this light: the 1960s and 1970s were an era of domestic consolidation, while the 1980s and arguably the 1990s were about improving quality and moving up the value chain to higher value-added products, as shown in Figure 3. To succeed in the next stage of development and to compete in the top league of nations will require innovation and creativity. To reach this new stage, we will need to push the boundaries of our mental and psychological space and to intensify the breadth and depth of our engagement in culture and the arts. These efforts will spur further development of well-being and engaged citizenship as well as groom a broader base of higher calibre citizens and workers to help Singapore move more decisively from a society of good learners to be one of innovators. (It will also produce better artists, performers, writers and designers — virtue brings its own reward.)

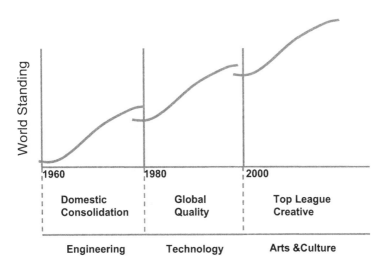

Fig. 3   Singapore's development

What Makes a Vibrant City?

Finally, referring to the theme of this dialogue session, Well-being Creates Vibrant Cities, how do we see the connection?

Vibrancy can be understood in several ways — not just the narrow and superficial perception of entertainment or "buzz", but in terms of physical, economic and mental vibrancy.

A good physical environment provides the foundation for a well-ordered city that can cater to the material and post-material needs of its citizens — the necessary conditions, in other words, for physical and economic vibrancy. This could aid us most of the way to "well-being" in the Gallup behavioural economic model. To ascend the heights of engaged citizenship and brain gain, we also need the creative ballast that culture and arts can provide. Economic and mental vibrancy will depend, in Richard Florida's words, not just on technological innovation and economic entrepreneurship, but also on artistic and cultural creativity.

The challenge for us now is to overcome our constraints and expand the mental and cultural space that we have, so that everyone who wishes to can find something that keeps them engaged and energetic in their work and their community, and in that way create a vibrant city. If we interpret vibrancy in these terms, Singapore should be on track towards brain gain and higher GDP, as well as greater happiness.

ACKNOWLEDGEMENTS

I am deeply grateful to Ms Koh Tsin Yen of Civil Service College. In a calm and confident manner, she helped me put the paper together, with a high level of accuracy in conveying important concepts and details, and with meticulous sensitivity in fine-tuning the nuances of meaning and elegance of the text. It was great to work with her.

REFERENCES

Arts Council, England (2006). *Final report of the World Summit on Arts and Culture. Transforming Places, Transforming Lives* England. August 2006. http://www.artsummit.org/files/FINALSummitreport.pdf?id=195, 1–13. Accessed 25 September 2008.

Clifton, J (2007). *Global Migration Patterns and Job Creation.* http://gmj.gallup.com/content/101680/Global-Migration-Patterns-Job-Creation.aspx. Accessed 25 September 2008.

Diener, E and Seligman, MEP (2004). Beyond money: Toward an economy of well-being. *Psychological Science in the Public Interest*, 5(1).

Dreher, C (2002). Be creative — or die. Interview with Richard Florida. 6 June. www.salon.com. Accessed 26 September 2008.

The Age of the City: The Challenge for Creative Cities

PETER HALL

This chapter addresses the key needs that will confront cities seeking to compete in the new knowledge economy. The most successful are likely to be world cities that are already integrated in different ways with the world economy. These cities and their challenges were discussed during the World Cities Summit 2008 session on Urban Planning and Conservation: Planning for a Distinctive and Vibrant City. In the global marketplace for jobs and investments, there has been extensive effort to make the city more creative, distinctive and liveable. The paradigm of the creative city is centrally important in understanding how knowledge, applied through human intelligence, has been central to the success of great cities throughout history and continues to provide the vital element today.

FOSTERING THE CREATIVE CITY

First, cities must foster the creativity of their citizens and attract creative people to live and work in their city. They need to learn from those cities that have been uniquely creative in the past, or are uniquely creative today. To take only Western or European culture, why was Florence so remarkable a place in the 15th century, or London at the end of the 16th, or Paris at the end of the 19th and the beginning of our century? Why in a different way was Manchester so remarkable at the end of the eighteenth century, or

Detroit around 1900, or Silicon Valley today? How exactly do these golden ages come about? Why is it that such golden ages do not last more than a few decades at a time? And why do so few cities have more than one such golden age? How is it that they fail to recapture the creative spark that once animated them? Perhaps most important, how do some cities occasionally bring off the trick? What forces are going to shape the fates of cities in the coming century — and what, if anything, can we as planners do about them?

The question is important for planners, because practical people, the ones whom John Maynard Keynes believed to be the slaves of some defunct economist, seem to be obsessed by the question of what we now call cultural industries. Nearly 70 years ago, in a marvellous essay, Keynes predicted that the world might eventually reach the position where we no longer need to care about the basic economic problem of survival that has plagued the human race since beginning of time, but are able at last to do only the things we find agreeable and pleasurable. He unforgettably wrote that we would face our "permanent problem — how to use ... freedom from pressing economic cares, how to occupy the leisure, which science and compound interest have won ... to live wisely and agreeably and well" (Keynes, 1972, p. 328). In the 70 years since he wrote that, in North America and Europe and other developed economies, we have almost arrived at that condition he described: we can guarantee at least a decent minimum level of existence. But, even Keynes never foresaw that these agreeable activities would themselves become sources of income and economic growth, generating new industries of a kind never known before. Rich, affluent, cultivated nations, above all their cities, can sell their beauty, philosophy, their art and their theatre to the rest of the world. During the 1980s and 1990s, cities across Europe — Montpelier, Nîmes, Grenoble, Rennes, Hamburg, Cologne, Birmingham, Barcelona, Bologna and Glasgow — have become more and more preoccupied by the notion that cultural industries (a term that 20 years ago no one would have understood, but that we no longer seem to think are anomalous or offensive) may provide the basis for economic regeneration. Culture, it seems, will fill the gap left by all the lost factories and warehouses, and will create a new urban image that would make cities more attractive to mobile capital and mobile professional workers.

But — and this is an important argument in the book I have written on this subject — it is not the only kind of creativity (Hall, 1998). Cities have always been the places where human creativity flourished; from them came not only the world's great art, not only the fundamental advances in human thought, but also the great technological breakthroughs that created new industries and even entire new modes of production. Ever since cities became large enough and complex enough to present problems of urban management, they also became urban laboratories, places that developed the solutions — technological, organisational, legal or social — to their own problems of growth.

So, the fundamental argument is that we can distinguish three main kinds of urban innovation: first, cultural/intellectual; second, technological-productive; and third, a relatively new phenomenon in history, the marriage of the cultural and the technological. During the 20th century, the first and second types of innovation have tended to fuse together into the third. And we should expect this to continue into the 21st century.

THE ARTISTICALLY-CREATIVE CITY

The six studies that make up the first part of *Cities in Civilization* (Hall, 1998) deal with cultural and artistic creativity. They are Athens in the fifth century B.C.; Renaissance Florence, between 1400 and 1450; Elizabethan London, the time of Shakespeare; Vienna during the 19th century, culminating around 1900; Paris between 1870 and 1910; and Berlin in the 1920s.

These cities became culturally creative long before they proved very adept either at technological advances, or in managing themselves effectively. They enjoyed their golden ages even while the majority of their citizens laboured in abject poverty, and most people lived in conditions of abject squalor — at least, by the standards of the 21st century. One question is why diverse urban societies should have set themselves this apparently odd order of priority. Another closely related question is whether this has anything to do with the kinds of urban societies they were.

There is not much in the conventional theory to explain the phenomenon of golden ages. There are, however, a few insights. One is France, where a now obscure professor of art, Hippolyte Taine, developed the idea of a creative milieu. Another is Sweden, where a professor of geography at the University of Lund, Gunnar Törnqvist, developed an identical idea (Taine, 1865; Törnqvist, 1983). They help to develop an explanation, which runs like this: these six cities varied enormously in size, but they were generally among the bigger and more important places of their time. More important, every one was on a course of rapid economic and social transformation, a city that in consequence had grown with dizzy speed. Athens was the first example in the world of a great global trading emporium with a complex system of exchange arrangements. The others were all capitalist cities, but interestingly, with strong precapitalist features: Florence and London were still essentially guild craft cities, Vienna and Paris likewise had strong *atelier* traditions; only Berlin was a full-fledged capitalist manufacturing city. They were all great trading cities; in the cases of Athens, Florence and London, they were the true global cities of their time. Out of trade came new ways of economic organisation and out of those came new forms of production. Their geographical position, as ports or as national or regional capitals, helped them. But this was no guarantee, because there were other similarly placed cities that achieved far less. In economic terms they were sometimes world leaders (Athens, Florence, London, Berlin), sometimes laggards (Vienna, Paris); there is no clear pattern. All we can say is that they led their respective polities and they were large by the standards of their day, and that made them magnets for the immigration of talent, as well as generators of the wealth that could help employ that talent.

Wealth is important. Athens was not a rich place, but by our standards its citizens had exceedingly modest personal needs, and there was wealth to spare; the other European cities were by far the wealthiest places in their respective domains, and however as seen — that wealth was concentrated in relatively few hands, usually that of the rising bourgeoisie and the more canny of the old aristocracy, who might (though not inevitably) intermarry. So it was true that, as DH Lawrence once said, culture was founded on the deep dung of cash. That meant individual patronage, but it also meant community patronage whether at the level of the city or (after the arrival of the nation in early modern times) the nation state. The role of the community was always vital, whether in creating the Florentine Baptistery or the court theatres of London or the Louvre or the Vienna Rathaus or the great Berlin theatres.

These were all high-culture cities, cities in which culture was fostered by a minority and catered for the tastes of that minority. Athens was the last case in history, or perhaps the last before mass television culture, where an actual majority of the population could share the same plays or poems; and even then, of course, the majority was a minority, because it did not include the slaves. But in any subsequent place and time, art had a bourgeois clientele. That had to imply a very unequal distribution of wealth, because that would be needed to foster individual consumption, and also to generate a surplus necessary for state support. So, most creative cities were bourgeois cities — but the reverse is not always true: by no means all, or most, bourgeois cities were creative; it was a necessary but not a sufficient condition.

So the talent may be more important than the wealth. A notable feature is that recent in-migrants — sometimes from the countryside, but often from far-distant places, provided both the audience and the artists: just consider the Metics of ancient Athens, the artists who came to Florence from the countryside or from further afield, the provincial musicians of Vienna and provincial artists of Paris, the Jews in *fin-de-siècle* Vienna. The creative cities were nearly all cosmopolitan; they drew talent from the far corners of the empires they controlled, often far-flung. Probably, no city has ever been creative without this kind of continued renewal of the creative bloodstream.

Talented people needed something to react to. Because these were all cities in economic transition, they were also societies experiencing a transformation in social relationships, in values and in views about the world. Most were in a state of uneasy and unstable tension: between a set of conservative forces and values — aristocratic, hierarchical, religious, conformist — and an opposing set of radical values: bourgeois, open, rational, sceptical. These were societies troubled about themselves, societies that were on the course of losing the old certainties but were deeply concerned about what was happening to them. We are prone to associate the first set of values with medieval feudalism and the second with modern capitalism, but it is more complicated: during the 19th century when the bourgeoisie might have become a brake on the development of new artistic forms and new values, as can be seen in Paris. It might take a near revolution and a total breakdown of the established aristocratic-bourgeois coalition, as in Berlin after 1918, to generate the creative spark.

What appears crucial is that this disjuncture is experienced and expressed by a group of creative people who feel that in some ways they are outsiders: they both belong and they do not belong, because they are young or because they are provincial or even foreign, or because they do not belong to the established order of power and prestige; quite often most or all of these things. That label applies to the Athenian Metics, the guild craftsmen of Renaissance Florence, young actor-playwrights of Elizabethan London, the court musicians and later the Jewish intellectuals of Vienna, the Impressionists and later the Cubists as well as producers and writers who flocked from the provinces into Berlin in the 1920s. Great art is not produced by insiders, even though the artists may be patronised by insiders (as many of these groups were) and may in consequence enjoy a fleetingly close relationship to them. A creative city will therefore be a place where outsiders can enter and feel that state of ambiguity: they must neither be excluded from opportunity, nor must they be so warmly embraced that the creative drive is lost.

They must then communicate their uncertainties, their sense that there is another way of perceiving the reality, to at least part of the class that patronizes them. That demands a widespread schism in the mainstream society, wide enough to provide at least a minority of patrons for the new product. Creative cities are almost certainly uncomfortable, unstable cities, cities in some kind of basic collective self-examination, cities in the course of kicking over the traces of the past and the stable.

That means that there must be traces to kick over. Conservative, stable societies will not prove creative; but neither will societies in which all order, all points of reference, have disappeared. Creative cities have been those in which an old-established order as well as a too-long-established order, was being challenged or had just been overthrown; Vienna in 1900, obviously, but likewise the London of 1600, Paris of 1860 or Berlin of 1920. There is indeed something subversive about most serious art; it is likely to express the forces of discontent and unrest that challenge the old order of doing things and thinking things, and at the same time help foster and give voice to those forces. That is self-evidently true of art with an explicit political purpose, such as Berlin theatre of the 1920s; but it can be equally true of art with no such purpose or with a merely incidental political aim, such as most Elizabethan dramas, Picasso's Cubist paintings or the work of the Viennese *Sezession*.

So, is the *milieu* purely a reflection of broad socio-economic forces in a particular place at a particular time, or does it spring from cultural traits that develop almost independently of the economic substructure? That is a very difficult question to answer. You can explain Athens' lead over the other Greek states in terms of Attica's central position and the consequent trading advantages within the eastern Mediterranean; but it seems difficult to express the scale of the difference. Likewise, 15th century Italy had developed as the most advanced part of Europe, and Florence as perhaps the most advanced city in Italy; but again, the Florentine achievement appears quite disproportionate in comparison with cities like Siena or Verona, let alone Bologna or Parma or Ravenna. I could give other examples: it seems that an initial economic advantage is massively transformed into a much larger cultural one. It is almost as if there is such a socio-economic explanation, but it is hardly enough to bear the weight of explaining why an Athens or a Florence, should have developed so uniquely.

THE TECHNOLOGICALLY-INNOVATIVE CITY

The technologically-innovative cities were in every sense different. Again, six cities can be considered: Manchester and innovation in cotton textiles around 1780, Glasgow and steamships between 1820 and 1880, Berlin and electrical engineering around 1870, Detroit and automobiles around 1900, the San Francisco Bay Area and electronics around 1950 and Tokyo in the same field in the last half of the century. They were not generally established cities, 20th century Tokyo was an exception; they were cities somewhat on the periphery of the established world, neither right at the centre (as the culturally innovative cities were) nor right at their periphery. They were middling cities, plugged into what was happening in the world much like world cities of today, but keeping their distance: they were emerging, upstart places.

The Japanese example apart, these case studies seem to show the continuing strength of bottom-up, individualistic innovation. The innovators were outsiders living in outsider cities. Most were middle class; though some of the early ones had little education, the majority was at least well grounded in basic technical skills. A surprising number were self-taught. All followed careers that taught them what they needed to know, in a related industry or field; they were well-grounded, so their success was no accident. They all relied on strong local networks, supplying specialised skilled labour and services, and creating a climate of innovation among small firms, even individuals, who shared knowledge while they competed with each other. More closely analysed, as a number of commentators have recently emphasised, in the late 20th century there seem to be at least two, perhaps three, models of capitalism, with different attendant models of innovation: the American model of bottom-up innovation in a *laissez-faire* environment, and German-Japanese model of state guided capitalism. The integrated model seems to have faltered in the West, and now massively in Japan too: the verdict is not in, but it seems likely that bottom-up, small-scale, networked innovation will always be necessary for real fundamental economic change, the process of "creative destruction" that Joseph Schumpeter wrote about half a century ago.

The innovative places could all be called edge cities: more accurately, they were not at the centre but neither were they off the edge of the world altogether. All had some strong previous tradition that proved critical. They were not trammelled by old traditions or ways of doing things. Most had egalitarian social structures: they lacked old wealth and were not class-hidebound; they were open societies in which careers were open to talents. They shared an ethos of self-reliance and self-achievement; they tended to have open educational systems, or at least apprenticeship systems, with a stress on the practical uses of scientific knowledge. They might well have recently acquired wealth, in the hands of adventurous people who were willing to take risks. Many of the infant firms in these places seem to have started by catering for a local market whose characteristics they understood. It might be a consumer market, but often it was a market of related producers; in this case, there might be a chain of interactions in which the demand spurred producers to come up with innovative solutions to overcome problems.

Primary innovation does not seem to have been crucial, indeed of decreasing importance: what was important was the downstream innovation, tuned to the market. New entrants like Ford could achieve this; so could established Tokyo corporations. Local demand helped here, but it does not provide a satisfactory total application. One can say that there was something else: continuing ability to innovate and ally technical knowledge to the changing demands of the marketplace. Geography relates to industrial organisation. Theoretically, as examples like GE and IBM show, the giant bureaucratised corporations can exist on a self-contained basis far distant from the city. Yet Japanese corporations continue to lock into Tokyo and its surrounds, apparently fearing the consequences if they move R&D too far from the city.

THE CREATIVE-INNOVATIVE CITY

There is thirdly, and importantly, a hybrid form: a phenomenon I called the marriage of art and technology, which is exceptionally important to the argument, because it points the way to the 21st century future. It is in fact a 20th century story. It happened especially in the United States, and that is not surprising. America was not outstanding in technological invention, but it was unique in its capacity to turn inventions into commercially useful innovations. At a very early stage, it developed traditions of mass production of standardised consumer goods for vast mass markets: the American system of manufacturing. It allied to this a populist concept of culture and entertainment, far removed from the European patrician attitude that public corporations should give the masses what was good for them; out of this, for good or ill, came Hollywood and Tin Pan Alley as well as commercial radio and television. The stories of Hollywood in the 1920s, and of Memphis Tennessee in the 1950s, were both stories of entrepreneurs, flourishing in a uniquely open society. These entrepreneurs were able to reach new audiences. The American media revolution was created by classic Schumpeterian new men, who fitted the classic definition of entrepreneurship given by one such entrepreneur, Henry Kaiser: *Find a need and fill it.* They discovered huge markets for new products. The industry was always market-led, but in turn it led the market. In particular, it identified new mass markets — the turn-of-the-century immigrant communities in the cities, the bored and rebellious teenagers of postwar suburban America — and produced a new product that catered directly for their deepest emotional needs.

Almost certainly, it could not have happened in any other country. What is puzzling, however, is why this should happen in two cities so far removed from the cultural mainstream and from the original New York powerhouse of the mass media revolution. Such huge innovative capacity does not come easily. It can happen only in a society in extreme flux, where new socio-economic or ethnic groups are defining themselves and asserting themselves. New York in 1900, America's quintessential immigrant city, was one such society, but it lost its touch, and its most successful entrepreneurs removed themselves to the opposite side of the continent.

Both the new industries existed in an uneasy relationship, half-symbiotic, half-hostile, with the forces that created them. Movies, once past their nickelodeon origins, were expensive, capital-hungry products that needed yet more capital to exhibit them nationwide and worldwide; so the industry was soon in thrall to the bankers. But the individuals who had forged it were archetypal small and opportunistic entrepreneurs. They retained the attitudes of their youth and they rebelled against their bankers. The resulting organisation of the industry, based on constant tension between producers and financiers three thousand miles apart, was in a sense logical; out of it came the legendary hostility between the two urban cultures, New York seeing Los Angeles as superficial and gimmicky, Hollywood viewing Wall Street as stifling and philistine, and the East Coast elite wishing a plague on both houses.

Oddly, Tin Pan Alley was essentially created by the same cultural-ethnic group as Hollywood. It grew up catering for a mass market it understood viscerally, because it was them. But it destroyed itself, because finally it could not come to terms with the generation gap: it became an industry peopled by old men, catering for a teenage market. Worse than that were the comfortable old men who had forgotten their origins, losing touch with the grassroots of poverty and alienation that had once inspired them. These grassroots were deep in rural America, in the one part that had retained deep folk traditions out of Africa and England and Ireland, ironically because it was too poor to share in the media revolution that New York and Hollywood had sold to the rest of America. New entrepreneurs who knew those grassroots, either because they had grown up with them or because they emotionally responded to them, filled the gap: a classic Schumpeterian situation.

Today, there may yet be another untapped market that no one properly understands or even knows. It may be the millions of children playing with their computer games. It may be adults bored with their everyday lives, and seeking solace in fantasy worlds as yet impossible to grasp. Someone will empathise with such a group and produce another industry, the outlines of which are still dim and uncertain. The likelihood is that this will happen in a special kind of city, a city in economic and social flux, a city with large numbers of new and young arrivals, mixing and merging into a new kind of society. It sounds like London or Los Angeles, New York or San Francisco as well as many of the world cities that are connected and integrated with the world economy. The places that achieved the revolution the last time round could be the ones that achieve it next time. This might not necessarily be the case since there are no absolute rules in this ultimate game; time and chance can happen to come together in other cities too.

THE NEXT INNOVATIVE WAVE — AND ITS GEOGRAPHY

The practical question now has to be: how will creativity manifest itself in the 21st century city? If there is to be yet another Schumpeterian burst of innovation, which may be beginning right now, and giving rise to a new long wave of economic growth based on new industries, what are the key new industries that will provide the basis for it?

There are at least three clear clues. One is the point with which this paper began: the huge expansion of the creative and cultural industries, which are no longer the playthings of a few rich patrons, but have become mass-consumption industries. The future Keynes predicted has arrived in the developed world, and during the next century it will happen in much of the now-developing world. In the UK, Andy Pratt has shown that the cultural industries employ nearly one million people, some 4.5 per cent of the workforce; they are as big as the construction industries, and of course they have grown far faster (Pratt, 1997).

The second is the one I emphasised earlier: that we are now seeing the convergence of artistic and technological creativity, two forms traditionally held to belong to different people and to opposite sides of the brain: Frances Cairncross calls such people "techno-bohos", and more recently Richard Florida has captured the same concept in his study of urban creativity (Cairncross, 1997; Florida, 2002). We have already noticed two outstanding previous examples, both American. It is no accident either that the United States has so far proved equally outstanding in the new multimedia industries that are developing through the marriage of computing and telecommunications. The basic technologies are the Internet, developed in the 1960s by the American armed forces for military purposes, and the World

Wide Web, actually created in Europe by an Englishman, Tim Berners-Lee. Yet, again it has been American ingenuity that has developed the many commercial platforms, which have exploited the new technologies in the 1990s, such as Netscape, Yahoo and Google.

What matters here is not the basic technology but the uses that are made of it. Of course, the steam engine was important, but more important was the network of railways and steamship lines that were built on it, spanning continents, and finally the world as well as in turn producing the first global division of labour. Likewise, the internal combustion engine was a key invention, but what mattered was the vast apparatus of mass-produced auto-mobility that was erected on top of it and the phenomena that it then generated, ranging from suburbia to fast food. We need to ask: what are the industries, this time round, that will develop on top of the new infrastructure of the net and the web?

We can see some of them: tele-medicine and tele-health care, tele-education and tele-learning, online information services, electronic publishing, financial services, trading and brokering, tele-shopping, entertainment of all kinds (film, video, theatre, music, multimedia pop, animation, virtual reality, games), electronic sports and competitions and virtual reality expressions, security and surveillance, earth resources information, environmental monitoring and control, digital imaging and photography, data mining and processing. Most share a characteristic, identified by Manuel Castells as central: what he calls "the application of ... knowledge and information to knowledge generation and information processing/communication devices, in a cumulative feedback loop between innovation and the uses of innovation" (Castells, 1989, p. 32).

Education is perhaps the most obvious of these applications, but the one with the most profound social implications. During the coming decades it will be transformed beyond recognition through the injection of informa-tion technology in every stage of teaching and research. As MIT professor William Mitchell puts it: "If a latter-day Jefferson were to lay out an ideal educational community for the third millennium, she might site it in cyberspace" (Mitchell, 1995, p. 70). In the UK, Douglas Hague has predicted that first-rate remote lectures will replace second- or third-rate direct ones; multimedia presentations will allow students to pace their own learning. Teachers will thus find themselves performing new roles: as "guides" or tutors; "communicators/interpreters" on TV; "scholars/interpreters", turning research into teaching material, and "assemblers" packaging this material into products; all working in teams, on the model set in the 1960s by the UK's Open University. Healthcare will be similarly transformed, forcing physicians, consultants and nurses to learn new roles.

One group of applications is in no doubt at all in the media, where the digital-fibre optic revolution will generate virtually unlimited capacity to send moving images into a computerised box in the home, whether TV or PC and interactive broadcasting in the future. We can already see the revolution described by MIT professor Nicholas Negroponte in his book *Being Digital*: "broadcasting" is being replaced by "broadcatching" whereby everyone picks what they want from cables full of digital information (Negroponte, 1999). There is however, a third and extremely relevant clue to the nature of the new industries that will form the foundation of the new economy. This is the application of scientific research and development to meet the challenge of global warming by the development of new renewable energy sources. Here, Germany and its cities provide the classic case study.

At the start of the 1990s, it was one of the first countries to present a national timetable for reducing carbon dioxide. It fully signed up to the Kyoto treaty, with a pledge to cut emissions of key greenhouse gases by 21 per cent by 2012; in fact it had already achieved 18 per cent by last year. (The UK, it should be said, has done it as well.) At the March 2007 EU summit, it persuaded the 27 members to cut CO_2 emissions by 20 per cent by 2020, by increasing energy efficiency by 20 per cent and raising the role of renewable energy by 20 per cent: the "3 times 20" formula. But Germany has pledged to do much better: a 40 per cent cut, from 880 million tones to 270 million tonnes.

For Germany, this is a win-win formula. Historically, the country's economic development came somewhat late, after unification in 1871, and was based on applying top-quality scientific research to what were the high-technology industries of their day: electrical and electronic goods, optical products like microscopes and cameras, chemicals, cars — many of which goods, like the motor car, they actually invented. *Vorsprung durch Technik*, the line that Audi so successfully used in their advertising in the 1990s, could have been a national slogan. After 1945, Germany lost the leadership in technological innovation to the United States and Japan. But companies like Siemens or Jena or Mercedes remained much stronger than their British equivalents, and the German economy has retained a much bigger element of advanced manufacturing than those of other advanced economies.

Now, Germany sees a real prospect of achieving global technological leadership in new industries again, creating yet another industrial revolution. This time, the great economic driver will be environmental technologies: solar power, wind and wave power, energy conservation techniques. Germany's Renewable Energies Act came into force seven years ago and has triggered a frenetic response: already, 12 per cent of all the electricity consumed in Germany comes from wind, solar and water power. The government is backing the drive with three billion euros of additional spending over the next three years.

The result, to quote Burkhard Schwenker of Roland Berger Energy Consultants, is that "Germany is rapidly assuming the role of world leader in this field". On behalf of the Germany Federal Government, these consultants interviewed almost 1,500 German environmental technology companies and evaluated a number of other studies in order to compile an eco-atlas of Germany that was officially published at the European Union's environmental summit in June 2007. They conclude that energy and ecology-related occupations are becoming Germany's number-one job engine. His colleague Torsten Henzelmann says that "By 2020, this sector will be employing more people than mechanical engineering or the automotive industry". He calls it "the boom sector of the 21st century".

Companies' order books are full, boosted by the Federal Government's target to cut greenhouse gas emissions by 40 per cent by 2020. This year, the German Renewable Energy Federation (BEE) expects turnover to grow by 17 per cent compared to 2006 to a grand total of 32 billion euros. At the same time, 15,000 new jobs are planned in Germany this year. According to the BEE, approximately 214,000 people were already employed in the industry in 2006. A study conducted by the Federal Ministry for the Environment projects that 150,000 new jobs will be created by 2020. The background is that German companies are already market leaders and are now benefiting from the increasing global demand for clean and innovative energy technologies.

Burkhard Schwenker forecasts that by 2030, green industries could be generating a turnover of one trillion euros. And he cites the areas where

Germany has already attained the lead: it has the largest installed wind power input, has the most modern power station technology, and leads the world in the output of efficient household devices. Germany produces one third of all the solar cells and almost a half of all the wind turbines in the entire world. Renewable energy exports rose to six billion euros in 2006: a 30 per cent increase on the previous year.

The export potential is huge. Already, Germany is systematically promoting sustainable energy in the developing world: solar energy in China, wind power in Egypt and Morocco, hydro in Indonesia, biomass in Nepal, geothermal in Kenya. This kind of deal, long pioneered by France in areas like transport technology (TGVs in Korea and Taiwan as well as the UK and Spain), makes huge economic sense: once a technology is perfected, it can be confidently sold in the certainty that it will work without hitches the first time (the Channel Tunnel Rail Link), and that each iteration will generate progressive economies of scale.

All this is creating a huge demand for new qualified workers: engineers, mechanical engineers, chemists, physicists and project developers. They have to be produced, and the German government is busy at work on the issue. Sigmar Gabriel, Federal Minister for the Environment, launched a training initiative: *Umwelt schafft Perspektiven* (The Environment Creates Prospects) last year. It too has been a success: companies and employers' associations have already promised 5,100 new training places. Many universities and colleges already offer special programmes or options in this area within their courses. For example, degree courses in mechanical engineering often allow students to concentrate or specialise in fields such as renewable energy and materials technology, energy supply and renewable energies for power generation. Similarly, traditional courses in electrical engineering and information technology now frequently offer specialisations in renewable energies and electrical energy systems. Universities and colleges offer further subdivisions such as technical building services, energy plant technology, power engineering, environmental technology and wind energy technology. In addition, there are numerous further training courses on offer, such as a solar or energy consultant. The degree courses are modular in structure and usually last seven semesters. They are very practice-oriented: and practical work — experience within a company is usually part of the main study programme.

The German government recently completed an evaluation of their 4th energy research programme, covering the period 1996 to 2005, in the field of renewable energy. They conclude that Germany has the most successful research promotion in the field of photovoltaics, is second only to Denmark in wind energy, and comes in joint top position with Austria in low temperature solar power research.

This underlines a rare historic irony: Germany's original rise to world economic power in the 1880s and 1890s was based on its ambition to rival the UK and France and Russia as a global military power. The fairly direct result, in 1914, was World War One. The indirect result, following the fiasco of the Versailles treaty and the rise of Hitler, was World War Two. Now, one could fairly say, we are witnessing the beginnings of World War Three. But this is a war like no other: it is a war of humanity itself, in a desperate struggle to save the world it inhabits.

IMPLICATIONS FOR CITIES

What are the implications for the location of the economic activities that will form the core of the new knowledge economy? One point is certain: reports of the death of the city have been much exaggerated. We sometimes hear the argument that cities have no future at all. Frances Cairncross has predicted the "Death of Distance": a world in which the traditional distance-deterrence effects, embodied in every locational model, diminish to zero and the entire world becomes a frictionless plain on which everyone will be free to locate in the place that best suits their personal preferences and whims, intercommunicating freely and at uniform cost with every other person in the world (Cairncross, 1997). Yet although telecommunications costs have fallen spectacularly and the internet is almost frictionless, it is surely significant that the leading cyber-gurus have finally rejected this hypothesis.

In fact, significantly, some of the key locations for the new industries are the cities: Los Angeles, San Francisco, New York City and London. That is because the development of new ideas demands serendipity and synergy between minds, and it is easier to find this in great cities. It is also because there is a special relationship between multimedia and other activities that have always been clustered in great cities: the media, including the live performing arts, advertising and public relations, and tourism.

As many civic leaders have found to their cost, cities, at least in the developed world, are no longer locations for mass-production manufacturing: they are places for high-technology R&D and prototype production, creative and cultural industries of all kinds from theatres and museums to publishing and broadcasting, tourism, for command and control functions in government and transnational corporations, and specialised finance and business services. In all these, creativity plays a crucial role: witness the innovations in the financial sector in the 1980s, such as securitisation and corporate bonds, and the role they have played in hugely extending the total volume of business.

The evidence shows that although telecommunications substitute for personal movement, they can complement and stimulate it. It was immediately after the invention of the telephone, in 1876, that we saw concentrations of high-rise business offices in the centres of New York City and Chicago; and evidence from France suggests that over a period of more than a century, roughly since the spread of the electric telegraph and the invention of the telephone, personal business traffic has grown at almost exactly the same pace as telecommunications traffic (Graham and Marvin, 1996). Consider the growth of personal business traffic by air and rail, and the development of the conference/convention industry: they strongly suggest that the more telecommunication we have, the more it will be followed by face-to-face meetings. The fundamental reason is that the advanced business services — financial and business services, command and control functions, creative and cultural services, and tourism — which are the real drivers of the new knowledge economy, depend vitally on information exchange, often with a very high degree of immediacy. The investment analyst trading shares, the lawyer offering advice, the board of a major corporation in a meeting, the television producer at work on a show, or the tour guide taking a group sightseeing all imply specialised information to be processed and transmitted by highly qualified people in real time. Further, much of this activity involves face-to-face exchange of information, either as a central feature or as an essential ancillary (as when the stock analyst has lunch and picks up important market information). These activities are highly synergistic: hotels, conference and exhibition centres are simultaneously business services and a part of tourism. Museums and galleries are creative/cultural but also parts of tourism. Advertising is both creative and a business service. For this reason, not only does each of the sectors have strong agglomerative trends set by the need to process and exchange information, but there are also strong agglomerative forces between the four main service sectors.

So communications — a major international airport hub, a key interchange on the fast-spreading high-speed rail systems of Japan and Europe, top quality telecommunications — are a must. But there is another key requirement: quality of urban life. Just as cities had to guarantee pure water and sewerage systems a century ago, they now compete to make their cities attractive to visit and to live and work in. Urban innovation matters as much as it did when city engineers were struggling with problems of pure water and sewage disposal.

In this scheme, there are no fixed rules: cities can lever themselves up or fall down. In particular, they can achieve several objectives simultaneously with the right kind of policies. They can clear the ruins of the lost industrial economy, provide new flagship buildings to act as symbols of an urban renaissance, and create a high-quality urban ambience for visitors and residents. Barcelona, Bilbao and Glasgow in Europe, San Diego and Seattle and Toronto in North America, are classic illustrations.

Of course, urban quality does not guarantee creative genius. Nobel Prizes can and do come out of slum laboratories, and great undiscovered artists will always languish in garrets. Increasingly however, universities build laboratories to retain and attract international star scientists, while the garrets of the starving artists soon become immensely fashionable and expensive. Creativity is no longer an incidental miracle that happens occasionally in exceptionally favoured cities; in a globalised economy where no place can rest on its laurels for long, it is now a central part of the business of being a successful city. This is a principle that no city can ignore.

THE CITY OF URBAN INNOVATION

It is for this reason that we now come to the second of the two basic requirements I outlined at the beginning, and to yet a fourth kind of innovation. Cities must promote "urban innovations" that will improve the quality of life in their cities and make them models of sustainable urban living. These are subtly different in kind from the three varieties so far considered. They consist of cities attempting, generally through public administration but also through private enterprise, to solve the emerging problems caused by their own growth: water supply and waste disposal, traffic and transport, police and criminal justice, provision for the poor and destitute. None of these problems is unique to large cities. The point is that in such large cities, roughly those with one million and more people, they attain a new dimension of complexity: local wells and cesspits no longer suffice, people have to move over long distances, crime can no longer be handled by informal means, destitution can no longer be managed within the extended family. In every case, cities have to respond through organisational innovation, and often through technological innovation as well. So the places that make urban innovations are usually the biggest and most complex places of their time: cities like ancient Rome, London or Paris in the 19th century, or New York in the early 20th century and Los Angeles at the mid-century, or London again in the 1980s; though we can legitimately include a much smaller city like Stockholm or indeed Helsinki, that made important urban social innovations after World War Two.

Such cities make urban innovations because they have to (though not all cities that need to succeed in doing so, as 20th century history plainly shows). This means that they have reached a certain threshold of size and complexity. Rome, London, Paris and New York were among the three biggest cities of the world when they first made urban innovations; with the exception of Rome (estimated at 650,000 in 100 A.D.), London (861,000 in 1801) and Stockholm (889,000 people in 1950). All had one million or more people within their city boundaries. Los Angeles, however, was the 27th city in 1925 and Stockholm the 80th in 1950, so rank or size in itself is no guarantee of innovative power.

What may matter more is the speed of growth. London had doubled in size in the century before 1800, Paris had grown by two and a half times in the century before 1850; New York had doubled in the quarter century before 1900 (albeit with a major boundary change) and Los Angeles grew 10 times in the first quarter of the 20th century. Such cities had to cope quite suddenly with a drastic increase in the scale and complexity of urban organisation. They had the capacity to do so, because all were in countries that were highly evolved economically and technically. Further, because they were well networked both nationally and internationally, there were only minor barriers to importing knowledge from other places. Knowledge of urban innovations like water aqueducts, collector sewers, streetcars, subways and motorways all diffused very rapidly, though there were significant differences in the rate of takeup from city to city; European cities, in particular, were relatively slow in absorbing technological and transport improvements like the telephone, the electric streetcar and the urban motorway.

Demographic growth often went hand in hand with economic growth, if only because aggregate growth was almost bound to increase in line with population. That meant buoyant demand for new services and a supply of surplus capital to fund infrastructure, whether out of municipal coffers or out of private pockets. There seems to be a relationship between urban innovation and long waves of economic growth: London was highly innovative at the start of the second Kondratieff long wave (1842–97), New York and Los Angeles at the start of the third (1897–1954), Stockholm at the start of the third (1954–); Paris fits less well, though its major urban investments were all made before the crash of 1873. Further, such periods of growth by definition brought the immigration of talented and energetic individuals, some of whom at least were major agents: Edwin Chadwick, architect of many of the London reforms, was a Mancunian by birth, Harry Chandler in Los Angeles was an Easterner, though other key players — like Haussmann in Paris and Veiller in New York — were native-born sons of their cities.

There is however a basic distinction: Rome, London and Paris were unambiguously at the centres of their respective worlds. New York was the emerging commercial centre of the most dynamic part of the world of 1900. Los Angeles in 1925, as already remarked in discussing Hollywood, was by any measure at the edge of the American urban system; and Stockholm was a relatively small city at the periphery of the European system. Los Angeles, a city that combined political conservatism with maverick capitalism and eccentric philosophies, seems to have been a very special case, a frontier city that had thrown off most of the trammels of older cultures. Stockholm may have been an equally special case, a Protestant society in the course of secularisation, in which particular ideas of social responsibility developed as a response to the depression of the 1930s.

Finally, London represents an equally specific development: its regeneration in the 1980s represented the quintessence of the Thatcherite vision in an urban context, and that vision represented a kind of cultural counter-revolution, a systematic attempt to demolish the established institutions of British life and to replace them by a return to unfettered entrepreneurial capitalism. Equally however, the Docklands enterprise represented the idea that property development in itself could equate with substantive economic regeneration, as if one would axiomatically produce the other. This was an assumption that many were to question, especially after the great crash at the end of the 1980s. Wrong or right or partially right, this view is consistent with the Thatcherite notion that Britain as a manufacturing economy was largely finished and that the aim was to rebuild a new service economy on the ruins of the old. This belief, never as consistently expressed as in Britain, nevertheless formed a belief underlying much radical right rethinking, worldwide, in the 1980s.

We can conclude that, while earlier urban innovations were directly driven by hard physical problems and had an element of the inevitable, more recently, innovation has come from a variety of far more specific conditions. Nevertheless, it remains a fact that once made, innovations tend to provide some kind of model to the rest of the world. Stockholm in the 1950s became the model of the socially-conscious city. Los Angeles in the 1960s came to be seen as model of a new kind of urban society, one based on style and mobility and hedonistic conspicuous consumption; London in the 1980s, even while it repelled some observers, became almost a television soap opera parody of itself, the city driven by creation of new forms of wealth and power against a background of a new high-tech urban landscape. All these urban images have powerfully persisted even while the attempts at imitation have often collapsed in failure and recrimination perhaps because urban archetypes do not lend themselves so easily to imitation.

The need however — as with the other kinds of innovation — consists in trying to identify what kinds of urban innovation, what kinds of resulting city, will most effectively provide a physical and social environment in order to foster the kinds of creativity that will prove most significant in the new knowledge economy. I believe that we can answer this by looking at cities worldwide, and asking what kinds of cities seem to be most effective at attracting talented and creative people to live and work in them.

It soon emerges that such cities are in fact quite varied in their past histories and their present potential. The first category is the *established metropolis*: leading older cities that have maintained their position as outstanding centres of both artistic production and consumption, like London, Paris or New York. They succeed simply because of their historic endowment of human and social capital. They have long been leading centres of consumption for theatre, music and the graphic arts. Partly because of this, they continue to attract creative people who live at the margins, as they always have. To this select group we can add a second category which we can call *sunbelt cities*: newer and emerging cities in new world locations like Los Angeles, San Francisco, Vancouver, Sydney, Auckland or Cape Town. These attract migrants because of their physical qualities — waterside location, mountains, climate — and resulting lifestyle. They are often major university cities and have strong local concentrations of cultural facilities. They are in effect commercial and cultural capitals for wide hinterlands around them. All this makes them attractive as alternative destinations for creative individuals who cannot or will not make the long migration to the older more established cities.

There is now a third category, the most interesting of all: *the city undergoing urban renaissance*. This is an older industrial or port city, usually the biggest city in its region that has recently suffered from decline of traditional manufacturing or port functions. Manchester, Glasgow, Barcelona, Bilbao and Baltimore are prime examples. All have regenerated themselves through intelligent investment in new cultural artefacts which in turn have helped generate urban tourism: museums, art galleries, concert halls, conference centres. Since they are also strong university cities, they attract young people, some of whom remain after completing their education because they have put down roots and find the city an attractive place in which to live. They have often invested considerable amounts in improving their physical environment, especially in and around their city centres and in neighbouring waterfront areas, so that they can consciously compete in life quality and lifestyle with larger longer-established cultural cities. In consequence, these are some of the most interesting cities in the world today, simply because they have been so successful in rapidly shedding their 19th century industrial image and replacing it with a 21st century cultural image.

All this indicates that traditional advantages and disadvantages are no longer fixed and unchanging. Cities can literally remake and remarket themselves. Perhaps not every city can do this: to achieve the change, a city must have certain necessary prerequisites — a certain size and scale, a previous history of cultural achievement and a strong university infrastructure. Yet many cities worldwide are not perhaps achieving all that they are capable of achieving.

Most important of all, history shows that achieving true eminence as a city of culture is not something that can be achieved instantly, or even in a few years. It is a long process taking decades or even centuries. Certainly, a city can open a new art gallery or concert hall and thus achieve instant fame as an attractive tourist centre. That, however, means the creation of a pure city of cultural consumption, which is not the same thing at all as building a truly creative city, a city of cultural *production*.

Maybe an initiative like that of Barcelona, which in the summer of 2004 held what it called a cultural Olympic Games — a five-month, 141-day series of seminars and cultural events, attracting over three million visitors directly and perhaps as many again indirectly — provides a possible model. The question has to be what permanent legacy will remain. I do not, mean physical legacy — there is a high-quality convention centre which will bring continuing year-long business tourism to Barcelona — but the deeper cultural legacy. The right strategy must be to build a physical infrastructure for cultural production, in the form of educational and training facilities at the same time as the centres for consumption, side by side, as they are now trying to do at Gateshead in Northern England with the new Baltic Centre for the visual arts and the nearby Sage Centre for music. Yet, we should not expect that as a result Gateshead will turn itself immediately into a new Paris or a new Florence. It could take a long time and it might not happen at all. Meanwhile, places for consuming art can be pleasant places in which to live and work, and may even be the way to attract new life, and new work, of other kinds into the city. Cultural strategies can thus become just one part of a multi-pronged approach to urban regeneration. For many cities faced with the challenge of economic transformation, that will prove the most successful strategy. The new model of the creative city remains of great significance as cities throughout the world — established global cities,

emergent cities, cities in the developed and developing countries alike —
seek to remake themselves by understanding and applying new economic
paradigm.

REFERENCES

Cairncross, F (1997). *The Death of Distance: How the Communications Revolution will Change Our Lives*. London: Orion.

Castells, M (1989). *The Informational City: Information Technology, Economic Restructuring and the Urban-Regional Process*. Oxford: Basil Blackwell.

Castells, M (1996). *The Information Age: Economy, Society, and Culture*. Vol. I, *The Rise of the Network Society*. Oxford: Blackwell.

Graham, S and S Marvin (1996). *Telecommunications and the City: Electronic Spaces, Urban Places*. London: Routledge.

Hall, P (1998). *Cities in Civilization*. London: Weidenfeld and Nicolson.

Keynes, JM (1972 [1930]). Economic possibilities for our grandchildren. In *The Collected Writings, Vol. IX: Essays in Persuasion*, London: Macmillan, 321–332.

Mitchell, WJ (1995). *City of Bits: Space, Place, and the Infobahn*. Cambridge, Mass.: MIT Press.

Negroponte, N (1995). *Being Digital*. London: Hodder & Stoughton.

Taine, H [1926 (1865)]. *Philosophie de l'Art*. 20th Edition. 2 Vols. Paris: Hachette.

Törnqvist, G (1983). Creativity and the renewal of regional life. In Buttimer, A (ed.), *Creativity and Context: A Seminar Report* (*Lund Studies in Geography. B. Human Geography, No. 50*), Lund: Gleerup, 91–112.

Integrated Sustainable Waste Management

ANNE SCHEINBERG*

The World Cities Summit in Singapore in June 2008, provided a large group of international urban management professionals with a forum for exchanging information and ideas about good practice in their specific fields. The session on solid waste was no exception, about 50 solid waste experts attended the meeting and listened to four different, but complementary presentations. In this chapter, we use two key concepts, the concept of Integrated Sustainable Waste Management, and the concept of modernisation, to frame the presentations and summarise their contributions.

UNDERSTANDING ISWM[1]

Integrated Sustainable Waste Management (ISWM), as shown in Figure 1, is a framework for understanding solid waste management. It was developed in the mid-1980s by WASTE, a Dutch Non-Governmental Organisation (NGO), and WASTE's South partner organisations. It is a systems approach for understanding the who, what, why and how of solid waste management

---

*Corresponding author. Email: ascheinberg@waste.nl; office@waste.nl. Website: www.waste.nl

[1] Text in these sections first developed for the 2008 VNG International — WASTE publication: *Closing the Circle, bringing integrated sustainable waste management home.* Copyright VNG International and WASTE, used by permission.

Fig. 1   The integrated sustainable waste management (ISWM) framework

Source: Scheinberg and IJgosse, 2004, based on Klundert and Lardinois, 1995.

and change. It has been used in many programmes for improving waste management in low- and middle-income countries. ISWM frames and supports good practice and the inclusion of all stakeholders in planning and decision-making. The ISWM framework recognises three important dimensions in waste management — stakeholders, waste system elements and sustainability aspects.

The 'integrated' in ISWM reflects that solid waste management consists of a variety of activities, including prevention, recycling and composting, being operated by a variety of actors at many scales. 'Integrated' also refers to the linkages between system elements, and suggests that not only technical, but also legal, institutional and economic linkages are necessary to allow the system to function. In ISWM, the choices made about set-out, storage, collection and transportation are interdependent with the frequency and timing of collection, as well as with routing and choice of vehicles and the relationship between primary and secondary collection. For example, many public works departments assume that, in tropical countries, it is necessary to collect waste every day. Even in hot climates, with appropriate containers for the volume and type of waste, this can often be reduced to two or three times per week, and sometimes, in combination with separation of organic waste, to once a week or less. This makes collection more affordable, while maintaining an acceptable hygiene standard, especially for low-income areas.

A 'sustainable' system in ISWM is robust and can continue without collapsing. Sustainability, as explained below, is considered to include operational, financial, social, institutional, political, legal and environmental aspects.

Stakeholders, the first of the ISWM dimensions and listed in the box in the upper third of the ISWM 'egg' shown in Figure 1, are people or organisations with a *stake*, or interest, in waste management. In most pre-modern urban waste systems, such as those in the US in the 1980s, or in the Netherlands, Germany, and Denmark in the 1970s, and in many OECD countries today, the main 'recognised' stakeholders include the local authority (mayor, city council, solid waste department), the national environment or local government ministry, and one or two private companies working under contract to the municipality. But in the developing (South) and transitional (Eastern European or emerging) cities, there are literally thousands of others living from, working with, and affected by waste management. In ISWM, these are referred to as 'unrecognised stakeholders.' Stakeholders can be male or female and, in some cases, different sexes have different stakes. Unrecognised stakeholders may include (female) street sweepers, (male) workers on collection trucks, dumpsite scavengers or 'waste pickers', some of whom may actually live on or at the edge of the dumpsite, and family-based businesses that live from recycling.

In addition, micro- and small recycling businesses (usually called 'junk shops') buy materials that have been extracted from waste containers, collected from households or bought from businesses. They sell these to medium and large recyclers, called 'dealers' or 'intermediate processors,' who, in turn, sell them to end-user industries. Industrial waste generators, households, institutions such as hospitals and schools, and government facilities like airports or post offices are also solid waste stakeholders, although they would not normally see themselves as such.

The second ISWM dimension is the waste system elements. These are the technical components of waste management. Part of the purpose of using the ISWM framework is to show that these technical components are *part of*, not all of the overall picture. In Figure 1, the boxes in the top row all relate to removal and safe disposal, and the bottom row of boxes relate to 'valorisation' (recycling, recovery) of commodities. This distinction is important for understanding how waste management and recycling work in practice.

The elements represented in the central part of the ISWM diagram become institutionalised in a management 'hierarchy', giving priority to waste prevention and recovery, shifting the destination of materials away from land disposal to formal and informal re-use, recycling and composting (Scheinberg, 2003). The principles of the solid waste management hierarchy, shown in Figure 2, were developed in the Netherlands and incorporated in Dutch legislation in the late 1970s and early 1980s in the early phase of modernisation. Today, they form an integral basis for the solid waste policy of the European Union.

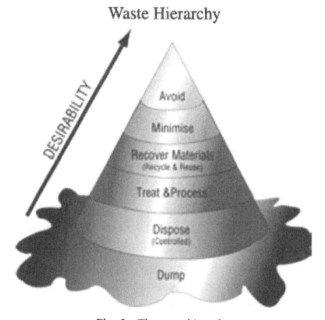

Fig. 2   The waste hierarchy

MODERNISATION OF WASTE MANAGEMENT, A SHORT ORIENTATION

Development co-operation programmes tend to assume that changes or improvements come about as a result of the *development intervention* — a project, programme focus or activities. In this chapter, the term '*modernisation*' is used instead to indicate a process which is under way in most countries in the world, even when there is no development co-operation or donor activity. 'Modernisation' of the solid waste sector is a global process, in line with the gradually increasing understanding of the negative environmental consequences of poorly managed waste. The most obvious aspects of modernisation relate to changing standards for dumping and landfill, based on increasing prioritisation accorded to environmental protection, and a political commitment to reducing water pollution related to the dumping of waste.

In Northern countries, the process of modernisation has been mainly driven by internal political events and has occurred gradually, as shown in Case Example 1. In countries of the global South, where solid waste competes with more urgent issues of water, sanitation, disease control, transport and housing for budgetary and professional attention, modernisation may take place after a period in which solid waste is pushed to the bottom of the priority list. There is a general tendency for local authorities to solve water and sanitation and housing problems first, and only then to turn their attention to upgrading and modernising solid waste facilities.

Modernisation really starts when there is a health or environmental crisis, or a push to clean up the city for economic or political reasons such as in Nairobi where, in 2000, economic and political pressures led to a push to close a central city dumpsite, so that the land could be used for housing. An essential feature of solid waste crises is that they both challenge and reinforce cultural ideas that waste is essentially unseen and also slightly shameful, 'private' or 'dirty,' and even a source of spiritual contamination in some cultures. This means that having a rational conversation about waste can be difficult, and also that those working with waste have low social status and little influence.

In the South, external drivers, such as donor interest or the opportunity to participate in city twinning or other international programmes, rather

Case Example 1: The AOO and modernisation of solid waste management in the Netherlands

In the 1980s, in the Netherlands, there was a great deal of pressure on municipalities to modernise their waste management systems. The direct driver was the goals for recycling decided upon in the National Environmental Plan (NMP) which meant that 50 per cent of municipal waste should be recycled by 2000. More importantly, waste had to be diverted from landfill, as the NMP included a target of landfilling no more than 3 per cent of the municipal waste by 2012. The recycling and (energy) recovery goals derived from this intital objective. The Ministry of Housing, Land Use Planning and Environment (VROM) initiated a platform, called the Waste Management Consultation Council (AOO), and financed its staff. This platform provided an institutional place for municipalities to discuss their ideas, problems and experiences, and to share these with the national policy-makers and regulators. The AOO operated from 1986 to 2004, when it was merged with Senter Novem, a regulatory agency financed by the Dutch government. The official ending of the AOO was a form of acknowledgement that the period of modernisation was coming to an end, and an implicit claim that the main policy work was done. Indeed, most Dutch waste stakeholders do consider the Dutch system to be complete, and mature, except for its response to new materials or new developments in EU law.

Source: Scheinberg and IJgosse, 2004 and experience of the authors.

than a crisis, can also stimulate the modernisation process. This can delay or hinder the commitment of political authorities to integrate planning and solid waste operations into municipal functioning. In most cases, it is usually not the crisis or the driver itself, but the political story about the crisis (the so-called 'crisis narrative') that sets the modernisation process in motion.

Modernisation changes the 'problematisation' of waste. Before modernisation, the presence of waste and the difficulties in removing it are seen as the main problems; during and after modernisation this changes to an understanding that the generation of waste, the overuse of materials and resources, and the impacts of waste on the environment are the important problems. Prevention, recycling and composting become priorities in waste management during modernisation, which usually includes the following developments:

1. Closing of local landfills and regionalisation of the disposal function (which is in itself a complex process, involving new stakeholders and institutional agreements).
2. A shift in institutional responsibility, so that, for the first time, supra-municipal entities have a role in solid waste management and are required to develop and manage regionalised disposal.
3. A rapid upward spiral in solid waste costs, due to (a) a large and sudden increase in costs of collection and the introduction of tipping fees, and (b) increased transfer and transport costs related to the regionalisation of disposal.
4. Strong pressures for the largely public municipal waste and public service sector to expand its activities to include recycling, composting and recovery activities, which previously were entirely under the micro-, small-, and medium-sized private recycling sector.
5. Prohibition and/or criminalisation of traditional solid waste practices, especially those relating to informal recovery at landfills.

The result of most modernisation processes is an 'integrated' system, following the hierarchy. In most cases, the integrated system includes more of the elements in the middle bar of Figure 1, above, and includes source separation, repair and re-use, collection, processing, composting, transfer, marketing of materials recovered from waste, and land or thermal disposal of the residues. Regionalisation changes power structures and implies shifts in responsibility, accountability and inter-municipal arrangements. In the Netherlands, Singapore, and in many developed countries, there is national legislation that governs this process, and the hierarchy is broadly accepted and depoliticised. In many South countries, in contrast, the push to diversify the elements of solid waste management may cause conflicts and tensions. National government policies and international trends and ideas about sound practice also push the modernisation agenda.

The ideas about integration originate from a global set of ideas about good practices in solid waste management. To understand the global nature of the modernisation process, as it affects municipalities in the South, we make a small detour to orient the reader to key points, which also help in understanding the presentations.

SERVICES AND COMMODITIES IN INTEGRATED SUSTAINABLE WASTE MANAGEMENT

In understanding change in the solid waste sector, both in the South and in the North, two concepts are critical:

1. providing solid waste *services*
2. trading recyclable *commodities*

Solid Waste Services: A Core Public Sector Activity in ISWM

Solid waste *services* are about the removal of waste or other undesired materials from their point of generation to a site — usually far away — where they are burned, buried or stored. Services are traditionally a public sector activity; and removal and disposal are considered a public responsibility. Various forms of removal are included in the 'core business' of solid waste service *providers*:

1. street sweeping *removes* litter from streets
2. waste collection *removes* household or industrial waste
3. drain clean-outs *remove* litter and organic materials from gutters, drains and ditches
4. green space maintenance *removes* branches and litter
5. sewer and latrine emptying are forms of human waste (excreta) *removal*

For removal to be effective, it requires a place to remove the waste to, a means of transport, institutions for organising the removal, and systems for covering costs and distributing benefits.

Most solid waste crises (including the one in Naples, Italy, at the time of the City Summit in June, 2008) are failures of *removal*. Either there is a lack of dumping capacity; or the existing landfills are closing; or the waste is not removed well or on time; or it is not transported efficiently or effectively; or the place it is removed to is not accessible, safe, or sufficiently removed from dwellings and businesses; or the neighbours living near the disposal site protest against the waste being or coming there, or there is contact between the waste and soil, air (through burning) or water which releases the 'removed' materials to the natural environment. Failures of removal cause water or air pollution, soil contamination, sickness or death of people, plants or livestock, and other environmental and health problems.

Commodities Trading: The Private Side of ISWM

The other aspect of solid waste management is about *commodities*. Valorisation (in Europe) or recovery (in North America) means claiming resources from the waste stream, upgrading and selling them. Effective recycling or organic recovery activities are based on capturing the value that remains in waste materials, preparing the materials for new use as an industrial or agricultural input, and selling the materials, so that they can be used to make new products.

Recycling is a private sector industrial activity which is globally organised. Prices and standards are set on the global level and applied by local private businesses in the *recycling supply chain*. The businesses in this chain are some of the most intensely private enterprises in the world. Before modernisation, recycling only occurs when the commercial value of the recycled materials covers the cost of extracting them from the waste stream. It is a private source of personal or business income. When modernisation raises the price of disposal, municipalities often become interested in recycling or composting because it (a) can reduce the amount of materials to be disposed of, and so lower their overall disposal costs; or (b) they think it will provide sufficient income to finance the rising cost of solid waste management.

While both of these are partly true, (a) is a win-win situation, whereas there are some difficulties with (b) since only a few municipalities know how to manage materials in a way that they are able to earn money in a competitive global marketplace. Further, the existing private recycling activities usually focus on the more valuable materials, specifically ferrous and non-ferrous metals and the more valuable grades of paper, as shown in Box 1. If the municipality wants to recycle these materials, it has to force private businesses out, and this usually creates a problem for the solid waste informal sector — the tiny, often family-based, businesses at the bottom of the recycling supply chain. There are millions of people doing this type of work: 40,000 in Cairo; 17,000 in Lima and at least several hundreds and sometimes even thousands in most small cities.

Box 1. Six levels of value-added in recycling paper

Paper is a manufactured surface for writing, and the highest conserved value-add is when it is re-used for the same purpose. When a sheet of paper is used on one side, the other side can be reclaimed and reused for writing something else. This is the first level. The second level is as a packing material, or in many societies (including in the Netherlands until quite recently) as toilet paper in emergencies. When there is no empty or unused writing surface left, the physical nature of paper still allows it to be used as a surface protector for other items, or as a filler. When paper is wet or dirty and no longer usable as paper, the wood fibres that hold it together can still be recovered and used as raw materials for new paper. Long fibres are thus a third level of value-added. When fibres are broken or short, they can be used as a fourth level material in certain low-grade forms of cardboard which do not require tensile strength, called 'boxboard' or 'corrugating medium'. The fifth level is used as a carbon source in composting, and the sixth level is that the carbon can be burned for heat and energy, or the resulting charcoal, ash.

RECOVERING ORGANIC WASTES, A HYBRID OF SERVICES AND COMMODITIES

There is a significant difference between *recycling* industrial materials and *recovering* organic materials as compost: recovery of organic wastes is highly localised. In some places, for example in West Africa, household waste consists largely of dirt floor sweepings, food wastes and excreta, and is itself a commodity that farmers are willing to pay for. In other places, organic waste can be recovered through separate collection and composting. An example is the situation in the Netherlands. In East Asia and Latin America, organic materials are collected as feeds to swine. India is one of the few countries where the informal sector is involved in composting; in other countries, compost is used but (prior to modernisation) it is not usually a marketable commodity. If there is interest in large-scale composting, the government usually has to be willing to use the compost in public places such as parks, cemeteries and green spaces; and in the process it 'creates a market' for the compost. When modernisation makes disposal more expensive; composting can be an attractive, lower-cost 'removal' option.

MODERNISATION, A "MARRIAGE" OF SERVICES AND COMMODITIES

Modernisation has one predictable effect everywhere in the world. When solid waste services are modernised, the public authorities become interested in recycling, and the private recycling sector has to, and will, respond. In this way, modernisation pushes — even forces — these two systems, with different rules and different cultures, to integrate with, or 'marry', each other. In rapidly growing countries like Singapore, the combination of scarce landfilling and global good practices, as well as standards have pushed this development but, in all cases of modernisation, this has become an issue.

When municipalities begin to investigate recycling, it is useful to first understand the existing recycling system, and then have the municipality target those materials not already being recycled to see whether it is worthwhile to target them in a municipal programme.

Prices, Costs and Expenditures in Commodity Activities: Is Recycling a Source of Financing for Solid Waste Management?

From a solid waste system perspective, the main value of recycling, composting and other commodity-based activities is the reduction in the amount that needs to be moved to a dump, landfill, or that is 'lost' and ends up in nature. Recycling is complicated and should not be seen as an easy way for municipalities to earn money from solid waste: not all materials are recyclable, and even some that are recyclable, cost more to recycle than they are worth. Table 1 presents a classification of recyclable materials according to their commodity, or economic, value. The handling of and the potential for recovery of these materials also changes quite substantially during and after modernisation. This information is highly relevant in combined planning and decision-making in the modernisation process.

Table 1 Understanding values of different types of materials in recycling

Type	Examples, incidence in waste	Pre-modernisation approach	Economic value	Modernised valorisation strategy
Type 1: high intrinsic value, globally traded commodities	High grades of waste paper, aluminium UBC, ferrous and other non-ferrous metals, approximately 10 to 15 per cent of household waste. In recent years, also PET (to China).	Recycled by individuals or enterprises through private initiatives and very rarely end up at dumping sites, except in extreme circumstances such as the global paper market crash at the end of the 1980s.	Price paid for the materials covers or exceeds the cost of labour and equipment involved in extracting or collecting them.	Prepare waste materials according to the specifications of the (potential) buyer in the recycling supply chain. Store them until there is a sufficient quantity to sell, then transport them and sell them.
Type 2: moderate intrinsic commodity value, locally traded commodities	Glass, tin, steel cans, rubber, non-PET polyolefines (PP, LDPE, HDPE), textiles, low-grade paper. Total is about 10–15 per cent of household waste.	Recycled by private enterprises only when there are local markets or a temporary shortage raises the price.	Have some value but not enough to cover the cost of extraction, processing and marketing. Recycling is not 'profitable,' or even able to cover costs on its own.	When the cost of disposing of materials reaches the local cost to collect and recycle, usually between €15 and €25 per tonne, recycling of these materials becomes less expensive than disposal, and it is worthwhile to cross-subsidise this with the so-called 'avoided cost of disposal'.

(Continued)

Type	Examples, incidence in waste	Pre-modernisation approach	Economic value	Modernised valorisation strategy
Type 3: non-commodity materials with local options for 'beneficial reuse', subject to 'market development'	Kitchen, garden and small livestock waste for composting (approximately 40 per cent of household waste); mixed waste with high organic content combined with high-density floor sweepings (as found in some West African countries approximately 60 per cent of household waste).	Small-scale private arrangements for removal by swine farmer, or by cultivators who use the waste in composting, or as a soil conditioner, with or without payments to generator or to remover.	Not a commodity, and so no intrinsic commodity value, but with some use value and some environmental value. May depend on willingness of government to 'purchase' compost for public uses: cemeteries, parks, sports fields, mine reclamation, erosion control, landfill cover and highways.	When the cost to dispose of materials (legally, for example, in a dumpsite or landfill) rises clearly above €40 per tonne, separate management of organic waste and compost recovery avoids the high cost of disposal, and this so-called 'avoided cost of disposal' helps finance recovery. Successes in Bangalore, Pune, India and in Lima, Peru combine a removal service with a price per kilogramme for selling compost.
Type 4: negative value materials that damage the environment ('highly negative environmental externalities')	Healthcare waste, hazardous wastes, chemicals, fluorescent light bulbs, used engine oil, end of life E-waste, automobiles, accumulators, batteries, white-/brown-goods, less than 5 per cent of household waste.	Illegally dumped or traded for parts or residual use value, often partially burned to more easily extract metals.	Some residual value-added, but not enough to cover cost of safe management with or without recovery.	Producer responsibility (EPR) systems that combine the maximum feasible recycling and guaranteed safe disposal with marginal repair, refurbishing and other recovery strategies, all financed by the avoided cost of disposal.

All percentages are estimates, and are based on weight, not volume.

Municipalities who believe that they can earn revenues from recycling usually focus on Type 1 materials. This creates a problem in that, in most countries of the South, it is precisely these materials which provide livelihoods for hundreds, if not thousands, of micro-entrepreneurs in the informal or semi-formal private recycling sector (GTZ/CWG, 2007). If the municipality wants to take over recycling, it usually gives itself an advantage by making informal recycling illegal, impossible, or even by labelling it a criminal activity and so stimulating or condoning police harassment, fining recycling businesses for violating zoning laws or not paying taxes etc. Such an approach may succeed in giving the municipality (or its formal private sector contractors) a form of monopoly in access to the more valuable materials. However, in terms of municipal policy it is a lose-lose situation, and can put thousands of people out of work unless deliberate measures are taken to include them in municipal recycling efforts. In the worst cases, a successful recycling programme in terms of the municipal solid waste budget can be a disaster in terms of the municipal social service budget.

A different approach requires the municipality to recognise and build on the existing recycling efforts, and also to support the private recycling sector in increasing its activities in keeping Type 2 and Type 3 materials out of landfills. In doing this the municipality can gain the benefit of extra tonnes of recycled or composted waste by the informal private sector. Some approaches include:

- contracting informal recyclers to remove recyclables on a sorting line (Bogotá, Columbia),
- stimulating informal recyclers to provide a home or business composting service (Jakarta, Indonesia and Delhi, India), or
- matching waste pickers with businesses who need cleaning and waste service and are not interested in recycling their own waste (Bangalore, India).

To summarise, recycling is not a guaranteed source of revenue, and cannot be relied upon to finance solid waste modernisation. Nevertheless, it is a source of benefits, and can lower the costs of modern, environmentally sound services.

ISWM PRESENTATIONS AT THE WORLD CITIES' SUMMIT, JUNE 2008

Solid Waste in Large Cities

Mr N C Vasuki, formerly from the Delaware Waste Management Authority in the US, gave an overview of solid waste management prior to modernisation. Most Asian cities, according to him, were not busy with modernisation and their focus was purely on removal of waste. They did not manage to do this effectively because they lack infrastructure, modern technology, and political will that would allow them to finance their solid waste systems sustainably.

Mr Vasuki focused on three ISWM aspects in Asian cities:

1. The financial-economic aspect was especially weak, as most cities did not do activity-based costing, and so did not know what their solid waste systems cost.
2. The technical and performance aspect was insufficiently organised, solid waste systems were dirty and did not make pleasant neighbours. By contrast, after modernisation, some cities had pleasant-looking facilities which did not attract resistance from their neighbours.
3. The socio-cultural aspect was under-emphasised. In particular, the workers did not receive training, even though they were one of the most important stakeholders for a well-functioning system.

The main conclusion, in Mr Vasuki's presentation, was that solid waste management was important, but that without specific education, citizens will not realise this, and so be unwilling to pay the costs, even though these were relatively minor. Consistent with the findings of Sandra Cointreau from the World Bank (1982), citizens in Delaware paid 0.5 per cent of their annual income for clean, effective, modern, solid waste management. This was a good target, and was enough, even for Asian cities to manage the costs.

Solid Waste Management: Sustainable Waste Management Choices

Mr Peter Woods, the Emeritus Mayor of Sydney, Australia, presented a typical solid waste system after modernisation. He showed how modernisation diversified the solid waste system, and changed the problematisation of waste. His presentation sought to redefine the whole business of solid waste management. It was not about removal of waste, but about reducing consumption and creating awareness. He brought the idea of environmental footprint and carbon emissions into the evaluation of the environmental problems caused by waste, even when waste was properly managed. For example, in New South Wales, he noted that there were up to 196 per cent more emissions from waste disposal than from electricity and vehicle use combined. Removal was the cause of this high impact, and so removal became the problem, rather than the solution. This was quite typical of the post-modernisation approach to waste management.

Mr Woods highlighted that with a modernised system, far less waste would go to landfill, and both 'soft' policy and 'hard' technical aspects would be more varied. His presentation showed clearly how the modernised integrated waste systems in New South Wales included separate collection of many different streams of waste, using different containers, vehicles, and management systems depending on the materials. For example, the local council had a role in separate collection of recyclables, in management of household hazardous waste, and in clean-up, but producers also had an important role in taking responsibility for their products and packages when these entered the waste stream. He emphasised the role of education and political choices in a modernised system.

Mr Woods' most important conclusion was that the more modern the waste system was, the more important it was to reduce consumption, prevent things from becoming waste, manage it responsibly, and choose the best approach for each item in the waste stream. He convinced us that New South Wales was a good example, even though they had yet to achieve zero waste.

Promoting Sustainable Cities through Sustainable Solid Waste Management, the UN–Habitat Initiative

This presentation by Mr Toshi Noda moved more into the realm of the ideal ISWM system that a city in a developing country should strive for. As part of UNDP, Mr Noda was responsible for supporting more than 66 cities in 10 Asian countries, with a portfolio of US$280 million. Many of these were about solid waste. The ideal of these cities was to have an integrated and sustainable modern system, comprising all of the main

ISWM elements:

- Waste collection
- Transportation
- Composting
- Waste composition
- Waste processing and disposal systems
- Land availability
- Landfill

Prevention and reduction of consumption, the hallmarks of Mr Woods' vision of a modern sustainable system, were not the main points for Mr Noda: for his client cities, removal is still the priority for health reasons. But removal was becoming too expensive, and so was disposal, so his focus was on pushing solid waste up the pyramid, towards recycling and reuse.

Sustainable waste management in his view depended on the waste composition in the cities, because most of his project cities had a waste stream which is more than 80 per cent compostable or degradable. For this reason, the focus in many of his projects is on demonstration projects and innovative initiatives for good and sustainable alternatives to disposal, which were also good for the environment. Many of these alternatives had to do with managing organic waste materials through composting, recycling, biogas, or animal feeds. Mr Noda said:

"At the moment, we are implementing several demonstration projects and try to transfer the best practices to other cities. We prioritise community-based solid waste management and to provide the education and training which is needed. Also, we are trying to make the people understand waste is a resource. This is quite an important issue.

In each demonstration project, we try to encourage this strategy by paying attention to four points. The first one is reducing collection costs. The second one is the collection option. The third one is the transport option and the last one is the disposal option. We have made the best combinations. This is one example of our demonstration project teams in Sri Lanka. First of all, we have to establish the strategies by paying attention to public awareness, knowledge management about solid waste, as well as strengthen the partnership with the community and private sectors and NGOs. Also, we have to reduce the volume of waste and we are introducing home composting. Based on these strategies, we are implementing several demonstration projects indicated on the right side, home composting bins and bio-diverse units, community waste collection, etc.

This is on one end and the other one is the Philippines. The strategy is almost the same. Based on these strategies, we are implementing demonstration projects as

indicated here — community-based solid waste management and sorting of waste and
shortage. Also knowledge management and information sharing is extremely important.
Accordingly, we are organising the stop-watch exchange so that people can understand
and study the best practices."

In addition to the community-level approach, UNDP is helping developing
countries understand and implement the Fukuoka method of fast
recirculation landfilling, a breakthrough in the technical and performance
aspect that originated in the UK in the 1990s. Japan has been a leader in
financing and installing this type of landfill, which avoids release of methane
by forcing underground aerobic digestion inside the landfill itself. It is a
hypermodern technical approach, and therefore it is expensive. But with
carbon financing, it may become more affordable.

The most important message in Mr Noda's presentation is that cities in
developing countries have to have practical strategies that they can afford,
and protect the environment. This is the ideal, and his programme helps to
do that. UNDP has had some successes with their project, and they have
information to share. For this reason, they are establishing a knowledge
management centre for Asia and the Pacific in order to disseminate the
information on best practices.

Integrated Sustainable Waste Management in Singapore[2]

Mr Joseph Hui's presentation crowned the Session by showing how
Singapore put all the elements of a modernised system together in an
efficient, innovative, and structured way. Singapore is between a developed
and developing country, and counts as one of the 'Asian Tigers', and as such,
it has important lessons for both rich and poor countries.

Singapore adopted the most important policy strategy for a modern
ISWM system: the goal of zero waste and zero landfilling, with 60 per cent
targetted for recycling by the year 2012. According to Mr Hui, the policy and
practice relate directly to local conditions. Singapore is a very small country,
with a total land area of about 700 square kilometres, high population density
and 4.5 million people living within this small area. The economy is highly

---

[2]This text is taken almost verbatim from the session transcript.

industrialised with few natural resources of its own and renewable energy resources and most important of all, they lack land.

Singapore made an early choice to commit to the environment along with their strong emphasis on economic development after independence. This fundamental commitment to environmental quality helped the island nation remain in the forefront of modernised and environmentally sound waste management.

Like most authorities, they began by improving their infrastructure in a pre-modern way, with an emphasis on simple removal to rather ordinary landfills. Over the years, although the infrastructure improved, decision-makers realised that they did not have space to continue building landfill after landfill to take care of the waste by removal. The decision to switch to incineration reduced the volume substantially. At present, Singapore's waste is handled by four waste-to-energy incineration plants located all around the island. Ash from these four plants are sent to an offshore ash and bulky waste landfill, which they called the Semakau Landfill. This accounts for a significant volume reduction — more than 90 per cent — but still it does not solve the problem when the waste stream keeps growing, because it is simply not sustainable to keep on removing and managing more and more waste.

Singapore, hence, modernised their policy, moving from a single strategy to a diversified, "modernised mxed" policy framework with four strategies to deal with the waste, according to its nature, composition, and economic characteristics:

1. volume reduction through incineration,
2. waste recycling to reduce the amount of waste that needs to go through the incinerator,
3. reducing landfilled waste, through finding beneficial 'down-cycling' uses for the incineration ash, and
4. reducing the amount of waste right at the very beginning. In other words, not generate waste in the beginning.

As is typical of modernised systems, the high cost of safe disposal has been the main driver, and in Singapore, this is intensified by the high cost of land. Thus, the first strategy, incineration for volume reduction, has been effective and affordable for 93 per cent of the waste that burns, in spite of its high costs, when combined with modest benefits from electricity generation which provides two to three per cent of peak electricity demand. In addition, scrap metal recovered magnetically from the ash is sent to a steel plant.

The second strategy is to focus on down-cycling and re-using all non-burnables. For example, construction waste can be recycled to components for making drains and road dividers and waste wood can be recycled into waste wood products. There is also strong encouragement for recycling of burnables, for their economic value, through house-to-house collection in flats, on a schedule. In addition, there is a recycling drop-off point within no more than 150 metres walking distance from any residence. This intensive and user-friendly system has resulted in increasing the participation rate for recycling from 15 per cent in 2001 to 63 per cent in 2007. Recycling in schools is another area which is being promoted and 95 per cent of the schools now have recycling corners within their premises. Currently, the overall recycling rate stands at 54 per cent and the goal is 60 per cent by 2012.

The third strategy is to recycle the seven per cent that would otherwise go to landfill. For example, the concrete from demolitions is actually recycled into other concrete products, rather than going to disposal.

The fourth strategy is to reduce the waste at the source. Singapore is amongst the very few countries outside of Europe that has negotiated an extended producer responsibility agreement with packaging manufacturers in which they use either recyclable materials or reduce the amount of materials that they used in packaging so that this does not end up as waste. And in this way, the amount that goes to the landfill is reduced. Singaporeans also have a habit of using plastic bags in their shopping but the good thing is that the bags are also used to pack their rubbish for disposal so it serves a purpose.

Mr Hui's most important conclusion, is that these four strategies have actually helped to meet the challenges of modernised waste management. But so far, the target of achieving 60 per cent of recycling by 2012 appears to be within reach. This highly organised 'modernised mixture' can serve as a model for many other develoing states, especially industrialised island states with relatively little land area.

CONCLUSIONS

Solid waste is not as complex as many other socio-technical systems, but it is not easy to do it well. There are many pitfalls: lack of political will; a singular focus on removal; the growing material well-being and associated growing waste generation; and high costs of a modern waste management system. The four speakers highlighted different parts of the problem and offered different accents to the solution. But they all agreed that modernisation was necessary, and that a modern state needs a modern waste management system. Such a system is based on a balance of economic, technical, institutional, social, environmental, and governance concerns, expressed in the ISWM 'egg'. The paradox is that the better the system, the more waste it prevents, and so the less it actually has to handle.

Singapore, an example of how 'less is more' in waste management, its modernised, mixed and pluriform system, demonstrates the way forward for other island states.

REFERENCES

Anschütz, J et al. (2005). UWEP City Case Studies. Advisers on Urban Environment and Development, Gouda, The Netherlands: WASTE.

Anschütz, J, J IJgosse and A Scheinberg (2004). Putting ISWM to Practice. Advisers on Urban Environment and Development, Gouda, The Netherlands: WASTE.

Chambers, R (1997). Whose Reality Counts, Putting the First Last. UK: Intermediate Technology Publications.

Chaturvedi, B (2006). Privatisation of solid waste collection and transportation in Delhi: The impact on the informal recycling sector. Paper prepared as partial fulfilment of course on Urban Issues in Developing Countries. School for Advanced International Studies, Johns Hopkins University. Washington DC, December.

Cointreau, S (2001). Declaration of principles of sustainable and integrated SWM. www.worldbank.org/solidwaste.

Cointreau, S (1982). Environmental Management of Urban Solid Wastes in Developing Countries: A Project Guide. Washington, USA: World Bank.

Dias, SM (2000). Integrating waste pickers for sustainable recycling. Paper delivered at the Manila Meeting of the Collaborative Working Group (CWG) on Planning for Sustainable and Integrated Solid Waste Management, Manila, 2000.

Doppenburg, T and M Oorthuys (2005). Afvalbeheer (Solid Waste Management). The Netherlands: SDU Publishers, Dutch order code: 9012110246.

Furedy, C (1997). Reflections on some dilemmas concerning waste pickers and waste recovery. Source Book for UWEP Policy Meeting 1997 (Revised April 1999), Gouda, The Netherlands: WASTE.

GTZ/CWG (2007). Economic aspects of the informal sector in solid waste. Research report prepared by *WASTE*, Skat, and city partners, principal authors Anne Scheinberg, Michael Simpson, Dr. Yamini Gupt, and Justine Anschütz. German Technical Co-operation, Eschborn, Germany (in press).

Ikonomov, LH (2007). *Training Materials Prepared for the IFC Recycling Linkages Programme, Private Enterprise Programme, South-Eastern Europe.* IFC Recycling Linkages Programme, Skopje, Macedonia and Consulting Centre for Sustainable Development Geopont-Intercom, Varna, Bulgaria.

ILO/IPEC (2004). Addressing the exploitation of children in scavenging: A thematic evaluation of action on child labour. *A Global Synthesis Report for the ILO*, Geneva, Switzerland: ILO.

IJgosse, J, J Anschütz and A Scheinberg (2004). *Putting Integrated Sustainable Waste Management Into Practice: Using the ISWM Assessment Methodology as Applied in the UWEP Plus Programme (2001–2003).* Gouda, The Netherlands: WASTE.

Ishengoma, A and K Toole (2003). Jobs and services that work for the poor; Promoting decent work in municipal service enterprises in East Africa: The *Dar es salaam* Project and the informal economy. Paper presented at the *Knowledge-Sharing Workshop Organized by INTEGRATION.* ITC Turin, Italy; 28 October–1 November 2003.

Keita, MM (2003), *Diagnostique de la Filiere de Recuperation de Dechets dans la Commune IV du District de Bamako*, Rapport Final, COPIDUC, and Bamako, Gouda, The Netherlands: WASTE.

Lardinois, I and A van de Klundert (1994). *Informal Resource Recovery: The Pros and Cons.* Gouda, The Netherlands: WASTE.

Lifuka, R (2007). City Report for Lusaka, resource document for GTZ//CWG 2007 "Economic Aspects of the Informal Sector". Lusaka, Zamnia: Riverine Associates.

Marchand, R (1998). *Marketing of Solid Waste Services in Bauan, The Philippines*, Gouda, The Netherlands: UWEP/WASTE.

Medina, M (1997). Informal recycling and collection of solid wastes in developing countries: Issues and opportunities. *UNU/IAS Working Paper No. 24.* Tokyo, Japan: The United Nations University/Institute of Advanced Studies.

Mitrovic, A and Z Gradimir (1998). Social position of the Roma in Serbia. *The Roma In Serbia.* Belgrade, Republic of Serbia and Montenegro, Council for Human Rights of the Centre for Anti-War Action, 9–68.

Mol, Arthur PJ and D Sonnenfeld (eds.) (2000). *Ecological Modernisation Around the World.* London and Portland, Oregon: Frank Cass Publishers (First published as a special issue of *Environmental Politics*, Spring 2000.)

Mol, Arthur PJ and G Spaargaren (2000). Ecological modernisation theory in debate: A review. *Environmental Politics*, 9(1), 17–49.

Mol, APJ. V Lauber, and D Liefferink (eds.) (2000). *The Voluntary Approach to Environmental Policy.* Oxford, UK: Oxford University Press.

Price, J, AR Rivas and I Lardinois. (eds.) (1998). *Micro and Small Enterprises, The Case of Latin America*, Gouda, The Netherlands: WASTE.

Robinson, M, M Simpson *et al.* (1990). *Unpublished Documents Related to Working With the Informal Sector to Develop Community Composting in Jakarta, Indonesia.* Cambridge, Massachusetts, USA: Harvard Institute for International Development (HIID), Massachusetts, USA: Cambridge.

Rosario, A (2004). Reduction of child labour in the waste picking sector, India: Review and findings of an evaluative field study in Bangalore and Kolkata. www.ilo.org/childlabour.

Rudin, V, L Abarca, F Roa, *et al.* (2007). *Systematisation of the Methodology for Managing Electronic Waste in Costa Rica.* Gouda, The Netherlands: WASTE.

Scheinberg, A (1999). Worse before it gets better — Sustainable waste management in Central and Eastern Europe. *Warmer Bulletin,* 68, 18–20.

Scheinberg, A (ed.) (2001). *Integrated Sustainable Waste management: Tools for Decision-makers,* Set of five tools for decision-makers — Experiences from the urban waste expertise programme (1995–2001), WASTE, Gouda.

Scheinberg, A and J Anschutz (2007). Slim pickin's: Supporting waste pickers in the ecological modernization of urban waste management systems. *International Journal of Technology Management and Sustainable Development,* 5(3), 257–270.

Scheinberg, A and J IJgosse (2004). Waste management in The Netherlands. *Report prepared for UNITRABALHO, Recife, Brazil.* Gouda, The Netherlands: WASTE.

Scheinberg, A, Dr A Mitrovic and V Post (2007). *Assessment Report: Needs of Roma Collectors and Other Stakeholders in the PEP SE Region for Training, Technical Assistance, and Financial Services and Recommendations for Programmatic Response.* Prepared for the Recycling Linkages Private Enterprise Programme South East Europe (PEP SE) of the International Finance Corporation, Skopje, Macedonia.

Scheinberg, A, J Ijgosse, F Praxn, V Post and representatives of LOGO South municipalities (2008). *Closing the Circle, Bringing Integrated Sustainable Waste Management Home.* July 2008, The Netherlands, Association of Dutch Municipalities, International (VNGI), The Hague.

Spaargaren, G and BJM Van Vliet (2000). Lifestyles, consumption and the environment: The ecological modernization of domestic consumption. *Environmental Politics,* 9(1), 50–77.

Spaargaren, G, P Oosterveer, J van Buuren and APJ Mol (2005). *Mixed Modernities: Towards Viable Environmental Infrastructure Development in East Africa.* The Netherlands, position paper, Environmental Policy Department, Wageningen University and Research Centre.

State of New Jersey (USA) (1984). *The New Jersey Recycling Act.* New Jersey, US, Law passed by the New Jersey State Legislature, Trenton,

State of New Jersey (USA) (1985–90). *Annual Reports of the New Jersey Recycling Act.* New Jersey, USA, New Jersey Department of Environment, Trenton.

Per Otnes (ed.) (1988). *The Sociology of Consumption: An Anthology.* New Jersey: Solum Forlag AS Humanities Press Inc.

UNDP-PPPUE (2003). *Toolkit for Pro-poor PPPs.* UNDP PPPUE, Johannesburg.

UNEP-IETC (1997). *The UNEP Solid Waste SourceBook.* United Nations Environmental Programme, International Environmental Technogy Centre (UNEP_IETC), Osaka, Japan.

UNESCAP (United Nations Economic and Social Commission for Asia and the Pacific) (1999). *Local Government in Asia and the Pacific, a Comparative Analysis of 15 Countries.* Report prepared for the International Union of Local Authorities Asia-Pacific Section. United Nations, New York, USA.

Urban Waste Expertise Programme Plus (UWEP Plus) (2004). *City Case Studies of Bamako, La Ceiba, Bangalore and Batangas Bay, the Four "PPS" Cities of the UWEP Plus Programme, (2001–2004).* Gouda, The Netherlands: WASTE.

Vilet, Bas van, H Chappels and E Shove (2005). *Infrastructures of Consumption*. London, UK: Earthscan Publications Ltd.
Wilson, Sir DC (2007). Development drivers for waste management. *Waste Management and Research,* 25, 198–207.

SOME RELEVANT WEBSITES

Website	Description
www.waste.nl	website of WASTE. Advisers on Urban Environment and Development, specialists on solid waste in South countries. Most documents available for free downloading.
www.cwgnet.net	website of the Collaborative Working Group on Solid Waste Management in Low- and Middle-Income Countries (the CWG). Has access to articles, conference proceedings, networking information, and a working group on the global informal sector in solid waste.
www.epa.gov	website of the United States Environmental Protection Agency. Has a publication called "full cost accounting for municipal solid waste management: a handbook" (ca. 60 pages); EPA 530-R-95-041, September 1997.
www.ilo.org	website of the International Labour Organization. The ILO has a wide variety of very useful publications on solid waste services by and for the poor, including "Start your own Waste Collection Service ; Business Plan."
www.iswa.org	website of the International Solid Waste Management Association. ISWA publishes Waste Management World, www.waste-management-world.com.
www.skat.ch	A Swiss NGO consultancy. Secretariat of the CWG, and specializes in the Brown environmental agenda.
www.worldbank.org/solidwaste	website of the World Bank. Contains a great deal of very good information on solid waste management in developing countries.
www.unep.or.jp/ietc/issues/Urban.asp	website of the former office of UN-International Environmental Technology Center in Japan, publisher of the UN Solid Waste Source Book.

GLOSSARY OF WASTE MANAGEMENT AND RECYCLING TERMINOLOGY

There are many different terms used for various parts of solid waste and recycling systems. The terms in this glossary are the ones that the project team has agreed to use. Wherever possible, these reflect standard English usage in the UK and in the USA.

Term	Other terms or abbreviations used	Working definition
Activities at source	Prevention, re-use, backyard burning, source reduction	The document refers to waste management activities by households and household-related personnel such as burning, burying, feeding waste to animals, segregation, re-use for own consumption.
AVI	WTE, incinerator	The Dutch term for a waste incinerator that generates energy.
Avoided cost of disposal	Diversion credit	The amount that would have been paid per kilogramme for disposing of materials in a controlled or sanitary landfill by paying the official tipping fee.
Broker	Stockist, dealer	A trader in one or more types or grades of recyclables who trades without ever being the physical owner of the materials, usually having no storage place.
Capital cost	Investment cost, capital, purchase cost	The amount it cost to purchase new equipment, facilities, space, buildings, etc.
Capture rate	Separation rate	A percent or ratio relating the amount of recoverable materials that are directed to processes of recycling or composting and the total amount collected.
CBO	Community-based organisation grassroots organisation	A group organised to provide a solid waste function or service in a community, often fully or partially staffed by volunteers.
Characterisation study Waste audit	Composition study	Describing the components of a particular waste stream: results in a list of materials and their percentage occurrence.
Coefficient	Ratio, parameter	A mathematical relationship that describes part of the waste system, such as kilogramme per waste picker per day.
Collection coverage	Coverage, effectiveness	The percentage of the total (household and commercial) waste generating points that have regular waste collection or removal.

(Continued)

(*Continued*)

Term	Other terms or abbreviations used	Working definition
Collection efficiency	Efficiency, collection coefficient	One or more measures of the performance of the collection system, usually expressed as households/vehicle/day or tonnes/litre of fuel used or distance travelled/litre of fuel.
Commercial waste	Business waste, shop waste, small quantity generator waste	Waste which comes from shops, services and other generators which are neither residential nor industrial. Sometimes includes institutional or public sector waste.
Community	Barrio, barangay district	A grouping within a city, it may be as small as a group of neighbours or as large as a sub-municipal division, and may or may not have formal governance functions.
Composition	Characterisation physical composition	See characterisation.
Composting	Treatment, organic waste management	The aerobic decomposition of materials from living organisms under controlled conditions and in the presence of oxygen.
Construction and demolition waste	Debris, construction and demolition, rubble, contractor waste	Waste from the process of construction, demolition or repair of houses, commercial buildings, roads, bridges, etc. Generally divided into commercial construction waste from construction companies, and do-it-yourself (DIY) waste from homeowners making their own repairs.
Co-operative	Co-op, buyers association, sellers association	An enterprise organised as a co-operative with multiple owners who participate in the activities. In some Latin American countries, co-operatives have a special tax status and so are a favoured form for establishing a business.
Coverage	Collection rate	See collection coverage.

(*Continued*)

(Continued)

Term	Other terms or abbreviations used	Working definition
Depot	Deposit, drop-off, community collection point, community container	A container, site or facility designed to receive waste materials and/or separated recyclables directly from the generator.
Diftar ("Differentiated Tariff", Dutch)	Volume-based fee, prepay bag system, sticker, pay-as-you-throw	A system for assessing the cost of removal and allocating it to users based on the volume or weight of the waste and/or materials handled.
Disposal site	Dumpsite, dump, depot	The site where solid wastes are deposited on land without precautions regarding human health or the environment.
Dry waste	Recyclables, packaging, inorganic waste	What is left after organics are separated at source. Alternatively, a way of describing a fraction that is to be further sorted into its components.
Dump picker	Scavenger, waste picker	Woman, man, child or family who extracts recyclable materials from disposal sites.
Dumpster	Container, skip	A vessel to contain waste, usually larger than $1\,m^3$ and used for more than one household.
Effectiveness	Coverage	See coverage.
Efficiency	Collection efficiency	One or more measures of the performance of the collection system, usually expressed as households/vehicle/day or tonnes/litre of fuel used or distance travelled/litre of fuel.
Fee	Tariff, solid waste fee	The amount paid by a user for a service, generally refers to what is paid for the combination of primary (from the house to the storage place) and secondary collection, transfer and disposal.
Ferrous metals	Iron, steel, ferro-metals	Metals which contain iron and which react to a magnet and are subject to rusting.
Formal sector	Official, government	Used to mean the official solid waste authorities and the activities they sponsor and operate.

(Continued)

(*Continued*)

Term	Other terms or abbreviations used	Working definition
Formal waste sector	Solid waste system, solid waste authorities, government, materials recovery facility	Solid waste management activities planned, sponsored, financed, carried out or regulated and/or recognised by the formal local authorities or their agents, usually through contracts, licences or concessions.
Generator	User, waste producer, household, business,	The source of the waste, that is, the first point it becomes waste.
GFT (Dutch terminology)	Kitchen and garden waste, organic waste, household organics, wet waste	Primarily plant waste from cooking, leftover food, flowers, plants, branches, leaves and other plant wastes from garden and yard.
Household container	Set-out container, bin, waste or garbage can, waste or dustbin	The vessel used by a household or commercial generator to store and set out waste materials, usually made of metal, plastic, rubber or a basket.
Household waste	Municipal solid waste, domestic waste, msw, non-dangerous waste	Discarded materials from households which are generated in everyday life.
Incineration	Burning, combustion	Controlled process by which solid, liquid or gaseous combustible wastes are burned and converted into energy, gases, and residues, including fly ash and bottom ash.
Informal sector	Waste pickers, rag pickers, scavengers, junk shops, informal private sector, micro private sector, micro private recyclers	Individuals or enterprises who are involved in waste activities but are not sponsored, financed, recognised or approved by the formal solid waste authorities, or who operate in violation of or in competition with formal authorities.
Itinerant waste buyer	IWB	Woman, man, child, family or enterprise that purchases source-separated waste materials from households, shops or institutions, usually focusing on one specific material or type of materials.

(*Continued*)

(*Continued*)

Term	Other terms or abbreviations used	Working definition
KCA (Dutch) HHW (English)	Household hazardous waste	Materials such as household chemicals, medicines, detergents, paints which are used in normal households safely, but are dangerous when disposed of in a dumpsite.
Landfill	Dump, dumpsite relleno sanitario	The engineered deposit of waste onto and into land.
Mass balance	Process flow diagram, materials flow diagram, chain analysis	A visual schematic representation of the movement of materials through the entire waste system or only the formal or informal waste system, which indicates the weight of each fraction at each stage.
MRF — Materials Recovery Facility	Ipc, ipf, intermediate processing centre/facility, recycling processing centre	An industrial facility of moderate scale that is designed for post-collection sorting, processing and packing of recyclable and compostable materials. It is usually of moderate technical complexity with a combination of automated and hand-sorting. The inputs are usually mixed recyclables rather than mixed waste. The outputs are industrial grade materials, usually crushed or baled and separated by type, colour, etc.
MSE	Micro- and small enterprise. micro-enterprise, junk shops, materials recovery facility	The smallest businesses, smaller than SMEs, usually with less than 10 workers.
Municipality	Local government authority, mayor's house, mayoralty, city, town, village	A unit of local government with its own level of governance, responsibility and representation.
Non-ferrous metals	Coloured metals semi-precious metals aluminium, copper, bronze, lead	Metals that do not contain iron and are not magnetic such as copper, aluminium, brass, bronze, silver and nickel.
O&M cost	Operating and maintenance cost, operating cost	Costs associated with ongoing operations, such as energy, supplies, labour and rent.

(*Continued*)

(Continued)

Term	Other terms or abbreviations used	Working definition
Organic waste	Bio-waste, green waste, wet waste, organics, gft, putrescibles, compostables, food waste	The decomposable fraction of domestic and commercial wastes, includes kitchen and garden wastes, sometimes includes animal products.
Organised re-use	Repair, re-use, product recycling	A commercial or livelihood activity focused on extraction, repair and sale of specific items in the waste stream. An example is the recovery of up to 20 different types of glass bottles in the Philippines.
PPP	Public-private partnership	A range of relationships between the public sector (including municipalities, public agencies such as the military or a public university, and parastatal organisations) and private sector businesses. The private sector element in a PPP can range from informal recyclers and micro-enterprises to multinational enterprises.
Pre-processing	Sorting, screening, sieving, compaction, densification, size reduction, washing, drying	Preparing waste materials for subsequent processing without adding significant value to them.
Primary collection	Pre-collection, house-to-house collection	Organised collection of domestic waste from households which is taken to a small transfer station.
Process flow diagram	Pdf, materials flow, chain analysis	A visual schematic representation of the movement of materials through the entire waste system, which does NOT indicate the weight of each fraction at each stage.
Processing	Beneficiation, upgrading	Manual or mechanical operations to preserve or re-introduce value-added into materials. Usually involves densification, size reduction, sorting, and then packaging or transport.

(*Continued*)

Term	Other terms or abbreviations used	Working definition
Provider	Service organisation, waste collection firm, public works department, hauler	The entity providing the removal service, either public or private, formal or informal, micro-, small, medium, or large.
Recovery rate	Capture rate	The percentage relationship between the amount of recoverable materials that reach recycling, composting or energy recovery and the total amount generated.
Recyclables	Recoverables	For the purposes of the document, 14 types of materials which have a value to the users and may also have a price.
Recyclers	Scavengers, waste pickers, mrfs, junk shops	Entrepreneurs involved in recycling.
Recycling		Processing and transformation of waste materials to be used in products that may or may not be similar to the original.
Recycling or composting market	End-user industry, buyer, dealer, broker	A business, individual, organisation or enterprise that is prepared to accept and pay for materials recovered from the waste stream on a regular or structural basis, even when there is no payment made.
Recovery	Resource recovery, energy recovery, re-use, materials recovery, recycling, or a combination of these	Process of extracting economically usable materials or energy from wastes. may involve recycling.
Residual waste	Rest-waste, rest-fraction, residue, rejected	The discarded materials remaining in the waste stream or on the sorting line because they are not recyclable or compostable or because they are perceived to have little or no monetary value.
Re-use	Second hand use	Use of waste materials or discarded products in the same form without significant transformation.

(*Continued*)

(*Continued*)

Term	Other terms or abbreviations used	Working definition
Sanitary landfill	Landfill, state-of-the-art landfill, controlled landfill	An engineered method of disposing of solid wastes on land in a manner that protects human health and the environment. The waste is compacted and covered every day. The landfill is sealed from the ground below, and leachate is collected. There is gate control and a weighbridge.
Sanitation	Solid waste, urban cleansing	In the 'French sense' it is used to refer to urban environmental activities including solid waste management.
Secondary collection	Transfer, small transfer station	The movement of wastes collected from households from their first dumping point to processing facilities, larger-scale transfer points or final disposal.
Separate collection	Segregated collection, collection of recyclables, organics collection, selective collection	Collection of different types of materials at different times, or in different containers or vehicles, or in another way so as to maintain the separation and maximise the recovery.
Separation at source	Segregation at source	Actions taken by a household to keep certain materials separate from others.
SME	Small and medium-sized business, small business	Businesses usually having between 11 and 50 employees or workers.
Solid waste	Garbage, trash, waste, rubbish	Materials that are discarded or rejected when their owner considers them to be spent, useless, worthless or in excess of the requirements.
Sorting	Classification, high-grading, selection	Separating mixed materials into single-material components, mechanically or manually. In some cases classifying a mixed single-material stream into specific grades or types of that material.
Source	Generator, origin	The point at which a material is defined as waste and discarded. Usually either a house or a business.
Source separation	Separation at source, segregation at source	Actions taken to keep and store certain materials separately from commingled (mixed) waste at the point of generation.

(*Continued*)

(Continued)

Term	Other terms or abbreviations used	Working definition
Street picker	Street scavenger, waste picker	Woman, man, child or family who removes recyclable materials from dumpsters, streets and public places.
Swine feed	Pig slops, swill, organic waste	Food wastes collected from the household and commercial sectors which are either sold or used to feed pigs.
Tariff	Fee, price of collection or other service	What a user pays for a service, generally refers to what is paid for the combination of primary (from the house to the storage place) and secondary collection, transfer and disposal.
Tipping fee	Dump fee, tip fee	Payment to discharge waste at a transfer station, composting facility, incinerator or landfill for the service of disposing of waste. Is usually assessed per tonne, per cubic metre, or per vehicle-load or 'trip'.
Transfer	Transit, collection point, depot	The movement of wastes from their first point of dumping to final disposal; it usually includes some very basic processing: compaction, pre-sorting or size reduction.
Transfer station	Transit point	A place where waste from collection vehicles is assembled before being transported to disposal sites or treatment stations.
Treatment	Decontamination, processing, composting, beneficiation, sorting, baling	Manual or mechanical operations to make discarded or disposed materials or mixed waste less dangerous, or to improve its physical characteristics so that it is easier to incinerate or landfill. In some locations, the term is also used to mean conserving value-added.
Valorisation	Recycling, recovery, conserving value-added	The entire process of extracting, storing, collecting, or processing materials from the waste stream in order to extract the economic value.
User	Client, household, business, waste generator, waste disposer	The entity that benefits from the service of removal or cleaning. In this document, usually a household, but can also be a business.

(Continued)

(Continued)

Term	Other terms or abbreviations used	Working definition
Waste audit	Waste assessment, walk-through	A visit to a factory, office or institution for the purpose of inventorying and analysing the ways in which waste is generated, handled, managed and removed.
Waste dealer	Junk shop owner, scrap trader, consolidator, waste buyer	Individual or business purchasing materials for recycling or composting, storing them, upgrading or processing them, and then reselling them, or someone who trades in recyclables and uses a dedicated storage place.
Waste picker	Scavenger, rag picker	Person who salvages recyclable materials from streets, public places or disposal sites.
Weighbridge	Scale, wheel scale, truck balance	A facility for weighing trucks, which produces a written record of the weight on the basis of which an invoice can be sent for the service of dumping.
Wet waste	Organic waste, green waste, organics	Used both for the physically wet part of the waste stream and to describe compostable waste separated at source from dry or recyclable waste.
Willingness to pay	Price elasticity for solid waste service	The level and rate at which users (or their proxies) are willing to pay providers (or their agents).

Transportation for Liveable Cities: Problems, Obstacles and Successful Solutions

VUKAN R VUCHIC

The 2008 World Cities Summit Congress in Singapore was an event held at the right time and at the right place. The time was right because the trend of urbanisation and growth of cities around the world requires a broad view and understanding of problems and development of policies and measures to cope with chronic urban problems. Cities' leaders are making increasing efforts to create liveable and sustainable cities. The place was right because Singapore has been one of the world's leading cities in using a systems approach in analysing and developing comprehensive policies to solve social, economic as well as environmental and urban problems. In particular, the focus has been on the relationship between efficient transportation and city's liveability.

This chapter focuses on urban transportation. It is written by the moderator of the session on Land Transportation. He asked the five speakers to report on positive achievements and challenges in their cities or countries. The chapter starts with the moderator's review of developments and trends in urban transportation and a summary of the five reports by participants presented in the session. It is followed by a brief review of the conditions in urban transportation and its impact on cities. Following a review of problems most cities face and mistakes in transportation planning many cities continue to make, this chapter places emphasis on progressive policies and successful solutions which feasibility has been demonstrated by a number of leading cities.

URBAN TRANSPORTATION DEVELOPMENTS IN THE 19TH AND 20TH CENTURIES

The process of industrialisation since 1800 led to urbanisation and rapid growth of cities (particularly in the industrialising West). A major problem in that process was that people could travel only as pedestrians, on horse-drawn coaches and, later, on inter-city trains. The cities were, therefore, being developed with high density for easy travel: this period resulted in "*Walking Cities*", that is, cities that were compact and walkable (Schaffer and Sclar, 1975).

The invention of electric tramways and metro systems in Europe and the US led to extensive building of rail lines and networks to meet the need for greater mobility and better quality of life. Following rail transit lines and networks, the cities grew spatially. Thus, from the 1890s onwards, cities could be described as "*Transit Cities*" for several decades.

Another major transportation development that greatly affected cities was a fast increase in automobile ownership, which occurred in the US during the 1930s, and in Europe, Japan and other industrialised countries during the 1950s and 1960s. Widespread ownership and use of private cars for urban travel caused a serious conflict in cities between personal convenience and transportation system efficiency. This conflict can be explained in very simple terms. For many trips, the private automobile offers the most convenient mode of travel, particularly if its direct out-of-pocket costs are very low. However, when most travel is performed by cars, the resulting chronic traffic congestion makes the transportation system inefficient and the entire city unliveable (Figure 1). Construction of freeways/motorways and parking garages can alleviate this problem, but it results in creation of cities which are not people-friendly (Figures 2 and 3). Moreover, large freeway networks induce longer trips and lead to even greater congestion. This phenomenon is often referred to as the "collision of cities and cars." Policies of accommodating and maximising automobile travel while sacrificing system efficiency and quality of life have been strongly supported by lobbies of highway builders, automobile manufacturers, oil companies and related industries. Many of these industries not only promote

Fig. 1 Traffic congestion and pollution in cities — negative side effects of unlimited motor vehicle use

Fig. 2 High-capacity freeways in central cities harm their liveability

Fig. 3   Large parking area requirements make cities less people-friendly

the use of cars, but work actively to downgrade transit services to the least
attractive mode — buses on streets.

Policies intended to create *"Auto-Based Cities"* led to the following
activities and results (Newman and Kenworthy, 1989):

- Extensive construction of freeways and parking garages that facilitate and
  encourage faster and longer trips by car;
- Transit services are inadequate, serving only captive riders;
- Resulting automobile dependency leads to increased driving and increased
  traffic congestion; 30–40 per cent of people who do not drive become
  second-class citizens;
- Pedestrians are neglected, limiting cities' liveability;
- Retail and many other activities relocated from central cities to suburban
  malls.

Another group of countries and cities, led by Germany and several
other European countries and Singapore, gave greater attention to defining
the goal in urban transportation planning: achieve liveable cities through

coordinated policies towards economic development, transportation, housing and other elements. By defining the types of services and impacts transportation should have, these countries clearly stated that they did not want to create automobile-based cities. To achieve greater efficiency and enhance urban liveability, they decided that the transportation system should consist of a number of complementary modes, including private and public transportation and also encouraging walking, bicycles and other modes. This led to the definition of "*Intermodally Balanced Cities*".

To achieve this goal, it became clear that a number of measures had to be implemented that will shift a considerable volume of trips from private cars to transit, walking and other more efficient modes from the systems point of view. Examples of these measures, divided into two categories, are presented here.

Incentives for Use of Transit, Paratransit, Bicycles and Walking

- Building metro, light rail or other medium-capacity modes with separate rights of way
- Coordinating transit modes and integrating their information and fare collection
- Creating attractive pedestrian streets and areas, often served directly by transit
- Coordinating land use with transit lines and stations
- Providing bicycle ways and other bicycle facilities

Disincentives for Use of Private Cars

- Eliminate subsidised and "free" parking in central cities
- Use parking charges to discourage commuting by car which requires eight hours of parking
- Use petrol taxes for financing all transportation facilities, including transit, pedestrian zones, etc., instead of roads only
- Use road pricing (for example, Singapore's Electronic Road Pricing — ERP) to reduce traffic congestion; it is an effective way of charging automobile users for social and environmental costs which they are not paying

- Provide park-and-ride and kiss-and-ride facilities at rail stations in major cities
- Review and reduce requirements for provision of parking space for residences and businesses in central cities

The following sections present highlights of the five presentations at the World Cities Summit.

KEY ROLE OF PUBLIC TRANSPORT IN INCREASING LIVEABILITY AND SUSTAINABILITY: GLOBAL EXAMPLES OF BEST PRACTICES

Mr Hans Rat, the Secretary General of the International Association of Public Transport — UITP, described the activities of his organisation. With over 200 transit companies as members in more than 90 countries, UITP serves and assists the transit industry with extensive data, reports on technical and organisational topics, from rail and bus vehicle specifications to enquiries on fare levels and collection methods, sources of transit financing and organisational aspects of transit operators.

In addition to this guidance and services for the industry, UITP very actively participates in international discussions about liveability and sustainability of cities as well as the role of public transit in achieving these goals. It publishes a journal and brochures on different topics, reporting on best practices in providing transit lines — the key element in creating pedestrian zones around metro stations or light rail lines in pedestrian malls.

Mr Rat reviewed several world trends that affect urban transportation and, particularly, transit. The wave of globalisation is reflected in the growth of multinational transit companies which operate transit under contracts with cities or umbrella transportation authorities. In Europe, about 40 per cent of public transit systems are now operated by multinational or other companies, which are not owned by the cities they serve. He mentioned that in some countries, there are also anti-globalisation movements. This situation is complicated by the unstable conditions in international monetary relations and volatile stock market conditions. The weakening role of the US dollar as the international basic currency, and the rapidly increasing price of oil on the world market also create financial uncertainties.

The increasing price of oil, which is affecting most countries' economies and international trade relations, can be expected to have a particularly strong interaction with different modes of urban transportation. With continuous growth in purchasing power of populations of large industrialising countries such as China, India, Russia and Brazil, automobile ownership will increase. This will add to the demand for oil and cause further increases in the price of oil, as well as in traffic congestion in cities.

While the increase in the price of oil and hence, operating costs of public transit agencies, affect private car users much more, this might result in significant shifts of travel from cars to other modes, particularly public transit. This has been demonstrated by significant increases in transit ridership in most industrialised countries, including the US. The attitudes toward public transit and demand for its improvements, particularly among the younger generations of citizens, have grown significantly. The support for policies that increase the role of public transit in urban transportation in industrialised countries is now much greater than it was in recent decades. However, in countries which are experiencing growth in automobile ownership now, the costly mistakes of favouring automobiles while neglecting transit made in industrialised countries several decades ago, are in many cases being repeated.

Countries and cities leading in transportation planning support the trend of increasing transit ridership as a development to meet the need for greater mobility without increasing congestion. This is reinforced by the increasing social consciousness for inclusion of different population groups, by income, age and travel patterns, as well as for the revitalisation of central areas in many cities.

In conclusion, the increasing requirements for population mobility in growing cities call for more effective control of traffic congestion and for massive investments in transit modes with high capacity, comfort, performance and permanence, i.e. public transit modes on mostly or fully protected rights of way. These modes with separate infrastructure strongly support urban forms with greater liveability and sustainability.

TRANSFORMING URBAN TRANSPORT
TO ACHIEVE LIVEABLE URBAN
ENVIRONMENT — EXPERIENCE
FROM BOGOTA

Mr Enrique Penalosa, former mayor of Bogota, Columbia, described major changes he introduced in transportation in Bogota as its mayor from 1998 to 2001. His most important innovation was to define the type of city and its quality of life, and then determine the roles which different transportation modes should have. He emphasised the fact that a transportation system should be adjusted to the specific conditions, needs and possibilities of implementation of selected policies. Hence, Mr Penalosa emphasised that "If we want to have a city similar to Amsterdam, we should not use the transportation policies used in Houston".

Referring to the experiences from Bogota, Mr Penalosa said that in a typical developing city with several million people and a large low-income population, transport is a very peculiar problem: it gets worse as society gets richer. Demand for construction of large highways and parking to accommodate private cars can directly conflict with the needs for better health, education, housing and other basic social needs.

Mr Penalosa asked how a democratic developing city should distribute road space among pedestrians, bicyclists, public transport and cars. To make the city friendly to people, a lot more space should be given to pedestrians and bicycles than had been the case in Bogota.

In developing countries, bicycles were accessible to large numbers of low-income people who do not own cars. Thus, building of bicycle ways represented an economical way of increasing the mobility of certain segments of the population, such as teenagers, students and in some cases even most age groups. This need not be considered only as an improvement for low-income groups, because in Germany, Netherlands, Denmark and many other European countries, bicycles were used extensively by all income and age groups.

In Bogota, a proposal for the construction of a 45-kilometre long urban highway submitted by Japanese consultants was rejected because it would intensify car use rather than decrease congestion and increase mobility. Mr Penalosa pointed out that if there were more space for cars in New York or London, there would be more cars, but not more mobility. Unfortunately, some cities did not understand this. Mexico for example, had just built a large number of huge elevated motorways which were environmentally disastrous for the city, its character and sustainability.

Bogota built a network of about 400 kilometres of bicycle ways that were being used by up to 350,000 cyclists. This was paralleled by restrictions on car parking and improvements of public transit. Great effort and many innovations had been used in building the Transmilenio Bus Rapid Transit (BRT) system which had four lanes, stations in the median lines, accessible in many cases by elevated pedestrian walkways. With its high capacity and frequent services, Transmilenio had attracted many people away from using their cars so that 20.7 per cent of its riders have cars but choose to use transit.

The Transmilenio BRT (Figure 4) had drawn international attention by its high capacity and design of bus stops with high-level platforms and simultaneous boarding at several doors. Mr Penalosa claimed that the investment cost for the Transmilenio was much lower than for rail systems and then made a strong generalisation that buses were the only feasible solution for high-performance transit in developing countries because the BRT was able to provide the same performance at much lower cost than rail. This statement was challenged as contrary to worldwide experience that for very high passenger volumes, rail transit provided much higher capacities at lower operating costs. Actually, in corridors with heavy travel volumes, rail transit was the only physically feasible solution because in many cities, particularly in developing countries, reserved busways could not be maintained. Even many newly built busways could not be defended from pressures to allow other vehicles in the same lanes, which practically eliminated the entire BRT.

Mr Penalosa's emphasis on the need for every city to define the goals for its transportation system was valid for any city. His strong support for better treatment of pedestrians also has general validity. Incentives for greater use of bicycles were also valid for many cities, but would depend on local conditions. He did not discuss in depth the difficult problem of implementing measures to create disincentives for automobile use with the exception of the elimination of curb parking in some city streets.

Fig. 4   Transmilenio BRT in Bogota attracted attention by providing high capacity on a four-lane roadway, but it created a barrier to pedestrians.

URBAN TRANSPORT CHALLENGES IN RAPIDLY URBANISING COUNTRIES: POLICIES AND INFRASTRUCTURE DEVELOPMENTS IN INDIA

Mr Sanjeev Kumar Lohia, Director of Urban Transportation in the Ministry of Development of India, reported that his country was experiencing rapid urban growth, resulting in 35 cities with population exceeding one million and seven cities exceeding four million. With automobile ownership growing even faster than its population, most cities suffered from chronic congestion of streets with pedestrians mixing among many types of vehicles, from bicycles and *rikshas* to buses and trucks.

Despite this trend of increasing urban congestion, transit development and financing were seriously neglected. In most cities, transit consisted of buses on streets. However, the rapidly deteriorating traffic conditions in so many cities led to an intensive national discussion about urban transportation and by the end of 2006 most cities began to change attitudes toward transportation policies and measures. Instead of focusing efforts on construction of roads and flyovers to accommodate increasing volumes of cars, it was recognised that mitigating problems of congestion, air pollution and traffic safety required policies that favour public transit as well as non-motorised modes over private cars (Agarwal and Zimmerman, 2008).

Improvements of public transit through operational measures were needed, but not sufficient for large cities. High-capacity rail systems had therefore been planned and built in several cities. Cities with extensive railway networks, such as Mumbai, Kolkata and Chennai, had extensive suburban (regional) rail networks. Mumbai had one of the world's largest suburban (regional) rail systems, carrying about six million passengers per day. Indian Railways reported that the country's suburban railway systems ridership increased from 23 trillion passenger-km in 1970 to 106 trillion in 2005.

The first metro rail system was opened in Kolkata in 1984, followed by Chennai and Delhi. Mumbai, Hyderabad and Bangalore were also building or planning new metro rail systems. The Delhi Metro is particularly recognised as an efficiently planned and built system.

In recent years a lot of attention had been given to BRT. Its promoters had been very critical of the high investment costs of rail systems and claimed that BRT would require much lower investment costs and easier implementation than metro systems. This claim had proven to be too simplistic. While upgrading of bus services can bring significant results in most cities, the claims that BRT can be effective in most Indian cities had proven to be unrealistic. In theory, BRT can operate efficiently on reserved rights of way, but in practice obtaining reserved lanes cannot be implemented in highly congested streets. Thus, the introduction of BRT in New Delhi and Mumbai led to serious problems which BRT promoters usually overlook: the ability to keep bus ways for buses only faced strong opposition in most cities. BRT was practically unfeasible in cities without strict police enforcement. Mumbai bought BRT buses, but could not organise the infrastructure for their operation.

Interestingly, light rail transit (LRT) which requires substantially lower investment than the Metro, but more effective than buses in its separation from general traffic had yet to obtain much attention in India. Considerable potential for upgrading old fashioned tramways in Kolkata into modern LRT had yet to be utilised.

The discussions about implementation of urban transportation policies that favour transit and pedestrians over cars in urban areas continued in India. The national government was considering a programme that would contribute 30 per cent of infrastructure investments for transit projects but the formulation of coordinated intermodal policies and their implementation were yet to be fully established.

PROMOTING PUBLIC TRANSPORT AS AN ATTRACTIVE MODE OF CHOICE — SUCCESS IN ADELAIDE

Ms Heather Webster, the Executive Director of the Public Transport Division in South Australia, described a comprehensive effort in promoting transit use in Adelaide by focusing on present and potential transit users. The city of Adelaide, with a population of 1.1 million, low population density, high automobile ownership and cheap gasoline — elements that create automobile dependence which transit must overcome to become competitive.

Facing these difficulties, coupled with the trends of increasing gasoline price and environmental concerns, the government of South Australia made a concerted effort to increase the role of public transit. Extensive surveys were undertaken to establish the features affecting transit use, such as service frequency, moderate fares, reliable services offered during evenings and weekends, as well as improving the image of transit by system symbols, vehicle colours and extensive, easily obtainable information. Explanation about potential savings acquired from switching from car to transit travel had further contributed to the success of the campaign of increasing the share of transit travel and strengthening its role in the city's pedestrian orientation and liveability, as well as improving economic efficiency of transit services.

BUILDING A PEOPLE-CENTRED INTERMODAL LAND TRANSPORT SYSTEM — SINGAPORE

Mr Yam Ah Mee, Chief Executive of the Land Transport Authority (LTA) in Singapore, described the development of a remarkably comprehensive and successful intermodal transport system in Singapore (Yam, 2008). Development of transportation in Singapore during the last three decades clearly showed that the establishment of LTA was key to the present efficient integrated transport system and liveable city. LTA was an agency that formulated and implemented transportation goals and policies in coordination with land use planning. The emphasis on public transport actually predated the establishment of LTA. The Urban Redevelopment Authority (URA) performed this latter function in close coordination with LTA, and that cooperation had been crucial to the success of land transport planning in Singapore.

Faced with the problems of a growing population and increasing automobile ownership, as well as the goal of achieving a sustainable city, LTA focused its efforts on changing modal split in favour of public transit by implementing three sets of measures:

i. *Make Transit a Choice Mode* — public transit-use incentives consisting of improvements to its network of Mass Rapid Transit (MRT), automated mass rapid guided transit as feeders to the MRT, and an extensive bus network. The current plan projected a doubling of the MRT to 278 kilometres in length and improvement of its intermodal transfers, improving service quality and its information system.

ii. *Manage Road Usage* — automobile travel disincentives consisted of expansing its Electronic Road Pricing (ERP) scheme to an extensive system across the island, coupled with disincentives to automobile ownership.

iii. *Meet diverse needs of people* — analyse and improve travel opportunities by adjusting to the needs of different groups of travellers and population categories by income, travel purposes and physical characteristics among others.

Singapore's example clearly showed a number of innovations that it had introduced over the last four decades, placing it in the forefront of comprehensive transportation and city planning that contributed to increasing liveability in spite of its population growth.

PRESENT CONDITIONS IN URBAN TRANSPORTATION

The preceding reports showed that while urban transportation has been a serious problem in most countries, significant progress with innovative policies and implementation methods has also been achieved in a number of cities. Selected aspects of the present transportation conditions and problems typical for many cities are described in the following paragraphs. Successful solutions are reviewed in the closing section.

- The complexity of urban transportation is yet to be fully understood in many cities, as such, the necessary transportation policies are missing in many cases. Actually, many cities do not have organisations that are in charge of developing and implementing coordinated intermodal policies and projects. This problem is particularly serious but not limited to developing countries (World Bank, 1996). Many cities in industrialised countries have not achieved adequate development of transportation policies and their coordinated implementation (Vuchic, 1999).
- In the absence of clear transportation goals, policies and implementation procedures, many cities appear resigned to chronic traffic congestion as an inescapable phenomenon of large cities — or even a sign of their economic vitality!
- When automobile ownership grows, cities and regions must adjust streets to handle higher traffic volumes; a freeway network serving major corridors is also needed. However, attempts to "meet the demand for travel" when automobile travel is underpriced by constructing more freeways into central cities and building multi-storey garages generally

result in increased automobile dependency and permanent decrease of cities' liveability.

- The relationship between private and public transit is mostly based on the short-term decisions of individual travellers rather than on efficiency of transportation as a system. As automobile travelers do not pay either social costs they incur (congestion, environmental deterioration, stress and accidents), or long term damage to cities' liveability, automobile travel becomes more attractive for many trips than use of transit. This condition results in chronic congestion with all its short- and long-term negative impacts on cities.

- In addition to the issue of excessive trip making, the low direct cost of driving gives the automobile competitive advantage over public transit and forces many cities to subsidise public transit fares. On the other hand, cities which have road user charges, high parking rates and other levies on car use, can have higher fares and lower operating subsidies for public transit (Vuchic, 1999; Shoup, 2004).

- Due to inadequate understanding of the complexity of urban transportation and absence of rational intermodal transportation policies, many cities do not provide adequate funding for public transit, particularly for construction of high-performance systems (rail and other systems independent of traffic congestion), which are competitive with private cars.

- These problems are aggravated in cities and countries where many special interest groups oppose innovations and improvements to present conditions and trends. Pursuing their own interests, these groups are often in conflict with transportation efficiency and city's quality of life. They include, for example, many automobile manufacturers, oil companies, public transit labour unions, jitney and taxi organisations (particularly, in developing countries), parking garage builders and owners, and many others.

- Rail transit, the highest quality of public transit mode, is often the subject of distorted criticism because it decreases use of cars and oil consumption. Pedestrians and walking as a mode — a basic element in any liveable city — are often not protected or promoted in agencies that are planning and operating transportation systems.

- Unfortunately, many cities, particularly those with growing automobile ownership, are repeating obvious mistakes made by the cities in the United States, Canada and Western Europe, where that phenomenon occurred several decades ago. Several examples follow.

Large and rapidly growing cities in developing countries suffer from increasing and uncontrollable congestion. Their public transit systems are so overloaded and often dangerous, that whoever can buy a car does that in order to avoid the slow, unattractive transit. Ironically, the addition of more cars leads to a decrease in mobility by all other modes of travel. Instead of investing in high-capacity metro rail, light rail and bus systems with separate roadways, these cities invest mostly in widening of roads and building of freeways.

- Many cities in China, India, Russia, other former Soviet republics and Eastern Europe are also repeating some of USA's and Western Europe's mistakes made a few decades ago as they now respond to the rapid automobile ownership growth:

  — Bicycle use is discouraged by converting bicycle lanes into motor vehicle lanes, resulting in increased vehicle congestion and parking demand;

  — Trolley buses are in some cases replaced by diesel buses, increasing environmental damage;

  — Tramway tracks are paved to "increase street capacity;" where in reality, person-carrying street capacity is decreased;

  — Tramways are replaced by buses, resulting in passenger losses, while their upgrading into light rail would make transit much more competitive and pedestrian-friendly;

  — Construction of metro and light rail systems is given less attention than construction of freeways;

  — Land use/transportation aspects in urban design are not given adequate attention. In some cities this leads to construction of large office and residential buildings without adequate transit services, street capacities for accessibility, or necessary off-street parking facilities and pedestrian ways.

These policies and activities have been used in many industrialised countries several decades ago, but the negative experience has led to their reversal. So today, bicycle use is encouraged, transit is separated rather than mixed with general traffic, electric traction modes are favoured over diesel-powered ones and transit improvements are promoted as an important element in reaching sustainability.

EMERGING SOLUTIONS LEAD
TO LIVEABLE CITIES

There are now a number of cities which have used experiences from recent decades to develop policies, organisations and procedures that have made them distinctly successful in achieving efficient transportation and city's liveability. Among the most progressive leaders are core cities like Berlin, Cologne, Copenhagen, Curitiba, Munich, Portland, Prague, San Francisco, Singapore, Tokyo, Toronto, Vancouver, Vienna and Zurich. Selected features which these cities have introduced with success are described in the following paragraph.

Cooperation between competent civic leadership, transportation and city planning experts enabled these cities to develop policies which define the goals for the city where development of efficient transportation system is a component for achieving a liveable and sustainable city. The roles of different transportation modes in achieving the cities' goals are also extensively and publicly discussed, so that innovative measures, including those restrictive in the short run, have been well received by the population. This public awareness is extremely high, for example, in Copenhagen, Munich, San Francisco and Singapore.

The basic problem in allocating roles to different transportation modes is achieving the optimal balance between individual or private and public transport, automobiles and public transit. In this respect, simply building more roads, parking and using more buses had proved to be inadequate, sometimes even counterproductive. In 1974 Singapore was the first city that introduced road use charges as an efficient means to prevent wasteful traffic congestion (Figure 5). Although this measure was obviously successful, it took more than 20 years before other cities began to use this method. Oslo, Stockholm, Trondheim and London followed suit so that road pricing is now a viable proposition for many cities.

A desirable balance between cars and transit is usually achieved by two sets of coordinated policies: incentives for public transit and disincentives

Fig. 5 Smooth flow of traffic on attractively designed streets, ensured by the Electronic Road Pricing (ERP) system, contributes to sustainability in Singapore

for automobile use. The key to providing transit incentives is to introduce high-performance public transit systems. In medium and large cities, public transit systems which are competitive with automobiles are those which operate on partially or fully separated rights of way. The number of cities with rail rapid transit or metro systems has increased from 20 in 1955 to about 110 today.

The metro rail system (Figures 6, 7 and 8) is a logical solution for basic transportation networks in large cities because it is by far, the highest performance (capacity, reliability, safety) transit mode that has positive impacts on urban development and liveability. However, their investment costs are very high, so that many medium-sized cities have found Light Rail Transit (LRT) to be fully adequate for medium-capacity lines with very pedestrian-friendly characteristics (Figures 9 and 10). LRT can provide high-speed services similar to those of metros on fully controlled sections, but they can also penetrate into city centres and pedestrian zones in central cities (Girnau *et al.*, 2000; Vuchic, 2007). Their investment costs are therefore substantially lower.

Fig. 6 Munich U-Bahn — one of the new metro systems built in recent decades in over 100 world cities

Fig. 7 Bay Area Rapid Transit — BART, a regional metro serving San Francisco and its region

Fig. 8 Regional rail systems in many cities are introducing double-decker cars to increase capacity and comfort

Fig. 9 Light Rail Transit (LRT) serves pedestrian zone in the centre of Karlsruhe, Germany

Fig. 10 Montpellier, France, introduced LRT as part of rebuilding the central city for increased liveability

Considerable progress has been made in recent years in bus technology. Many types of hybrid buses have lower energy consumption and produce much less air pollution than traditional diesel buses. Hundreds of hybrid diesel/electric buses have shown good results in New York City, while Rome and Naples have introduced trolley buses which obtain electric power from overhead wires or from powerful batteries. These vehicles (Figure 11) produce virtually no noise and no air pollution on urban streets.

The BRT (Figure 12) has been aggressively promoted in many countries, including India and China. BRT is usually built at a lower cost and in shorter time than LRT, and its successful operations in Sao Paulo, Curitiba and Bogota have been widely recognised. Caution is however needed because the advantages of BRT over LRT are offset by serious disadvantages. BRT described in theory often cannot be implemented in real world conditions. A number of bus ways and BRT systems in the United States were built during the 1970s, but they were later degraded into high-occupancy vehicle lanes or discontinued completely.

Fig. 11 New trolley bus capable of using power from overhead wires or battery, introduced in Rome to avoid air pollution

Fig. 12 The Bus Rapid Transit (BRT) in Mexico, a low-cost improvement attracted many passengers from cars and mini buses

Many conceptual and numerical facts quoted widely about BRT systems are grossly distorted and divorced from real world facts. For example, the Institute for Transportation and Development Policy (ITDP), which has done excellent work on encouraging development of pedestrian, bicycle and transit systems, particularly in developing countries, in the case of mode comparison presents many inaccurate statements in the case of mode comparison — promoting only BRT systems and negatively distorting facts about rail systems. ITDP claims, for example, without any documentation, that BRT requires 10 times lower investments than LRT. This claim ignores, for example, the fact that the BRT Silver Line in Boston had required about five to 10 times greater investment on its core section than average investments for LRT systems in many US cities.

Hensher (2008, p. 30), also a strong promoter of BRT and opponent of rail, quotes that in Bogota, peak ridership of 35,000 passengers per hour is achieved, "with recent claims of up to 45,000 passengers with maximum peak headways of three minutes" and articulated buses with capacity of 160 spaces. Simple computation shows that headways of three minutes, i.e. a frequency of 20 buses per hour, offers a capacity of mere 3,200 spaces per hour, i.e., only 9 per cent of the claimed actual provided capacity and 7 per cent of the "recent claims of 45,000 passengers capacity." In addition to incorrect computations, the concepts of offered and utilised capacities are mixed here.

These examples show that many claims about BRT capacity and performance are highly inaccurate and based on unrealistic theoretical assumptions about operating conditions in the real world. This kind of misinformation has been very damaging when many cities have been led to believe that BRT is very easy to introduce and that it can provide better performance than rail. Such misguidance has set back transit improvements in a number of cities.

The success of BRT systems depends greatly on the efficiency of police enforcement on streets and intersections. It also depends on the culture and public behaviour. Several BRT or bus way systems were terminated by courts after legal challenges or by local governments under pressure from highway lobbies. Thus, the implementation of BRT in many cities, including New Delhi, Mumbai and Jakarta, has been very different from the systems which their promoters proposed without analysis of local conditions.

Most bus, trolley bus and tram way services around the world can be significantly improved, but that can be achieved only if there is careful planning and cooperation between public transit agencies and the city's traffic departments in giving transit priorities. Such priorities are easily justified by the greater efficiency of transit compared to private automobiles, but that principle must be politically adopted and supported.

Leading cities also demonstrate the importance of giving attention to different categories of travellers (see the above cases of Singapore and Adelaide). Public transit use greatly depends on the attraction and convenience of transit stops and stations, easy transfers, ample information and urban design that provides for human environment. So public transit and pedestrians, when planned to be mutually supporting, create the basic element of urban liveability; they also decrease the need for use of vehicles and provision of freeways and parking which tend to have negative impacts in central areas of cities and major activity centres throughout urban regions.

Recent developments show that the challenges of introducing coordinated intermodal transportation policies and improving liveability of cities have been successfully met in some cities, mostly in industrialised countries. Cities in developing countries face similar challenges and even greater obstacles. They face more rapid urban growth, but must meet greater social needs with much smaller financial resources.

Learning from the past decisions of industrialised countries, including many serious mistakes, developing countries should greatly increase investments and planning efforts in high-capacity transit systems, which provide high transporting capacity that can decrease the chronic congestion of streets. Provision of public transit ways that are separated from general traffic is the most important step in that process. Simple and durable rail systems should be secured for all large and rapidly growing cities. BRT systems can be very effective if their rights of way can be permanently protected. The least costly, but organisationally most difficult and often least durable measure is to control street traffic by giving preferential treatments for buses on streets.

All leading cities in transportation innovations have paid increasing attention to pedestrians. Movement of pedestrians should be planned and promoted not only by providing greater safety, but by making walking attractive. Cities can be liveable only if they provide for a good and attractive environment for pedestrians (Figures 13 and 14).

Fig. 13   Large pedestrian area in the centre of Munich gives the city a reputation for liveability

Fig. 14   San Francisco Market Street is a pedestrian haven and it is served by cars, taxis and five transit modes

REFERENCES

Agarwal, OP and SL Zimmerman (2008). Toward sustainable mobility in urban India. *Transportation Research Record 2048*, 1–7. Washington, DC.

Girnau, G, A Müller-Hellmann and F Blennemann (eds.) (2000). *Light Rail in Germany* (in German and English). VDV, Cologne, Germany, Verband Deutscher Verkehrsunternehmen.

Hensher, DD (2008). Frequency and connectivity. *Journeys*. Singapore, Land Transport Authority (LTA) Academy, November, 25–33.

Newman, P and J Kenworthy (1989). *Cities and Automobile Dependence, an International Sourcebook*. UK: Aldershot.

Schaffer, KH and E Sclar (1975). *Access for All: Transportation and Urban Growth*. UK: Penguin, Hammondsworth.

Shoup, DD (2004). *The High Cost of Free Parking*. USA: American Planning Association, Chicago, Il.

Vuchic, VR (1999). *Transportation for Livable Cities*. Brunswick, NJ, USA: CUPR, Rutgers University.

Vuchic, VR (2007). *Urban Transit Systems and Technology*. Hoboken, NJ, USA: John Wiley & Sons.

World Bank (1996). *Sustainable Transport*. Washington, DC, USA: World Bank.

Yam, AM (2008). Building a people-centred land transport system. *Paper presented at The World's Cities Summit, Singapore*.

7 Biodiversity in Sustainable Cities

LOKE MING CHOU

INTRODUCTION

Environmental sustainability is a fundamental concern for the survival of human society on Earth where limited resources are expended at an increasingly alarming pace. A city's high demand for resources imposes enormous strains on the environment. Is there a role for biodiversity in a city's quest for sustainability? This and other questions concerning the impact of biodiversity on the quality of life for city residents, city planning and governance were discussed during the "Biodiversity in Sustainable Cities" session of the World Cities Summit 2008 held in Singapore, and highlighted in this chapter.

This chapter examines what biodiversity is and what it means, and how it can be utilised to raise sustainability levels in cities. There are strong but not insurmountable challenges for biodiversity to perform such a role in cities. Required is the willingness to try clever ideas and test creative approaches that may go against some of the basic principles and wisdom of conventional ecology, architecture and urban planning. The challenge of society's acceptance of biodiversity at the doorstep is also addressed, particularly when it comes to dealing with pests and dangerous species. Cities that are ready to accept these challenges will progress faster in becoming model 'eco-cities'.

RESPONDING TO ENVIRONMENTAL
DEMANDS: GLOBAL TRENDS

The year 2008 was significant in that for the first time, half of the world's population is settled in cities. The United Nations Population Division estimates that the urban population will continue to increase to 60 per cent (five billion) by 2030. For the cities of Asia, 44 million people are added to the population each year (Roberts and Kanaley, 2006). Cities occupy 2 per cent of the Earth's surface but the urban population uses 75 per cent of global resources and generates a high amount of waste. If not carefully managed, urbanisation and the demands of city dwellers could accelerate the loss of biodiversity.

Cities have developed as people aggregate to interact and synergise their contribution towards economic expansion. Supporting infrastructure have expanded as large concentrations of people allow for more efficient and pragmatic economies of scale. Culture, history, education and entertainment all become embodied in the character of the city, which symbolises civilisation. Housing and jobs are needed for the growing population. These provisions necessitate massive change to the landscape as the area transforms from a natural to a built environment (Figure 1). Dr Ahmed Djoghlaf, Executive Secretary of the Convention of Biological Diversity, reminded the World Cities Summit 2008 that large populations living in megacities consume massive amounts of energy, thus contributing to climate change, which has been identified as one of the most important driving force today in the loss of biodiversity. Planning is essential to arrest this loss and ensure an acceptable living environment.

The consumption patterns of cities make it impossible for them to be sustainable as the environmental footprint is simply too large, but achieving some level of sustainability is better than none. This means that cities can be far more sustainable than they are today. Smart planning can help to reduce the environmental footprint by lowering resource demand. Human behaviour, processes and systems that drive a city can be regulated to reduce wasteful resource loss. Can biodiversity be used to improve a city's sustainability? In the development and rejuvenation of cities, the relevance of biodiversity is increasingly being examined. Should biodiversity be incorporated in city planning and governance, and does it have a positive impact on the quality of life and attractiveness of cities?

Fig. 1 The built environment encroaches menacingly on the natural environment. Foresighted planning can merge both without complete loss of the natural system

The benefits of biodiversity are now better known, but not fully utilised, especially in inner city planning (Figures 2 and 3). Parks, nature reserves and wildlife centres are, and have been considered as useful social, recreational and educational amenities. However, in dense city centres, biodiversity remains a remote and unrealistic option as it stands in the way of city development, occupies expensive real estate and for economic considerations, is certainly dispensable. This attitude towards biodiversity is changing, which underscores the evolutionary phases of urbanisation that have gone from "destroy nature to build" to "restore and re-introduce nature". With rapid urbanisation, efforts are directed at clearing land together with whatever biodiversity it supported and replacing nature with built structures that leave no room for biodiversity. The need to improve environmental quality and to allow people to enjoy nature has led to increasing nature restoration activities in recent decades.

Major river systems in different parts of the world have been cleared of pollution and restored to improve their functionality. They include the

Fig. 2   An urban jungle dominated by concrete, steel and glass. Can biodiversity make a difference?

River Thames (London) in 1963, Singapore River (Singapore) in 1977 and Cheonggyecheon River (Seoul) in 2004. In all three cases, biologically dead rivers have been transformed from repulsive and wasted environments into clean and attractive water systems filled with aquatic life and open to a diversity of use options. The restored Singapore River provides an avenue for the staging of water sports and water-related cultural events (Chou, 1998). The restoration of London's Ravensbourne River has likewise enhanced its amenity and recreational potential, apart from improving its ecological and conservation value (Tapsell, 1995).

Aquatic biodiversity in turn contributes to a balanced ecosystem that has helped to maintain a river's water quality and perpetuate its cleansing service at no financial cost. The improved environment exposes the river banks to all types of development opportunities that generate economic growth. Restoration of the Cheonggyecheon River has required the removal of the Cheonggye Expressway, which was built to cover the river during the earlier days of rapid economic development. The massive restoration project

Fig. 3   High density living with evidence of an appreciation of plants by some homeowners

is meant to revive the historical and natural heritage of Seoul and become a major tourist attraction (Kim, 2005). At the same time, it is meant to reduce the city's 'heat island' effect. Kajikawa *et al.* (2005) argue for the revival of Tokyo's covered rivers based on similar reasons of providing recreational space for city dwellers and lowering trapped heat. During the World Cities Summit 2008, Deputy Mayor Jeong of Pusan Metropolitan City shared Korea's effort at increasing urban biodiversity which is not limited to Seoul. Pusan has implemented forestry, conservation and natural actuary policies to sustain and manage biodiversity conservation. The city has started nature plans to establish wildlife centres and a wetland recovery project along the Nakdong River.

In addition, artificial wetlands have been created and degraded ones restored worldwide with the realisation that these habitats perform a useful role in wastewater treatment and filtration. Reforestation activities have also been increased to help with temperature regulation, erosion prevention and better maintenance of the hydrological cycle. With greater awareness and appreciation of the full value of biodiversity, including its role in conditioning and maintaining environmental quality, the emerging challenge is to plan cities around nature instead of artificially forcing nature into cities. This approach allows human society to benefit most from the 'goods and services' provided by nature right in the heart of cities themselves as well as being a far less expensive alternative to restoring or re-introducing nature. It also helps to prevent unnecessary loss of the natural heritage and avoids the opportunity cost of a degraded and sick environment. However, the present situation for most cities is that the built environment is extensive, and bringing nature back remains about the only option. Tilting the balance towards more biodiversity has benefits that are economically sensible and socially more acceptable.

At the Curitiba meeting on Cities and Biodiversity held in March 2007, 34 mayors adopted the Curitiba Declaration on Cities and Biodiversity. Their commitment to integrate biodiversity into urbanised areas endorsed the realisation that urbanisation and biodiversity are mutually supportive. The Mayors Conference on 'Local Action for Biodiversity' held in Bonn in May 2008 affirmed the importance of urban biodiversity with an understanding that it is more than just the presence of plants and animals but how people depend on this natural capital. These are all encouraging signs of a growing perception that cities can contribute towards reversing biodiversity loss, while at the same time benefiting greatly from it.

WHAT IS BIODIVERSITY?

The Millennium Ecosystem Assessment (2005) concluded that 65 per cent of ecosystem services are already degraded from biodiversity loss. Biodiversity refers to the living component of the environment. All plants and animals, including microbes, make up the biota that interacts with the abiotic physical components of soil, water and air. In this natural system, the fundamental role of the living component is to facilitate the flow of energy and raw materials in efficient cycles without continuous demand for more materials.

The significant continuous input into the natural system is solar energy. Plants, as primary producers, harness this energy during photosynthesis to convert inorganic materials into organic matter, a process which locks in carbon. Plants are next consumed by animals, which do not possess the ability to produce organic materials. This sets off an entire suite of trophic relationships as different species of animals prey on the plant consumers and on each other. The food web of a habitat endowed with a rich mix of species gets extremely complicated as energy and materials flow along different pathways but what is most important is that there is a flow. In a species-poor habitat, the flow moves at a slower rate, is more restricted and makes less efficient use of the continuous solar energy supply.

When plants and animals die, their remains are converted by bacteria into nutrients that are once again available for assimilation by plants in an unending natural recycling of materials. The materials are repeatedly looped through the food web as plants are again eaten by herbivorous animals, which are in turn preyed on by carnivorous animals. Energy and materials are kept moving through the system. The waste of one species becomes the food of another and as the saying goes "there is no such thing as rubbish in the natural world". Without the biotic component, solar energy is not used, soil continues to lack nutrient enrichment and becomes exposed to erosion, and the water cycle as well as the cycling of the atmosphere's component gases, remain largely curtailed. Such scenarios are provided by densely built-up areas where there is little choice but to rely extensively on technology to generate the natural ecosystem processes so as to maintain some acceptable standard of environmental quality. Garbage, for example, has to be managed and much effort is required for its removal. When left to accumulate, the environment deteriorates quickly from the offensive stench and human health risks. Sewage management requires investment in extensive infrastructure to move the waste to a treatment plant. Solar energy falling on cities is largely wasted. Instead, fossil fuels are burned to provide energy and this enlarges the carbon footprint.

Natural habitats comprise a whole mix of many plants and animal species. Ecological systems such as a forest, scrubland, grassland or wetland, contain species that are most suited to the environmental conditions prevalent in each. A rich biodiversity confers some degree of resilience to the habitat. Since biodiversity is about variety where different species exhibit different responses to changes in the environment, it follows then that the presence of more species will ensure that an impact will not eliminate too many species to the extent that the system's ecological integrity breaks down and its functions are severely compromised. A species-rich habitat is much better at tolerating impacts. But to what use is a natural habitat rich with species to people and to cities? The answer lies with the ability of the habitat to provide ecological goods and services.

All living systems are highly productive, driven by energy from the sun. Unlike managed habitats, natural habitats develop with whatever is available and recycle everything with incredible efficiency. Managed habitats require external inputs such as fertilisers, pesticides and herbicides as people have their own ideas of which species are desired and where they should be confined to. This is evident in landscaped parks and gardens where nature looks neat and orderly (Figures 4 and 5). In this type of managed setting, the artificial mix of selected species disrupts the natural flow and recycling of materials and energy that prevails in a natural system and biological productivity is relatively depressed. People who live off the land appreciate and depend on biodiversity for their survival. A natural species-rich system provides the basic needs of people. Food, building materials, medicinal and

Fig. 4 Flowering plants add beauty to the built environment but this planter requires continuous maintenance that includes frequent input of fertiliser, water, herbicides and pesticides

Fig. 5 A landscaped park has less biodiversity than a natural system and needs to be maintained

ornamental products are all obtainable from natural habitats. Apart from providing the basic needs of people, habitats perform valuable environmental services such as carbon sequestration, erosion prevention and the regulation of environmental quality.

CAN BIODIVERSITY MAKE A DIFFERENCE TO CITY SUSTAINABILITY?

What can we reasonably expect from biodiversity in built-up cities? Biodiversity in natural systems provides a range of goods and environmental services. Whatever biodiversity that is brought back into cities is at best scattered, fragmented and restricted. In such a situation, the exploitation of city biodiversity poses an interesting challenge. The limits posed on biodiversity by a built environment need to be understood so that people's expectations of city biodiversity under such circumstances are more realistic.

The provision of goods from a city's biodiversity to its human population is definitely constrained and unsustainable. To achieve sustainability, large tracts of plantations are needed and the economics of real estate value makes this a difficult proposition. Besides, it is impossible for cities to provide the global average per capita ecological footprint of 7.2 hectares. In the unlikely event that cities open up such land even in rural areas, these plantations have to be amply provided with fertilisers and pesticides to boost food production. However, small-scale cultivation of crop plants by individual households in their own gardens or community-managed gardens in shared public plots can collectively help to increase self reliance for food and lower external market demand. Farming techniques such as aeroponics and hydroponics that are suitable for flat rooftops or concreted ground could be seriously considered. While this approach enters the realm of intensive farming rather than biodiversity preservation, it shares the same purpose of improving sustainability by reducing the demand for food from beyond the city. The downside is that these practices require the necessary infrastructure to be put in place like plantations together with a constant input of labour, nutrients, water and pest management measures. Such inputs can result in non-sustainable production (Schmidheiny, 1992) but this should not totally dismiss opportunistic farming. Research can focus on increasing biodiversity in conjunction with crop planting to see how biodiversity can help to reduce the inputs.

The environmental services provided by biodiversity appear more appropriate for cities. Such services appear to be less constrained by size. People have a natural affinity for nature. City dwellers make it a point to get in touch with nature occasionally in order to escape from the harshness of a built environment. Parks and nature areas are important recreational amenities and are described as a city's lungs. The aesthetic quality of nature gives some sense of enjoyment and relief to many people and helps to refresh and rejuvenate the mind. Having biodiversity right in the heart of cities provides a soothing and calming atmosphere and city planners adopt the most efficient manner by designating specific areas for parks so that they stay out of the way of further development. Manicured parks for people to enjoy at leisure have limited biodiversity but are still an avenue for some biodiversity to exist in a built environment (Figure 6).

Fig. 6 A healthy mix of nature and buildings create a relaxing atmosphere for people to enjoy

Tall trees provide welcome shade in hot weather while flowering shrubs add color and vibrancy to any city landscape (Figure 7). The cooling effect of plants is a useful service that can reduce energy demand needed to lower the temperature in buildings all year in the tropics and during summer in the higher latitudes. Rooftop gardens are effective at preventing excessive overheating of buildings (Figure 8). The careful integration of planters in building facades and positioning of tall trees can provide maximum shading and keep the ambient temperature down. Vertical greening is also an option that can be explored. Exploited in this manner, biodiversity has a role in creating more suitable environmental conditions for people. It also helps to improve sustainability by lowering energy demand.

The rooftop garden concept has been adopted by cities throughout the world, e.g. in Germany, Switzerland, Japan and United States of America. In Singapore, a study showed the numerous benefits of establishing biodiversity on flat exposed rooftops that can reach 58° centigrade during the day

Fig. 7   Creative use of flowering plants does help to beautify and add colour to the cityscape

(National Parks Board and Centre for Total Building Performance, 2002). Rooftop gardens lowered roof surface temperature to 31° centigrade and reduced ambient air temperature by 4° centigrade. The insulation against heat transfer to the interior of a five-storey commercial building resulted in a 15 per cent net annual energy saving.

The city of Chicago, set on becoming a green city, has targeted more than 2 million square feet of rooftop gardens, more than that allocated by all other US cities combined (Ferkenhoff, 2006). The first rooftop garden on its City Hall kept roof temperature on a cloudy summer day at 22° centigrade, similar to the air temperature, while the exposed rooftop of an adjacent building reached 66.6° centigrade. The plants also added to the aesthetic value and are recognised for filtering the air, reducing pollution and improving air quality. Over 30 species of birds are attracted by the 150 species of plants. In addition, economic opportunities have opened up with some rooftop gardens supporting the planting of simple crops such as herbs, tomatoes and onions, and the keeping of beehives for honey. Chicago's

Fig. 8 Rooftop gardens increase biodiversity in cities while at the same time reduce heat transfer to the interior of buildings

green movement is expected to save billions in reduced energy costs and new businesses.

Apart from terrestrial biodiversity, there is aquatic biodiversity to be considered for freshwater habitats such as ponds, lakes and rivers, and marine biodiversity for coastal cities. Rivers and aquatic bodies add a welcome change to the scenery and offer different recreational possibilities. Similarly, the marine environment opens up a range of leisure opportunities. Such are the service values of natural habitats that keep city dwellers occupied and removed from boredom. Like the terrestrial habitat, the health of the aquatic habitat is also dependent on its biodiversity. Water bodies are considered downstream habitats and receive much of land-based pollutants washed out during rainfall. Species richness promotes better cycling of materials and enables the habitat to better assimilate the degradable pollutants at more efficient levels. Aquatic biodiversity also attracts attention as people do not get to see aquatic species as much as terrestrial species.

Biodiversity certainly has positive roles in the urban environment. It provides healthy recreational outlets and offers an important social amenity. Hence, biodiversity contributes to sustainability by maintaining good environmental quality and especially for cities in the tropics or during summer, helps to keep buildings cool and reduces dependence on energy required for air-conditioning. The role of biodiversity in the built environment has until recently been under-estimated. Biodiversity was then considered to be standing the way of development and it was more efficient to wipe it clean off the land designated for construction. Another contributory factor is that biodiversity has seldom been viewed as a resource system and hence eliminating it was never considered a big deal. The perception of developers is that biodiversity can easily be brought back based on the impression that biodiversity can be symbolically represented by a few trees and plants. Sustainability-wise, this approach makes no sense. A more enlightened approach is to consider the biodiversity value of the habitat that is to be sacrificed and plan the development to avoid destroying species of high conservation value or implement effective mitigation measures. During the development of the facilities for the 2000 Olympic Games in Sydney, discovery of the rare Bell frog (*Litoria aurea*) on the site of the tennis centre prompted the construction of special tunnels to allow them safe access to nearby creeks and ensure the frog population's viability.

ECOLOGICAL CONSIDERATIONS RELEVANT TO THE CITY ENVIRONMENT

There is now better understanding of the benefits of biodiversity to the environment and to human society. Targets were set at the 2002 World Summit on Sustainable Development in Johannesburg to substantially reduce biodiversity loss by 2010. This set the pace and direction for the implementation of numerous initiatives by many agencies globally to reverse biodiversity degradation trends. The role of cities in biodiversity maintenance came more into focus in recent years. The 2007 "Curitiba Declaration on Cities and Biodiversity" resolved to integrate biodiversity into urbanised areas. At the 2008 Biodiversity Summit in Bonn, a Steering Committee for an initiative on "Cities and Biodiversity" was established to develop a full fledged integrated work programme for adoption by 2010 where cities can contribute effectively to conservation, sustainable use and the sharing of benefits.

Biodiversity represents a country's natural heritage. It is a possession that raises national pride, improves the sense of national identity, and can be used as symbolic gifts in diplomatic exchanges. Well known are China's giant pandas and Japan's cherry blossom trees. Endemic species especially have increased values in this respect. Singapore's National Parks Board launched the Heritage Roads and Heritage Tree Schemes in 2001 to conserve unique and established trees along some roads. Trees species are indigenous and give a pleasant forest ambience to road users. Dr Geh Min, who is the former President of Nature Society (Singapore), noted during the World Cities Summit 2008 that the National Parks Acts were amended to give better protection to Singapore's nature areas and the first Singapore green plan was introduced in 1993, which identified 19 terrestrial and four marine areas. Outside the nature reserves, as Ng Lang, CEO, National Parks Board recounted, Singapore has developed a green network of parks and park connectors. Plans are being implemented to build signature world-class gardens. The outcome is that there are now more than 360 bird species in Singapore, representing about 60 per cent of the species of birds in the UK and 70 per cent more than France. There is a growing partnership among the different sectors to sustain the positive trend in bringing up the city-state's biodiversity conservation. Elsewhere, as mentioned earlier, in South Korea's second largest city of Pusan, a concerted effort is made to protect the Nakdong River estuary, recognised as supporting the city's richest biodiversity. Declared as a national monument in 1966, it is now managed as a wetland conservation area in spite of strong development pressure. Measures to maintain the ecosystem's integrity include the re-alignment of the new Myungji Bridge.

A stronger argument is that the economic value of the genetic material when found to have application in the biomedical sector is enormous. For this reason, many countries have taken steps to preserve their genetic bank and in doing so are keeping intact a valuable resource with a large commercial potential. This is commonly done by protecting natural areas. The larger they are the better their functioning since large areas ensure a sizeable core with less edge effect. Fragmenting a large habitat into smaller fragments immediately erodes the core area as containing boundaries lengthen together with increased exposure to edge effect. This makes it more difficult to preserve species that are vulnerable to disturbance. However, a series of natural reserves selected on the basis of biodiversity and location can function quite effectively for biodiversity preservation. Such an arrangement adopted in Costa Rica (Boza, 2002) has the advantage of management ease. For smaller countries, this approach makes sense and is easier to accept. The underlying ecological consideration is that a minimum size has to be met for a fragment to function in the role of biodiversity protection.

If habitat fragmentation is unavoidable, then the next consideration is to link them into a network to reduce isolation and facilitate movement of species between the fragments. Powell *et al.* (2000) suggested that the establishment of linkage zones can improve ecological connectivity between the protected areas. Natural corridors can improve connectivity but the advantages and disadvantages will continue to be open to debate. Isolation curtails migration of species, restricts them to the resources within a fragment and provides no bail out opportunity should the fragment be heavily degraded. Connectivity on the other hand, increases the risk of spread of disease and other disasters such as a forest fire. The scientific basis of ecological corridors is still being debated but policy and practice have been more receptive (Van Der Windt and Swart, 2007).

Ideally, if cities were planned and built around nature, high levels of sustainability can be achieved as less will be spent on technological and engineering interventions to maintain environmental quality and improve its carrying capacity. In high density cities, full sustainability is not possible, but the ecosystems services provided by biodiversity can help to lower the cost of environmental rejuvenation by purely technological means. Cities that incorporate biodiversity have the option of utilising a combination of biological and engineering solutions in pursuit of sustainability. The dependence can tilt more in favour of ecology. Not only is it a less costly alternative, but also one that allows people to enjoy and relax. Wetlands for example, can be exploited to purify water to levels at which it is less expensive and less carbon demanding to clean it fully by technology. Aquatic plants along the banks of water bodies help to remove pollutants from the water for free (Figure 9). Concreted banks simply prevent this first level

Fig. 9 Biodiversity performs a water cleansing role. Aquatic vegetation provides the first stage filtration by absorbing pollutants from drainage water

filtration. In Singapore, a pilot project to use gardens to filter rainwater was completed in 2008 by the Public Utilities Board. Called a 'rain garden', the plant species were selected for their ability to trap soil contaminants from surface runoff. This first stage natural treatment makes the final treatment less expensive.

The cost of free services offered by ecosystems is not widely appreciated. Nutrient cycling by tropical forests are valued at US$3,800 billion annually, while climate regulation and waste treatment by temperate forests reach US$894 billion a year (Costanza *et al.*, 1997). Swamps give an annual US$3,200 billion worth of services in terms of water supply and disturbance regulation. These figures translate into substantial savings. Destroying a natural system means loss of these savings as more will be spent on providing the technological fixes to replace these services. In this respect, biodiversity has a role in financial sustainability, but is seldom accounted for. Cities should plan to include biodiversity, not exclude it. The development of an Urban Biodiversity Index, proposed by Singapore's Minister of National Development, Mr Mah Bow Tan, can serve as a measure of a city's progress in biodiversity conservation. While details of the Index have yet to be finalised, the concept gives biodiversity the deserved recognition. It will focus attention to the value of biodiversity and its role in making sustainability less remote, and encourage stronger measures to increase urban biodiversity. In addition, Singapore will be hosting in early 2009 an expert meeting on guidelines for the preparation of a cities and biodiversity plan of action for the implementation of the three objectives — conservation, sustainable use and the sharing of benefits.

In cases of a built environments where biodiversity was not central to the planning, the re-introduction of biodiversity is at best *ad-hoc* and requires a lot of creativity in making plants and animals adapt to demands that are commonly beyond ecological norms. This less efficient approach should not be dismissed. Under the circumstances, it will be an acceptable compromise if biodiversity is brought back to serve specific functions. For cities, enhancing biodiversity to cleanse waterways, to reduce indoor temperature (rooftop gardens), to increase food production even if on a limited scale, to improve air quality and to provide recreational relief, should be considered appropriate. Ecologically, this approach is not suitable for biodiversity conservation because the best strategy to protect species requires protection of the entire ecosystem, which is not pragmatic for built-up areas. However, with careful planning, biodiversity enhancement can be maximised despite the limitations.

Another approach to enhance biodiversity with little external input is to allow natural colonisation of abandoned or public land within cities. Without any human intervention, such areas will be colonised by pioneer species and through ecological succession, develop into a maintenance-free 'wild' habitat with a good mix of species. Biologically, such areas are more productive and can accommodate a greater species diversity compared to one that is managed and maintained. Social acceptance of this approach will be the major obstacle. People remain wary of such places because of the untidy look and the possibility of dangerous creatures that may spill out. These are acceptable for a nature reserve, but not within a built environment. The nature reserve is usually far removed from human dwellings and people feel secure from unwelcomed creatures. Homes next to 'wild' areas are vulnerable to snakes and other creepy crawlies. What people are comfortable with is to be able to enjoy nature and its services but without the 'threat' from such creatures. This demand is met by parks and landscaped gardens.

Nature reserves in or close to cities have to cater to large numbers of visitors. They are easily accessible and many city dwellers want to be close to nature. This raises the problem of impact from the high visitor traffic. Fixed trails are needed to regulate and contain the impact. Boardwalks and elevated access ways are essential for nature areas in cities to keep the ecology intact and removed from visitor traffic (Figures 10 and 11).

Fig. 10   A boardwalk through a mangrove confines the impact from visitors and at the same time makes it easier for city dwellers to appreciate the habitat

Fig. 11 Specially constructed bridges allow visitors to admire biodiversity at the tree canopy level of forests

THE CHALLENGE OF BIODIVERSITY ENHANCEMENT IN CITIES

Biodiversity has an important role in cities. It can reduce a city's environmental footprint which translates directly into cost savings. In return, cities can contribute to the reversal of ecosystem degradation by implementing effective biodiversity enhancement programmes. Countries with large wilderness areas can afford to set them aside for protection, but cities everywhere can enjoy biodiversity services. Biodiversity and cities are compatible and the benefits of biodiversity are known. Proper and enlightened planning can increase biodiversity in the built environment and raise its sustainability level.

Restrictions within the built environment require a new look at ecological principles to see how best the obstacles can be addressed. Fragmentation is inevitable and ecological knowledge indicates that this is not good for biodiversity preservation. However, this is still better than having no diversity at all. Network corridors can be established to overcome this restriction. At the same time, planners should accept biodiversity as a resource system and understand its full value and potential to improve sustainability. Biodiversity enhancement is really an investment for better environmental quality over the long term.

Enhancing and protecting biodiversity in cities requires ingenuity, creativity and the willingness to test novel ideas. The most popular approach to establishing nature in cities is to plant trees, mainly for their shading effect. This common response can be expanded to improve biodiversity by simply considering what species should be planted where and what species of animals they are likely to attract. Tree planting is one of the simplest of options and has been adopted by many cities (Roberts and Kanaley, 2006). New innovations include rooftop gardens, vertical greening, and the use of biodiversity for services such as water filtration, air purification, food security and carbon sequestration.

Political will is crucial and cost-benefit analysis should take into account the environmental services inherent in biodiversity. Biodiversity restoration should be cost-effective but many planners perceive this as the cheapest means available. Cost-effectiveness should not be equated with the lowest cost. Millions of dollars are spent in developing infrastructure to ensure that environmental quality is maintained at a certain level. Spending millions of dollars on habitat restoration is still largely unthinkable for the simple reason that there is little awareness of the service benefits that biodiversity provides over the long term. Investing large sums of money on habitat restoration and biodiversity enhancement requires strong and committed political will.

Social acceptance of biodiversity for what it is can be a challenge. Car owners want to enjoy the shade provided by large trees in outdoor car parks, but cannot tolerate bird droppings because these dirty their cars. People want to be close to nature to enjoy its tranquil atmosphere, but cannot tolerate 'wild' creatures entering their homes.

Another great challenge of enhancing biodiversity in cities is for everyone to be able to accept nature not only for its ecological function but also for its social function (Eden and Tunstall, 2006). Cities are for people but nature can provide both functions to create a more livable environment.

The process initiated at the "Curitiba Declaration on Cities and Biodiversity" has strengthened the network of political leaders committed to the reversal of biodiversity degradation in the urban environment and the strong role that cities can perform in addressing the target set at the 2002 Johannesburg World Summit on Sustainable Development of substantially reducing the rate of biodiversity loss by 2010. At the 2008 Bonn Local Action for Biodiversity meeting involving 50 mayors and representatives from 30 countries, a roadmap was established to develop measures of biodiversity and an action plan for adoption at the Nagoya Summit on Cities and Biodiversity was planned for 2010 to coincide with the International Year on Biodiversity. All these activities confirm the belief that cities can be a solution and not just the problem to unprecedented biodiversity loss. Dr Ahmed Djoghlaf, Executive Secretary of the Convention on Biological Diversity emphasised the role of cities very succinctly at the Biodiversity in Sustainable Cities session of the Singapore World Cities Summit 2008 when he said, "Indeed, the fight for life on Earth will be won or will be lost in cities of tomorrow. The hearts of citizens must be won. The local authorities have a major role to play as global change starts at the local level".

REFERENCES

Boza, MA (2002). Conservation in action: Past, present, and future of the National Park System of Costa Rica. *Conservation Biology*, 7(2), 239–247.

Chou, LM (1998). The cleaning of Singapore River and the Kallang Basin: Approaches, methods, investments and benefits. *Journal of Ocean and Coastal Management*, 38(2), 133–145.

Costanza, R, R d'Arge, R de Groot, S Farber, M Grasso, B Hannon, K Limburg, S Naeem, RV O'Neill, J Paruelo, RG Raskin, P Sutton and M van den Belt (1997). The value of the world's ecosystem services and natural capital. *Nature*, 387, 253–260.

Eden, S and S Tunstall (2006). Ecological versus social restoration? How urban river restoration challenges but also fails to challenge the science-policy nexus in the United Kingdom. *Environment and Planning C: Government and Policy*, 24, 661–680.

Ferkenhoff, E (2006.) The greening of Chicago. *Time*, May 12.

Kajikawa, A, Y Masuda, M Sato, N Takahashi and T Ojima (2005). A field study on revived conditions of covered rivers in Tokyo's 23 wards. *Journal of Asian Architecture and Building Engineering*, 4(2), 489–494.

Kim, NC (2005). Ecological restoration and revegetation works in Korea. *Landscape Ecology and Engineering*, 1, 77–83.

Millennium Ecosystem Assessment. (2005). *Ecosytems and Human Well-being Biodiversity Synthesis*. Washington, DC: World Resources Institute.

National Parks Board and Centre for Total Building Performance, School of Design & Environment, *Handbook of Skyrise Greening In Singapore*. National University of Singapore. 2002.

Powell, GVN, J Barborak and S Rodriguez (2000). Assessing representativeness of protected natural areas in Costa Rica for conserving biodiversity: A preliminary gap analysis. *Biological Conservation*, 93(1), 35–41.

Roberts, B and T Kanaley (eds.) (2006) . *Urbanization and Sustainability in Asia; Good Practice Approaches in Urban Region Development*. Asian Development Bank, Philippines.

Schmidheiny, S (1992). *Changing Course: A Global Business Perspective on Development and the Environment*. Cambridge, MA: MIT Press,.

Tapsell, SM (1995). River restoration: What are we restoring to? A case study of the Ravensbourne river. *London. Landscape Research*, 20(3), 98–111.

Van Der Windt, HJ and JAA Swart (2007). Ecological corridors, connecting science and politics: The case of the Green River in the Netherlands. *Journal of Applied Ecology*, 45(1), 124–132.

8 Liveable Cities

ANDREW TAN

INTRODUCTION

The first East Asia Summit on Liveable Cities Conference (EAS LCC) was held in Singapore on 22–25 June 2008, in conjunction with the World Cities Summit (WCS) and the Singapore International Water Week (SIWW). The EAS LCC aims to create a platform for East Asian cities to network and contribute to the global effort to address climate change.

The inaugural EAS LCC brought together mayors and governors from East Asian cities, who shared challenges, best practices and expertise in developing sustainable and ecologically-friendly cities. Delegates from 25 cities representing all 15 East Asian participating countries attended the Conference (Annex 1). The Conference also featured practitioners and thought leaders with insights and experiences in the areas of public governance and sustainable development of cities.

The highlight of the EAS Conference was a plenary session on 25 June 2008. It was chaired by Mr Mah Bow Tan, Minister for National Development, Singapore, who in his welcome remarks, noted that East Asian cities are experiencing large population growth. As cities become more crowded, congested and polluted, policy and decision-makers who are responsible for the development of cities and the well-being of their citizens must face and overcome a major challenge — that of developing and growing their city while still making it liveable for the people.

Governors/Mayors or their representatives from four East Asia Summit cities — Jakarta, Foshan, Melbourne, Tokyo — shared their cities' experiences in balancing modernisation and urbanisation with sustainable development and environmental protection. Thereafter, the EAS Conference delegates discussed the common challenges facing East Asian cities, and exchanged views on how East Asian cities could work together to develop sustainable and ecologically-friendly cities. This chapter aims to consolidate the different ideas exchanged and lessons learnt.

LIVEABILITY AND SUSTAINABILITY

All too often, liveability is confused or identified with sustainability. According to the Amsterdam city council, "liveability, in contrast to sustainability, does not refer to the future but to the current state of the environment, which must offer an acceptable quality of life" (de Roo, 2003, p. 40). In parallel, a government discussion paper of Victoria — Australia's most densely populated and urbanised state — drew a distinction between liveability and sustainability. Amongst one of the key messages of this paper is that most liveability and quality of life measures are a weighted index of locational characteristics, which are believed to contribute towards the liveability of a place. Sustainability indicators extend beyond economic indicators to include environmental and equity goals (Victoria, Australia, 2008).

Yet, there are those who feel that the two go hand in hand. According to Mr John So, Mayor of Melbourne, "to be liveable, we must be sustainable". He stressed that cities should, like the City of Melbourne since 1997, make sustainability a core consideration in city planning has done and operations — the goal is to provide the world's best quality of life for all citizens, now and in the future. Melbourne's mix of culture, low cost of living, job opportunities and green spaces has seen the city voted by *The Economist* as the world's most liveable city three times in the last decade. Singapore, too, was ranked as the most liveable city in Asia in 2008 by Mercer, and consistently recognised to be amongst the top liveable cities in the world (http://app.mewr.gov.sg/web/Contents/ContentsSSS.aspx?ContId=1039).

The World's Most Liveable Cities is an informal name given to any list of cities as they rank on a reputable annual survey of living conditions. The most commonly known liveability measures are the Economist Intelligence Unit's Liveable Cities Index and Mercer's Quality of Living Survey, which are composite measures of weighted characteristics (Measures of Liveability and Sustainability, 2008). It should be noted, however, that the choice of measure may provide different rankings in the liveability of cities. According to the Measures of Liveability and Sustainability 2008, the difference in rankings is a result of the subjective nature of the inclusion of factors relating to liveability, the weighting of these factors, and the vastly different indicators being included. There is a lack of theoretical underpinning for these measures, particularly with respect to composite measures. As such, it is questionable whether any of the available composite measures is directly relevant towards the formulation of public policy. Nonetheless, the measures are based on factors that people consider representative of quality of living (Mercer Human Resources Consulting Quality of Living Survey 2008).

It may be instructive to have an insight into Melbourne's successful approach towards achieving 'liveability'. The five principles that Melbourne views as major components for achieving liveability and sustainability — and also has abided by since 1997 — are discussed below.

First Principle: Retaining Local Character

With urban architecture and branding going global, it becomes increasingly important for cities to protect their local identity and retain a point of difference, that is, there is a need to retain the city's distinctive identity which is what attracts visitors and keeps residents satisfied. Hence, an effort must be made to capitalise on the city's unique characteristics. Heritage controls are essential in retaining the city's physical history, heritage and identity.

Second Principle: Ensuring Connectivity

Connectivity is the glue that holds a city together. Good connectivity will improve access and movement within and out of the city. A comprehensive network of walking, running and bike paths are driving a shift towards sustainable transport. Well-defined places of work, entertainment and leisure — coupled with good quality public facilities — help community members connect with one another.

Third Principle: Higher Density Living

By increasing the concentration of population and activity in central urban areas, vehicle usage, pollution and carbon emissions are reduced. This is because higher density living is believed to (i) reduce the consumption of land, which thus preserves public space; (ii) reduce distances travelled and traffic congestion; (iii) improve efficiency of infrastructure and promote public transport; and (iv) reduce energy consumption.

Fourth Principle: Diversity in Land Use

Ensuring a diversity of accommodation, businesses and infrastructure is the cornerstone of healthy, vibrant and sustainable communities. Mixed land use offers people convenience, choice and opportunities to build a sense of community. It reduces dependency on cars, encourages more walking and cycling, increases the viability of local businesses and reduces crime. In fact, when high-density urban development enables diversity to occur, the results may seem to be disorganised from outside but they demonstrate a kind of flexibility and resilience in the everyday living environment that is essential to sustain a city in the long run (Heng and Malone-Lee, 2008).

Fifth Principle: Ensuring a High Quality Public Realm

Everyone likes to live in a place that is clean, green, welcoming and safe. A high quality urban environment attracts people, increases economic performance and encourages activity at street level. In addition, it builds community pride by getting people in public places and improving social interaction. To create such an environment, the city can plant trees and potted plants, improve streetscapes, create new public spaces and improve pedestrian lighting.

Indeed, it appears that cities are generally adopting initiatives in line with the principles outlined above. The city of Foshan is an example. Mr Tianming Zhou, Vice Mayor of Foshan, People's Republic of China, shared Foshan's aim to develop the city into an advanced manufacturing base, a modern service centre for production, a city reputed for its culture and a home of great beauty and wealth. In particular, Foshan implemented five initiatives — consistent with Melbourne's Principles 1 to 5 — to achieve this goal:

- *Implement a comprehensive administration of the environment.* The construction of environmental protection infrastructural facilities has been accelerated in an attempt to restore the natural ecological environment of the water body. In addition, with energy conservation and emission reduction as the focus, air pollution prevention and control will be reinforced. The plan is to phase out enterprises or production processes with backward production facilities or that cause heavy pollution, and develop clean industries in their stead.
- *Preserve its heritage.* The aim is to achieve harmony between man and nature and enhance nature's ecological protection and construction. Tree planting will be encouraged, the greening of the construction of the city landscape will be promoted — generally, a move towards an ecological city which is suitable for living and working.
- *Establish a modern industrial system.* Foshan aims to strengthen cooperation with *internationally* advanced cities in areas of urban planning, construction of logistics parks and industry development so as to elevate standards and modernise industries.
- *Promote the city's internationalisation.* Accelerate the construction of a comprehensive modern transportation system and urban public infrastructure by reinforcing comprehensive urban administration and drawing upon the developmental experiences of *advanced* cities across the world so as to promote the internationalisation of the city.
- *Construct a wealthy and harmonious city.* In accelerating economic development, greater *importance* will be attached to the development of social enterprises such as education, culture, sanitation, sports and social security.

Foshan's aims took into account "sustainable development and international competitiveness for its industries", while noting the "great pressure in protecting the resources environment and the heavy task of conducting energy conservation and emission reduction, environmental administration, and construction of an ecological city" (Centre for Liveable Cities, 2008, p. 12).

The significance of sustainability was also shared by Dr Ing Fauzi Bowo, Governor of Jakarta, Indonesia, who keenly felt that "a city developed on a basis of sustainability will bring prosperity and better socioeconomic conditions to its people". Prosperity will mean that citizens can enjoy a better level of education, better socioeconomic conditions, and can more effectively participate in making the city a sustainable one, thereby guaranteeing their own future in the process. Dr Ing Fauzi Bowo clarified the influence of the following factors in sustainable city development:

- *Size of population.* The greater the city's population, the more complicated the steps needed to *establish* a sustainable city. The influx of immigrants and the city as a place where people travel to work will threaten the sustainability of the city. Large populations and their economic activities are factors to consider in urban sustainability. A common way in which population growth can be influenced is through family planning programmes.
- *Income per capita.* The lower the average income per capita, the more difficult it is to work towards a sustainable city. Indeed, a city requires substantial funds to be able to provide a *suitable* level of public service to its citizens and to develop in a sustainable fashion. However, without subsidy programmes from the central government and with a low average income per capita, this task will prove rather challenging.
- *Level of education.* It is easier to promote the concept of sustainability, publicise awareness of its *importance*, and encourage public participation in working towards it when the community is better educated.
- *Availability of space.* The more scarce the land or space is, the more complicated it is to *establish* a sustainable city. Cities with a high population density, limited land and intensive economic activity will experience high land prices because of competing land uses.
- *Administrative competence.* The lower the competence and autonomy of the city administration, the more difficult it is to emphasise sustainability in a city's agenda. If the power still resides at the national level, decisions on river management, planning and other strategic areas at the local level cannot be made easily.

Dr Ing Fauzi Bowo also highlighted that big cities need to take a different variety of actions from smaller cities. Purely technical solutions must be combined with social engineering as a developmental approach. With strong commitment and continued support from all stakeholders (community, city government and central government), a sustainable city can be established.

CHALLENGES FACING CITIES

Faced with many serious environmental issues that include global warming, the Earth is presently in a critical state. While being a driving force behind the development of civilisation, cities — where the majority of the world population is expected to reside — are also consumers of vast quantities of resources and energy and are becoming a heavy burden on the global environment. As such, 'sustainable development' has been gaining prominence in recent times, with more attention focused on the need for cities to grow in a responsible manner. In addition, the climate is changing, putting stress on the natural environment and water sources. More and more people use the city every day, posing serious challenges in terms of access to transport, pollution, waste, energy-use and carbon emissions. The rest of this section illustrates some of the sustainable development initiatives adopted by cities in the face of various challenges.

Environmental Management

In this respect, Mr Hiroshi Mori, Senior Director, Tokyo Metropolitan Government, shared Tokyo's success in implementing regulations on diesel vehicle emissions as well as compulsory greening on rooftops for new construction projects in metropolitan areas. Tokyo aims to have the lowest environmental burden on the world through reduced carbon emissions and increased use of solar energy. Tokyo has taken the initiative ahead of the national government and implemented its own regulations on diesel vehicle emissions, achieving a momentous improvement in the quality of Tokyo's air. Furthermore, the compulsory greening of rooftops at new construction projects resulted in the creation of approximately 90 hectares of new greenery inside the metropolis. In "Tokyo's Big Change: The 10-year Plan", Tokyo's urban development strategy, two goals with "environment" as the keyword have been included. One goal is related to greenhouse gas emissions, while the other revolves around the physical environment.

By 2020, Tokyo aims to "realise a city model with the lowest environmental burden in the world" and hopes to reduce "greenhouse gas emissions by 25 per cent from their 2000 levels". A bill to be resolved by the current session of the Tokyo Metropolitan Assembly is calling for an emission trading scheme and a mandatory cap on large emitters to reduce their emissions. This will be the world's first emission reduction scheme that also targets office buildings that abound in large cities. Furthermore, Tokyo, as the first member from Asia, is now participating in the "International Carbon Action Partnership (ICAP)" and presenting its new cap and trading scheme to the world.

In addition, Tokyo will establish a system to purchase the environmental value of solar energy, with the aim of increasing the use of solar energy to approximately one million kilowatts through the promotion and distribution of solar-generated power and solar-powered devices. Tokyo established the Asian Network of Major Cities 21 in 2001. In this association, 11 large Asian cities, including Singapore and Tokyo, are jointly attempting to resolve common issues generated by big cities through various initiatives, which focus on the environment, crisis management, and industrial promotion, among others. With respect to the environment, efforts are being made in areas that deal with automobile emission countermeasures, global warming and the education of human resources. In October 2008, cities participating in "The Large Cities Climate Leadership Group: C40" and the member executives of the Asian Network of Major Cities 21 were invited to Tokyo to the C40 Tokyo Conference on Climate Change. With the necessary expertise and a mutual sense of crisis, measures against the heat-island phenomena, drought, and other environmental severities were studied.

The EAS LCC delegates also noted various other initiatives such as Yokohama City's programme by which citizens actively sorted out garbage as a contribution towards preserving the environment, as well as Chennai's efforts to use bio-degradable packaging material, and also regenerate its rivers. Cities should also look into practical, affordable changes that make buildings cleaner and more efficient. Melbourne's experience holds some important lessons. Two years ago, Melbourne completed the construction of CH2, Australia's greenest office building. Apart from being the winner of the United Nations design awards, it has become an international case study in sustainable urban development. Home to city employees, it uses natural light and ventilation to create an inviting and productive workplace. Indeed, its smart design reduces energy use and emissions by over 80 per cent, saving the city council over $1 million annually. With an estimated environmental technology payback period of seven years, it stands as a replicable development to other governments and businesses. Energy use in residential and commercial buildings accounts for 95 per cent of greenhouse gas emissions from the municipality. CH2 demonstrates what is possible in the construction of new buildings.

However, Melbourne's greatest current challenge is the reduction of emissions created by existing city buildings. The performance of *existing* building stock must be improved to make a difference. To attain this goal, Melbourne has embarked on programmes in the following three core areas:

- Education of city users, particularly hotels, in energy and waste reduction;
- Changes to planning regulations;
- Partnership with the Clinton Climate Initiative to develop financial models for the retrofitting of old buildings.

Melbourne has adopted the Energy Efficiency Building Retrofit Programme. The programme provides cities and private building owners with access to lower cost funds for retrofitting existing buildings with energy efficient products. A landmark programme which realises energy savings of up to 50 per cent, this programme brings together four of the world's largest energy service companies, five of the world's largest banks, and sixteen of the world's largest cities.

In 2003, Melbourne installed over 1,300 solar panels on the roof of the city's largest market, Queen Victoria — the largest solar grid of its kind in the Southern Hemisphere. It generates 250,000 kilowatt-hours of electricity each year, which compensates significantly for the Market's electricity use. Apart from the above initiatives, Melbourne now purchases green energy produced from renewable sources. Moreover, the city invests in emerging technology, thereby creating a local 'clean technology' industry. For instance, Melbourne currently trails the 'active reactor', groundbreaking energy-efficient street lighting engineered by a local technology company.

Sustainable Transport Solutions

With public transport being the most efficient means of transporting passengers, Jakarta employs a mass rapid transportation project which involves the mass rapid transit, Light Rail Transit, as well as extending the bus way network. The objective of the project is to expand passenger transport capacity by constructing a mass rapid transit system in the Jakarta metropolitan area where traffic is heavier (Japan Bank for International Cooperation, http://www.jbic.or.id/en/oeco-mrt.php). This initiative, 'Energy Efficiency in Transportation', also serves the additional function of improving air quality. Apart from encouraging greater use of the public transport system, non-motorised means such as cycling can be explored. In the effort to pursue sustainable transport solutions, Melbourne has actually created safe pedestrian and bike paths for its citizens.

Water Management

In Jakarta, the 'Water for Life' initiative is implemented in response to their water management issues. An unprecedented increase in extreme weather events meant that programmes/projects had to be implemented towards the sustainable development of Jakarta. These events included floods due to longer rainy seasons and droughts due to lack of water resources and scarcity of water resources in terms of quality and quantity, as well as sea water intrusion due to the overuse of artesian wells creating land subsidence. The programmes/projects that had to be implemented included:

- Flood control projects (construction of canals, ponds and dams, and dredging existing rivers, canals and dams);
- Sanitation improvement projects (large- and small-scale solid waste management and treatment);
- Improvement in water supply and control of the use of artesian wells.

The city of Tokyo too has been supplying world-renowned safe and superior quality tap water to much of the metropolis, made possible through its advanced water treatment technology. Tokyo's innovative water management methods include advanced waste water reclamation technology and an outstanding water supply technology, which boasts an extremely low leakage rate of approximately 3 per cent.

Quality of Physical Environment

Improving the quality of the physical environment ensures that the city continues to be a clean, green and attractive city, with green and blue spaces for all to enjoy. In the attempt to beautify Jakarta, the city has implemented the 'Going Green' initiative, resulting in green areas being developed. New green open spaces — both large- and small-scale — and interactive parks have been created.

Tokyo, too, aims to restore the city's beauty as a "city of water and greenery". For that purpose, it intends to create a Tokyo bay area through reclamation and green initiatives. Tokyo has embarked upon a project to transform reclaimed land in Tokyo bay made of waste and soil from construction sites into 88 hectares of abundant natural greenery, to be known as "Umi-no-Mori (Green Island)". In addition, Tokyo is doubling the number of roadside trees in the metropolis to one million. Similarly, a thousand hectares of new greenery will be created by greening up rooftops and refurbishing city parks. The aim is to achieve the image of a comfortable Tokyo with plenty of greenery and cool ocean breezes.

The People Aspect

Dr Ing Fauzi Bowo emphasised that a key challenge in making cities more sustainable is a 'mindset change' towards encouraging progress rather than simply changing for change's sake. Apart from bureaucratic change in the Provincial Government itself, the mindset of all citizens must also be aligned. A shift in thinking will result in better cooperation and synergy among stakeholders. The community, government and private sector will then play a significant role in making Jakarta more sustainable. As such, Jakarta strives towards people-oriented policies via implementing initiatives such as 'Listening to the People's Voice'.

Jakarta believes it can realise this sustainability by:

• Empowering the community via awareness and activities. Awareness can be increased significantly at the community level. Target groups include neighbourhoods, school students and religious associations, where information can be promoted and disseminated via face-to-face dialogues. Activities that involve the community include the construction of ground water wells, the planting of trees and mangroves as well as the introduction of local public transport powered by natural gas.

• The role of the City Government. This includes enforcement of regulations for better quality of life (e.g. car and motorcycle emission controls, smoking bans and car-free days).

LESSONS APPLICABLE TO EAST ASIAN CITIES

There are numerous learning points that can be observed from the EAS LCC participating cities. East Asian cities can learn from the experience and success of other cities' initiatives. In the formulation of any policy, cities could keep in mind Melbourne's five principles in promoting liveability and sustainability as well as Jakarta's efforts to bring about a "mindset" change. Likewise, with respect to the creation of sustainable buildings, CH2, Australia's green office building could provide a good working example. This 10-storey building has sustainable technology incorporated into every aspect of its design. In addition, the building's energy-efficient features and fixtures show that conflicts regarding incentives can be reduced. CH2 has demonstrated that environmental sustainability and commerce do not have to be opposing forces; with the right approach and aligned thinking across all responsible parties, sustainability and commerce can be mutually reinforcing.

Being a small city-state with no natural resources, Singapore has more than its fair share of challenges. Although strong economic growth has improved the standard of living over the past 40 years, maintaining what has been achieved and making further improvements will be challenging. On the domestic front, greater economic and population growth will strain the living environment as well as its scarce land, water and energy resources. On the global front, rising fuel costs and higher demand for resources present uncertainties for the international economy, which will impact Singapore's small and open economy. Climate change further compounds the challenges as it requires early action by all countries to reduce carbon emissions, which cause global warming. It is therefore important for Singapore to be more efficient in the use of scarce resources such as water, energy and land, and thus contribute towards reducing carbon emissions in its bid to prepare itself for a more carbon-constrained world.

Resource efficiency is one of the three priorities identified by the Singapore Inter-Ministerial Committee on Sustainable Development (IMCSD), which was set up in February 2008 and is responsible for Singapore's sustainable development in the next 10 to 15 years. Here, the ideas shared by the other East Asian cities can be used as reference. Cities can promote resource efficiency amongst industry and businesses as well as within the transport sector.

The second area of priority is pollution control. Like many other cities, Singapore is not yet able to meet the US Environment Protection Agency (USEPA) standard for Particulate Matter 2.5 (http://app.mewr.gov.sg/web/Contents/ContentsSSS.aspx?ContId=1043). Diesel-driven vehicles such as goods vehicles and buses account for about half of the PM2.5 present in ambient air. In this aspect, Singapore can learn from Tokyo's success in implementing regulations on diesel vehicle emissions, which resulted in a momentous improvement in the quality of Tokyo's air.

Last but not least, the third priority lies in the quality of the physical environment. With the constant increase in population density, innovative measures to maintain cleanliness and enhance the physical environment of the city are required so as to ensure that residents can continue to have attractive spaces for leisure and social activities.

On the whole, East Asian cities could work with one another to share knowledge, influence change and develop solutions with global impact. As for cities that have formed strategic relationships with international sustainability groups, they are able to directly tap on the research and development achievements of larger cities, and thereby share the insights with other East Asian cities. Participating East Asian cities can then utilise the knowledge, and develop a tailored approach to deal with the challenges in their own cities.

Some East Asian cities are participating members of the C40 Cities climate leadership group — a group of the world's largest cities committed to tackling climate change. Through C40, participating cities struck an agreement with the Clinton Climate Initiative in August 2006, which allows them direct access to best practices in the reduction of carbon emissions and the increase of energy efficiency. Such knowledge, if shared with the rest of the East Asian cities, would certainly prove immensely valuable.

CONCLUSION AND FUTURE DIRECTIONS

Cities in East Asia are witnessing a phase of most rapid population growth in history. Two million new dwellers are expected in East Asian cities every month for the next 20 years (Gill and Kharas, 2007). City authorities will need to judiciously plan the development of their cities so that urbanisation and growth can be sustained.

Large cities including those in Asia, such as Tokyo, have the power to lead their countries and to come together in mutual cooperation to solve the challenges, including environmental ones, that they are all facing. The EAS Conference showed that there is a strong political will on the part of the participating cities to tackle the challenges of energy security, climate change and sustainable development. East Asian cities could play a key role in improving their country's energy efficiency, resource conservation, and help address the effects of climate change through pragmatic and practical measures. Simultaneously, the Conference recognised that every city is unique in its political, economic, cultural, geographic and climatic circumstances, and any measure must consider the diversity inherent in cities.

Despite their differences — in terms of economic development, size and resource endowments — East Asian cities face common challenges in catering to rapid population growth. These include ensuring access to clean water, addressing high carbon emissions and climate change effects, as well as redressing poor urban planning. The Conference agreed that the region should work together more actively to promote sustainable and ecologically-friendly communities. Events such as the EAS Conference provided good opportunities to share experiences and explore areas for collaboration.

Delegates agreed that the sharing of experiences and insights could pave the way for greater cooperation among the East Asian cities. According to the Governor of Tokyo, this is "an extremely noteworthy conference promoting teamwork among the cities of Asia and allowing them to work together towards the goal of realising cities which exist in harmony with the environment". In his concluding remarks, the Mr Mah Bow Tan noted, among other issues, Jakarta's key challenge of ensuring 'mindset change', and Foshan's desire to internationalise the city. He also highlighted that promoting public awareness and education, community-based initiatives, and the participation of citizens remain a paramount concern among cities. He further suggested that all cities could learn from Melbourne's success,

Tokyo's sense of urgency and its various contributions to making cities more sustainable.

In addition, Mr Mah suggested that Singapore could help facilitate the development of an informal network of like-minded cities through international conferences, workshops and pilot projects in collaboration with other cities, institutions and international organisations, to sustain these discussions and learning. Possible projects and programmes could include areas such as R&D, transfer of technology, joint test-bedding of projects, benchmarking and adopting best practices, creating an index or "star-rating" system for rating cities as well as cooperating on specific issues such as waste management and increasing citizen participation. Think-tanks could play a role in sustaining linkages, and Singapore's Centre for Liveable Cities (CLC) could serve as one such platform.

The CLC — jointly set up by Singapore's Ministry of National Development (MND) and Ministry of the Environment and Water Resources (MEWR) — is aimed at bringing together and building up competencies on sustainable urban planning, development and environment management across the public, private and people sectors. The establishment of the CLC was officially announced by Mr Lee Hsien Loong; Prime Minister, Singapore, during the World Cities Summit 2008. The CLC is set up with the intention of developing Singapore's expertise in the area of 'sustainable development'. The collated knowledge will be used for training, to influence the formulation of policies and further develop research in areas such as housing, recreation and transport. The aim is to complement and not to duplicate the work of various agencies already performing these functions. The CLC will host an integrated body of knowledge on the liveability of cities, encompassing areas such as urban planning, environmental management, sustainable transport solutions and effective resource management. The aim is for the CLC to be a centre of global excellence that brings together the best ideas and practices that support efforts in building liveable cities that are dynamic, vibrant, cohesive and sustainable.

EAS LCC cities recognised the need to balance economic growth and the environment in their development. They were all committed to addressing these challenges and had adopted somewhat similar strategies in energy efficiency, infrastructural solutions and the social and recreational needs of their citizens. There was also an awareness of the urgency and a sense of crisis for cities to develop in a more sustainable manner.

REFERENCES

Centre for Liveable Cities (2008). *Summary Report of the East Asia Summit Conference on Liveable Cities*. Singapore: Centre for Liveable Cities. http://www.clc.org.sg/pdf/EASLCC%20Plenary%20Summary%20Report.pdf

de Roo, G (2003). *Environmental Planning in the Netherlands: Too Good to be True: From Command-and-control Planning to Shared Governance*. Ashgate Publishing Ltd.

Greener Commerce and Community (2005). *Eco Voice*, 20, http://www.ecovoice.com.au/issues/issue%2020/EV20pg8Council.pdf

Heng, CK and LC Malone-Lee (2008). *Liveability, Density and Sustainability, Liveable Cities for Tomorrow, Centre for Liveable Cities Report*. Singapore: Centre for Liveable Cities.

Mercer Human Resources Consulting (2008). *Quality of Living Survey*. http://www.mercer.com/referencecontent.htm?idContent=1306640

Victoria, Australia (2008). *Measures of Liveability and Sustainability, Staff Discussion Paper* http://www.vcec.vic.gov.au/CA256EAF001C7B21/WebObj/Roundtable1-Staffdiscussionpaper-measuresofliveability/$File/Roundtable%201%20-%20Staff%20discussion%20paper%20-%20measures%20of%20liveability.pdf

Gill, I and H Kharas (eds.) (2007). *An East Asian Renaissance: Ideas for Economic Growth*. Washington DC, World Bank.

ANNEX 1: LIST OF PARTICIPANTS AT EAS LCC

Country	City	Name	Designation
Brunei	Bandar Seri Begawan	Pg Haji Mohd Ali bin Pg Haji Othman	Chairman of Municipal Board
	[Counterpart Ministry]	Pehin Dato Adanan Yusof	Minister of Home Affairs
	[Counterpart Ministry]	Dato Hamdillah H. A. Wahab	Dy Minister of Industry & Primary Resources
Cambodia	Phnom Penh	Trac Thai Sieng	Vice Governor
	Siem Reap	Sok Leakhena	Dy Governor
Indonesia	Jakarta	Dr Ing Fauzi Bowo	Governor
	Aceh	Irwandi Yusuf	Governor
Laos	Vientiane	Sinlavong Khoutphaythoune	Mayor
	Luang Prabang	Bounheuang Duangphachan	Governor

(*Continued*)

(*Continued*)

Country	City	Name	Designation
Malaysia	Malacca	Dato Latiff bin Tamby Chik	Chairman of Local Government and Environment Committee & State EXCO member
	[Counterpart Ministry]	Yeo Heng Hau	Dy Sec-Gen, Ministry of Housing & Local Government
Myanmar	Nay Pyi Taw	U Tun Kyi	Secretary
Philippines	Quezon City	Belmonte Feliciano	Mayor
	[Counterpart Ministry]	Austere Panadero	Under Secretary, Dept of Interior & Local Government
Thailand	Chiangmai	Piroj Saeng Poowong	Vice Governor
	Nonthaburi	*Churdvit Ridhiprasart*	*Governor (was represented by the Mayor of Nonthaburi)*
Vietnam	Ho Chi Minh	Nguyen Trung Tin	Vice-Chairman
	Hai Phong	Nguyen Van Thanh	Vice-Chairman
India	Ahmedabad	Kanaji Thakor	Mayor
	Chennai	*Ma. Subramaniam*	*Mayor (was represented by his Senior Comissioneri)*
Japan	Tokyo	Hiroshi Mori	Snr Director
	Yokohama	Hiroshi Nakada	Mayor
	Nagoya	—	Director, Mayor's Office
China	Tianjin	Lin Xue Fang	Vice Chairman, Eco-city Administrative Committee
	Guanzhou	Wang Dong	Director, Urban Planning Bureau
	Foshan	Zhou Tianming	Vice Mayor
New Zealand	Wellington	Ms Kerry Prendergast	Mayor
	[Counterpart Ministry]	Ms Tanya Perrott	Chief Advisor, Ministry of Economic Development
Australia	Melbourne	John So	Mayor
Korea	Busan	Jeong, Lakhyeong	Dy Mayor
	[Counterpart Ministry]	Young Geun, Lee	Dir-Gen, Ministry of Land, Transport and Maritime Activities
ASEAN		Dr Seoung Rathchavy	ASEAN Dy Sec-Gen

Collaboration between the Public and Private Sectors for Urban Development

SOCK-YONG PHANG

INTRODUCTION

In market economies, the government acts in many ways. In traditional public finance literature, the government taxes and provides public and merit goods. In addition, it regulates the behaviour of firms and individuals. In the context of market failures such as natural monopoly, high risk situations or long life projects, the government may choose to act as producer. In the past two decades, however, public sector collaboration with the private sector to achieve socio-economic objectives has become widely utilised as a method for the provision of the myriad of services that has come to be expected of governments.

There is a diversity of definitions and meanings (resulting in some confusion) for what constitutes collaboration between the public and private sectors. Collaborative arrangements may mean different things in different contexts. The range of perspectives and perceived desirability of these arrangements are affected by ideology, national, political, and socio-economic circumstances.

A broad definition of collaboration between the public and private sectors would be the state and private sectors (firms, individuals and non-government organisations) working together to achieve societal goals. An example of an 'informal' collaboration is the energy saving 'Cool Biz' campaign in Japan, initiated by the Mayor of Yokohama, Mr Hiroshi

Nakada, which enjoyed the support of the business sector.[1] Yokohama city has also established some 158 'goodwill' agreements with companies to provide goods and services at cost price in the event of a disaster.[2] Another example of informal collaboration is the Bombay First Society, which was established by prominent businessmen and citizens to facilitate engagement between the government, business and civil society with the objective of transforming the city into a better place to live, work and invest in.[3]

For purposes of international comparisons of trends and outcomes, we adopt a more formal definition of collaboration as contractual relationships or Public Private Partnership (PPP) arrangements between the public sector and the market. Grimsey and Lewis (2004) make the following distinction between privatisation and Public Private Partnerships (PPP):

> within a PPP the public sector acquires and pays for services from the private sector on behalf of the community and retains ultimate responsibility for the delivery of the services, albeit that they are being provided by the private sector over an extended period of time (i.e., 25 years or longer). In contrast, when a government entity is privatised the private firm that takes over the business also assumes the responsibility for service delivery ... A PPP is a formal business arrangement between the public and private sectors .... regulation through contract and the lack of government disengagement define much that is distinctive about a PPP.

PPPs have deep roots in the US where the scope of state owned enterprises have been limited; PPPs have covered transport, technology, water, prisons, health, welfare and urban regeneration (Grimsey and Lewis, Table 1.2). In the 1980s, privatisation of state-owned enterprises and assets started in the UK under the Thatcher government and subsequently became a worldwide phenomenon. Recognising that complete privatisation was not possible or desirable in some sectors, PPPs were first popularised in the early 1990s in the UK as Private Finance Initiatives (PFIs) for

---

[1] The campaign encouraged dressing 'cool' (no suit and neckties) during the summer months in order to cut down on air conditioning bills. Speech by Mayor of Yokohama Hiroshi Nakada at the World Cities Summit Conference, 25 June 2008.

[2] These agreements cover emergency supplies of food, transportation, coffins, shelter, publicity, health and even veterinary services in the event of a natural disaster. Speech by Mayor of Yokohama Hiroshi Nakada at the World Cities Summit Conference, 25 June 2008.

[3] Speech by Mr Narinder Nayar, Chairman of Bombay First and Managing Director of Concast (India) Ltd., at the World Cities Summit Conference, 25 June 2008.

asset-based infrastructure. PPPs have since been widely embraced as well by governments all over the world as vehicles for the delivery of a wide range of services, many of which are under the purview of local governments.

Section 2 of this chapter will review the reasons for the recent popularity of PPPs. In Section 3, we examine the main forms of PPPs that are used for urban development, focusing on the areas of land conversion or greenfield developments, urban redevelopment or brownfield developments, infrastructure provision, and operating concessions. Section 4 concludes with an evaluation of the usefulness of PPPs.

THE RATIONALE FOR PPPs

Kumar and Prasad (2004) succinctly describes PPPs as a strategy that combines the best of public and private sectors: "Through PPPs, the advantages of the private sector — innovation, access to finance, knowledge of technologies, managerial efficiency, and entrepreneurial spirit — are combined with the social responsibility, environmental awareness, and local knowledge of the public sector in an effort to solve problems." However PPP detractors have raised concerns over the high transaction costs, potential abuse of market power, lack of transparency and potential for corruption of these arrangements.

Given that the debates on the issue are more often driven by ideology, how are governments to assess if PPP can be an efficient mechanism for the delivery of services in a sustainable manner? In this section, we review the recent literature on the public procurement versus PPP decision and provide a careful analysis of the issues involved to help shed light on the issue.

Hart (2003) and Bettignies and Ross (2004) provide a general framework for thinking about the economics of public–private partnerships. A PPP project, according to Bettignies and Ross, may be seen as a simple extension of vertical disintegration or contracting out by government. However, it differs from simple contracting out in that, first, the number of tasks contracted out is larger, and secondly, in the privatisation of the finance function. A PPP project may be roughly broken down into four principal 'tasks': (i) defining and designing the project; (ii) financing the capital costs of the project; (iii) building or procuring the physical assets; and (iv) operating and maintaining the assets in order to deliver the product and service.

The following sequential questions arise with regard to the PPP decision which we will examine here: (i) Should the project or service be provided by the public sector or through a PPP? (ii) If the decision is for PPP, what are the considerations in choice of PPP strategy?

The answers to the above depend on a detailed understanding of the transaction costs involved in contracting out, the risks involved, an objective assessment of whether the private or public sector is better able to manage the risks (which differs according to local environment or contexts), and finally, a policy decision as to how the tasks and risks should be allocated.

In deciding which tasks or combination of tasks to allocate to the private sector via a long-term contract, Bettignies and Ross (2004) have adapted Crocker and Masten's (1996) comparison of the firm's choice between long-term contracts versus vertical integration diagram to fit the PPP versus public provision context (see Figure 1). Without relationship specific investments the context is simple — there are no switching/transaction/contracting costs and spot market provision is the better solution as it allows more flexibility relative to long-term contracts and it permits the efficiencies associated with competition and private provision.

Where assets are relationship specific as is the case with most infrastructure and real estate, outsourcing in a complex and uncertain environment gives rise to the risk of incomplete contracts and its associated problems of bargaining and opportunistic behaviour. Long term contracts (PPPs) are the best alternative when the relationships remain relatively simple. When transactional complexities and costs become too large, they

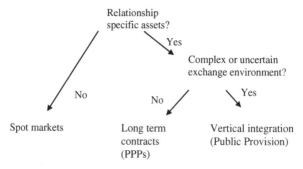

Fig. 1   Public provision or PPP decision

Source: Bettignies and Ross (2004).

can overwhelm benefits of private sector involvement, and government provision is then the preferred option.

Since the 1980s, policymakers have developed better understanding of complex urban environments and infrastructure sectors in order to introduce competition and/or private sector participation. The resulting vertical disintegration or unbundling of entire industries has been evident in sectors such as telecoms, power, water, rail and transport. In this exercise of 'taming complexity'[4] for privatisation of the infrastructure sector, Britain has been the pioneer. Designing long-term PPP contracts in an uncertain macro environment, however, remains a challenging task for both the public and private sector partners.

Public sector specific risks. Entering into a partnership with a private monopoly to provide services perceived to be government's responsibility requires the public sector to bear a diverse set of risks including:

— risks of interruption to works program and service delivery;
— risks of cost overruns;
— political risks with respect to residents and users;
— risks of project buyout;
— risks of non-performance;
— risks of absence of potential concessionaire replacement;
— risks of relinquishing future site planning and development options.[5]

While policy makers and the private concessionaire may try to anticipate every risk and ensure that each risk is properly allocated or shared in the partnership, there are limitations to foresight and it is impossible to plan for every potential contingency. There is, therefore, a need to establish a regulatory framework and/or build flexibility into such contracts to allow for renegotiations and contract extensions.

Renegotiation and bargaining outcomes, however, become dependent on *ex post* bargaining power, which itself is dependent on the alternatives in the event of negotiation breakdown. These uncertain 'payoffs', in turn, are affected by the nature of pre-contractual power relations, relative commercial resources, relative 'politicisation' of decision making within the

---

[4]This term is borrowed from Barabasi (2005)'s article 'Taming Complexity' on complex systems and networks in the sciences.
[5]Aoust *et al.* (2000, p. 59).

two parties to the transaction, relative salience of the transaction to the two parties, and the relative switching costs faced by the two parties (Lonsdale, 2005).

Lonsdale (2005) warns of post-contractual lock-in in the context of the UK, where the public body becomes asymmetrically locked-in to the private sector provider. Risk that is transferred to the private sector under the PPP contract and specified in the original agreement is transferred back to the public sector by opportunistic self-interested suppliers. While opportunistic behaviour may be tempered by the desire to obtain future business, this is dependent on the probability of significant future business within a reasonable time period. Moreover, it cannot be assumed that mobile managers will act rationally in the long term interests of the firm.

Private sector specific risks. For the private sector, Wells and Gleason (1995) and Irwin *et al.* (1997) warn of the continuing relevance of Vernon's perils of the obsolescing bargain for foreign investors venturing into infrastructure in developing countries (Vernon, 1971). Infrastructure investments, once made, are not potable and run the risks of expropriation at the worst, or the gradual erosion of investors' rights and privileges. The private partner in a PPP bears 'political risks' which include expropriation risks (nationalisation, confiscation, embargo); and appropriation risks. Appropriation of the investor's profits without causing it to leave can arise from changes in government priorities or policies, inability to transfer or convert project-generated revenues, as well as public sector partner's failure to comply with specific commitments made under the PPP. Wells and Gleason (1995) suggest that paradoxically, while high risk for private investors may justify high returns, for infrastructure projects, high returns may result in higher risk of expropriation or appropriation.

In projects requiring relationship specific investments and where the environment is highly complex and uncertain, governments that do not have the expertise to manage complex PPPs and that do not wish to risk loss of control through having to negotiate with potentially opportunistic private sector partners may decide on public sector provision as the preferred alternative.

It has been the norm for large-scale public sector construction in most market economies to be contracted out through competitive tendering to the private sector. Bettignies and Ross (2004) attribute this to the bidding process common for construction contracts which allows competition for the market, optimal allocation of risks as well as scale and/or learning economies of the construction process.

Hart (2003) makes a further distinction between incomplete contracts in building and operations and argues that the choice between PPPs (defined by Hart as build and operate) and conventional provision (private sector builds only) turns on relative contracting costs. Here, the builder can make two types of unseen investments which affect operation costs: investment in building quality which is productive and investment in 'corner-cutting' which is negative. Conventional procurement is preferred if the quality of construction can be well specified and corner-cutting investments are relatively easy to monitor, whereas the quality of service cannot be (e.g., prisons and schools).

PPP is good if the quality of the service can be well specified in the initial contract (there are good performance measures which can be used to reward or penalise the service provider) whereas the quality of building cannot be (e.g., hospitals). In developing country cities where projects are often of tremendous strategic importance, local authorities that are unfamiliar with the complexities and which do not have the expertise may be better off relying on private consortiums that have worked on similar projects in other cities, thus tapping on their economies of scale. However, this lack of technical expertise may have to be balanced against the lack of knowledge of PPP project management in those same cities.

Related to Hart's relative contracting costs is the often-cited benefit of Build, Operate and Transfer (BOTs) activities that arises from the complementarities or economies of scope between design, building and operations. For complex infrastructure projects, a broad range of technical skills is required to drive a project successfully, from conception to completion. Designing an integrated system with sophisticated system interactions and interfaces and its eventual efficient and safe operation will require the involvement of a diverse set of professions. The consortium that has to build the project has strong incentives to ensure that it is well designed. If it has to operate and maintain the system, it has strong incentives to ensure that it is designed and built such that operation and maintenance costs are minimised over the length of the contract.

The recent wave of PPP arrangements differs from conventional procurement or DB contracts in the involvement of private finance, and its *combination* with construction and/or operation/maintenance tasks. It has frequently been argued that the public sector by itself simply does not have the capacity to provide the amounts of needed funding for quality public infrastructure and services. Hart (2003) suggests that it is 'strange' for policy makers to argue that PPPs are good because the private sector is a cheaper source of financing or insurance than the public sector, as 'it is hard to imagine an agent that is more able to borrow or to provide insurance than the government (with its enormous powers of taxation)'.

Bettignies and Ross (2004), however, suggest that it is not at all clear that the government (especially sub-national ones) will be able to borrow at a lower cost than the private sector, or even to borrow at all in the case of some cities. One of the most frequent reasons governments employ PPP is that they are cash-strapped and too debt-laden already; it is not surprising that Hammami *et al.* (2006) find that PPPs tend to be more common in countries where governments suffer from heavy debt burdens. While that is true for many developing economies, the argument is increasingly made by developed country governments as well. Factors to consider in the evaluation of relative costs of financing would include (i) the credit worthiness of the private borrower and the protections offered in its contract with the public sector partner; (ii) the extent to which tax savings or subsidies may come from other levels of government if privately financed; and (iii) the marginal versus average costs of borrowing for governments.

Packaging the financing function with other tasks also recognises the complementarities that can exist between private financing and building, in particular that of reducing the risks of construction delays and project costs overrun (Bittignies and Ross, 2004). Under public procurement, public sector managers are so far removed from their principals (taxpayers) that project costs overrun may be more likely. Moreover, if delays are caused by the government (design changes, environment and zoning issues), under a PPP, the private partner may recover damages thus reducing the risks of such delays.

The benefits of a PPP (that include private sector financing, expertise, efficiencies and complementarities across tasks) will thus need to be weighed carefully against the transaction and governance costs of setting up a PPP, including the risks of loss of government control to a private monopoly, the need to renegotiate incomplete contracts and dealing with potentially

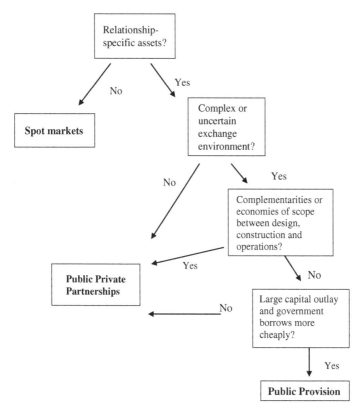

Fig. 2   Public provision or PPP decision

opportunistic private sector partners. In order to incorporate the above arguments so as to better understand the recent wave of PPP contracts in the sector, we extend Figure 1 to incorporate Hart's relative incompleteness argument as well as the possibility of lower private sector financing cost (see Figure 2).

Having considered the benefits and costs of entering into a PPP, the government that decides in favor of a PPP will next have to consider the appropriate strategy to adopt. The choice of strategy is essentially a risk preference decision on the part of the public sector decision makers. The potential to transfer risk to the private sector is often cited as one of the main reasons why PPPs are an effective procurement mechanism. The crux of PPP contract design and the eventual success of the partnership lie in a careful analysis of the inherent risks involved in each of the project tasks and how best to manage them.

Risk management involves four successive stages:

— risk identification;
— quantitative and qualitative evaluation of potential project impacts due to risk occurrence;
— risk mitigation;
— allocation of each residual risk to the most relevant partner.[6]

Risk identification involves distinguishing risks intrinsic to the project from exogenous project environmental risk. The latter category of risk does not pertain to either of the two parties, yet may have serious repercussions on various aspects of the project. They include risks of *force majeure* (acts of God), macroeconomic risks as well as risks of changes to the legal environment that are not specific to the sector. In general, it is impossible for any one party to bear the entire risk and the contract will need to be sufficiently flexible to allow for renegotiation and compensation.

Two critical factors determine whether a particular risk should be shifted to the private sector: the degree to which it is able to influence or control the outcome that is risky, and its ability to bear the risk (Irwin *et al.*, 1997, p. 8). The government should transfer a particular task or risk to the private sector if such a transfer of responsibility or property rights leads to a net efficiency improvement.

Under the PPP contract the government will have to provide guarantees against risks that are not allocated to the private sector. Inappropriate allocation of risks and poorly designed guarantees can result in adverse selection and moral hazard problems that undermine the benefits of private sector involvement. Guarantees also impose hidden costs on the public sector, consumers or taxpayers some of which may not be immediately apparent at the early stages of the project. These costs have budgetary implications that may not be immediately apparent and if not properly understood, will increase the risk of societal and political rejection of the PPP at a later stage (Engel *et al.*, 1997; Irwin, 2007). The existence and/or

---

[6]Aoust *et al.* (2000), p. 59.

development of public sector technical expertise and regulatory capacity are thus crucial for the success of PPPs.

The next section reviews PPP approaches that have been utilised in urban development in various cities.

PPP STRATEGIES FOR URBAN DEVELOPMENT

There is no simple paradigm for how PPPs should be structured and the choice of strategy appropriate for local requirements requires great care as the consequences of the wrong choice can be costly and long lasting. A broad range of PPPs strategies have been utilised in urban development and include partnerships for urban real estate development and inner-city regeneration, urban infrastructure projects and operating and maintenance concessions.

The literature on PPPs has grown rapidly and include Gomez-Ibanez and Meyer (1993), Daniels and Trebilcock (1996), Perrot and Chatelus (2000), Gomez-Ibanez (2003), Grimsey and Lewis (2004), Halcrow (2004), Perez (2004), Hammami *et al.* (2006), Phang (2007), Irwin (2007), Peterson and Annez (2007) and Yescombe (2007). Web links to PPP resources include those hosted by the World Bank, the European Commission, the European Bank for Reconstruction and Development, the Asian Development Bank as well as by governments (e.g., Partnerships UK).

URBAN REAL ESTATE DEVELOPMENT

Local government's ownership of land and its power to create new supplies of urban land through acquisition or conversion of rural land are perhaps the most strategic instruments in driving urban expansion. A recent *Newsweek* (May 26/June 2, 2008) story on China's megacities concluded that "No single factor has been more powerful in driving urban expansion than the freedom cities have had to buy and sell land." In 1988, China's constitution was amended to permit land leasing to the private sector while retaining public ownership of land. By 1992, Beijing and Shanghai had adopted land leasing as a local practice, where the purchaser can acquire land rights for a period of 40–70 years (Gao, 2007; Peterson, 2007). The practice has since been adopted by the rest of the country. This Chinese model of land leasing has been adapted from that used in Hong Kong where the government owns all the land; land leasing for urban development and for public housing is also widely utilised in Singapore where the government owns 90% of the land (Phang, 2005).

PPPs have also proven useful as a strategy for the transformation and regeneration of inner city spaces. Land and government buildings are hugely valuable assets on any municipal balance sheet. Moreover, local governments with planning and conservation powers, as well as *eminent domain* authority to purchase land can play a strategic role in the transformation of central city spaces. To attract private sector investments in urban real estate, a clear vision and commitment from the local government, and confidence in its ability to bring the vision into reality is essential. Revenues from land sales or leasing can be used to finance infrastructure assets. A comprehensive masterplan that has been developed with private sector inputs would create certainty and predictability, and harness the tremendous synergies amongst various developments.

Melbourne is an excellent example of a city that has utilised PPPs to bring about a major transformation marked by the rejuvenation of urban landscapes, strong tourism and vibrant cultural diversity.[7] It has become recognised internationally as a leader in urban sustainability. The Melbourne Principles for Sustainable Cities were developed in 2002 and has become a framework for sustainable development for many cities around the world.

QV, described as 'an urban village', 'a city within a city', is the successful redevelopment of Melbourne's historic Queen Victoria Women's Hospital site. The vibrant area, located in the centre of Melbourne's business district, was unused and abandoned for most of the 1990s as the hospital closed in 1987. It was returned to the City of Melbourne in 1999 which subsequently awarded the tender to develop the site to private developers in 2000. Contract conditions included sub-division, restoration, public open spaces, community services and the commissioning of multiple architects to ensure diversity. The 1.8 hectare site attracted more than A\$600 million of investments — creating 45,000 retail spaces, as well as two commercial towers which house amongst others, the headquarters of BHP Billiton.

---

[7]Speech by Mayor of Melbourne John So at the World Cities Summit Conference, 25 June 2008.

Another PPP project, the 66,000 square metre A$1.3 billion Melbourne Convention Centre Development, is scheduled for completion in 2009. The Victorian Government has committed A$370 million towards the construction of the new centre which is being developed through the Partnerships Victoria model. The private partner for the project is a consortium led by Multiplex Constructions and the Plenary Group. The Melbourne City Council's A$40 million contribution has been directed towards the public green leading to and surrounding the convention centre and the construction of a footbridge over the river.

On the private side of PPPs, an example of a private sector player in industrial and business real estate is Ascendas Private Limited, a Singapore incorporated company wholly owned by the Jurong Town Corporation (a Singapore government statutory board).[8] Ascendas has been active in PPP projects as a business space provider in over 11 countries and 30 cities in Asia.[9] Some examples of real estate PPP projects that Ascendas has been involved in Singapore include the Biopolis, a biomedical R&D facility, the Institute of Technical Education College West, a 27-year Design, Build, Finance and Operate (DBFO) contract and the Sports Hub (a 25-year DBFO contract).

Ascendas is also involved in the development of possibly India's first PPP in real estate infrastructure — the International Tech Park (ITP) Bangalore. The ITP Bangalore is a 26-hectare integrated work-live-play environment initiated as an Ascendas-Tata State Government joint venture. In China, Ascendas has partnered the Hangzhou government to develop the Singapore-Hangzhou Science and Tech Park, a 43-hectare integrated park.

Ppps FOR INFRASTRUCTURE PROVISION

Other than real estate development and redevelopment, PPPs have been widely used in the infrastructure sectors, in particular the transport and water sectors. This is not surprising, given the rapid expansion of the urban population worldwide and the often inadequacy of local government

---

[8] As a state-owned company, one might question whether Ascendas should be categorised as a 'private' partner in these PPPs.

[9] Speech by Ms Chong Siak Ching, President/CEO Ascendas Private Limited at the World Cities Summit Conference, 25 June 2008.

resources to meet the demand. The involvement of the private sector in the implementation of new infrastructure can take many forms, the most usual being BOT/BOO, joint ventures, leasing, contracting out or management contracts. In addition, the list of acronyms (details of which may be found in Grimsey and Lewis, 2004, Table 3.1) include BLT, BLTM, BTO, BOOT, LROT, and DBFO.[10] These contracts are usually long-term (25 to 30 years being common), have detailed provisions on payment, service standards and performance measures, provide objective means to vary payment depending on performance, and with the concessionaire usually having to assume substantial risk.

While Design-Build allows transportation agencies to gain access to technologies beyond their current organisational capabilities thus saving time and money, DBFOs can help assure the development of a system that could be economically maintained and operated. DBFOs can turn initially financially non-viable projects into viable ones by bringing private investors into the transit industry as partners. Many of the risks and much of the project management responsibility is also transferred from the authority to the private contractor. DBFOs have been widely utilised in highway construction and increasingly in the urban rail sector. It has also been utilised in the water, sanitation and electricity sector, as well as in the social services sector for health, education, sports, cultural facilities, government buildings, and prisons.

Competitive tendering concession is another PPP strategy that has been implemented in numerous sectors where services were formerly operated by the state. These include waste disposal and management, highways, bus transit, rail transit, and water supply and sanitation.

As compared to DBFOs, operating concession partnerships are less complex with risks associated with operations and maintenance potentially transferable to private partners. Often, competitive tendering is utilised in the award of concessions. Depending on the complexity of the task, coming up with an ideal bidding rule is not an easy task. Toll road concessions, for example, may utilise award criteria such as lowest toll, highest lease fee, least net present value, least cost to government, least subsidy, shortest

---

[10]Build Operate Transfer (BOT), Build Own Operate (BOO), Build Lease Transfer (BLT), Build Lease Transfer Maintain (BLTM), Build Transfer Operate (BTO), Build Own Operate Transfer (BOOT), Lease Renovate Operate Transfer (LROT), Design Build Finance Operate (DBFO).

term, lowest present value of revenue with variable term or multiple criteria (Estache *et al.*, 2000).

The term of the concessions can be relatively short such as five years to as long as 25 years. What are the relevant factors in deciding between short-term contracts or long-term contracts for concessions? Short-term contracts handle cost and demand changes through recontracting, making renegotiation due to unexpected changes less necessary. However, depending on the nature of the concession, the concessionaire may have been required to invest in specific rolling stock and would certainly have invested in the specific training of managers and workers. The cost of transfer from a current concessionaire to the new one could be fairly substantial and would be required to be managed carefully. If assets are highly specific, shorter contracts, especially when the number of potential bidders is limited, could prove less efficient than long-term contracts.[11]

The long-term contracts overcome the above problems, with the trade-off being that contingencies would need to be handled through negotiation and implicit understandings (Viscusi *et al.*, 2000), with the attendant risks. Given the need for the private sector to make or administer substantial investments, the long-term contract also provided the concessionaire with the proper incentives to ensure that investments made also minimise operation and maintenance costs over the length of the contract.

The UK was and remains an important testbed for a wide range of PPPs. Partnerships UK (web site at http://www.partnershipsuk.org.uk/) which provides support to the public sector for individual PPP projects before, during and after procurement, maintains a database with details of 885 projects. The extension of the Docklands Light Railway into the City's financial centre, one of the earliest UK PPP project, was partly funded by the major private developer in Docklands. In the 1990s, a decision was taken to extend it across the river Thames to Lewisham, and to turn the operation of the entire system to a private concession. This involved awarding the design and build concession for the 4 km (£200m) cross river concession and a seven-year operating concession in 1997 to the SERCO group. The current franchise, held by Serco Docklands Ltd., is due to expire in April 2013.

---

[11]Viscusi *et al.* (2000), Chapter 13 contains a comprehensive discussion of franchise bidding and the different types of contracts to handle future unanticipated events.

The United Arab Emirates has preferred to keep public establishment and utilities owned by the government, and involve the private sector mainly through concession contracts.[12] Dubai City has successfully attracted the private sector to participate in projects such as Jebel Ali Area, Knowledge Village, Internet Dubai, Dubai Port and Dubai International Airport.

The Kingdom of Saudi Arabia has recently embraced PPPs in several urban development projects. Other than contracting services for cleaning and concessions for operation of parks and public utilities, it has adopted BOT methods for some fundamental municipal services in addition to privatisation of communication, electricity and water services. On a different scale, Saudi Arabia has, in recent years, made plans to establish entire economic cities through PPP arrangements with several international companies and consultants. Examples include the King Abdullah Economic City, Jazan Economic City, and the Economic Knowledge City at Al-Medina Al-Munawara. The King Abdullah Economic City is the largest urban development project in Saudi Arabia with work starting in 2005. With a total development area of almost 2 billion square feet (173 square km), the city is estimated to cost about US$27 billion to build. The city design includes resorts, hotels, marinas, financial island, and university campuses, industrial and port zones.

Ppps: AN EVALUATION

The high costs inherent in developing sustainable cities have provided strong motivation in many developing countries for governments to seek private sector co-financing. Recent cases mentioned in the previous sections suggest that real estate developments, DBFOs and concessions can be designed in such a way as to attract the private sector. PPPs have been embraced as the means of financing infrastructure without burdening fiscal accounts while simultaneously allowing governments to access private sector capabilities and to improve on the efficiency, quality and reliability of urban services.

A recent World Bank review, however, concluded that Private Participation in Infrastructure (PPI) in developing countries 'has disappointed, playing a far less significant role in financing infrastructure in

---

[12]Speech by H.E. Abdullah Al Ali Al-Nuaim, President of the Arab Urban Development Institute, at the World Cities Summit Conference, 25 June 2008.

cities than was hoped for and which might be expected, given the attention it has received and continues to receive in strategies to mobilise financing for infrastructure' (Annez, 2007). Drawing from a World Bank database of developing country PPI transactions, Annez (2007) found that private investment flows into urban infrastructure to be geographically concentrated in Latin America and East Asia and the Pacific. Urban PPI investments accounted for only a 10% share of the total investment in infrastructure. Of these, 25% of total transactions in urban areas were classified as problem transactions, as opposed to 10% in total.

The main reason cited for the lukewarm private sector interest is the perceived high risks of the sectors and environments. The risks include political regime changes, political risks of shifting from subsidies to cost recovery, poor contract design, unexpected setbacks leading to contract cancellation (in particular unexpected currency devaluation), over optimistic demand forecasts, limited regulatory capacity, as well as the use of the price cap regulation that shifts excessive risks to the private partner (Annez, 2007).

Another problematic aspect of large complex PPP procurement is often the lack of transparency and the particular vulnerability of real estate and infrastructure deals to corruption. There is a clear need for accountability and good governance in order to attract private sector funding and ensure value for money and project sustainability. The UK, Canada, and Australia are examples of developed countries which have established specialised institutions to address PPP governance issues in an explicit and comprehensive manner (e.g., Partnerships UK, Partnerships BC, and Partnerships Victoria). Most developing countries however have yet to do so. Best practices for PPP that would limit corruption would include competitive bidding, disclosure policies, transparent process and public reporting as opposed to unsolicited bids and direct negotiations. Hodges and Dellacha (2007) are optimistic that if well implemented, PPPs can be used as an effective anti-corruption instrument.

Notwithstanding the problems that have arisen, PPPs have played a useful role in urban development. There are no unique solutions or templates to follow. Each PPP procurement will reflect the needs and characteristics of the city including its capacity to formulate, manage and regulate, as well as its risk preference given the multiple trade-offs involved. PPPs are not 'best practice' institutions but rather 'second-best' institutions — they take into account context-specific market and government failures that cannot be removed in short order.[13] In arriving at a decision, policy makers will need to have a clear vision of objectives and a deep understanding of context[14] in order to fully appreciate the advantages and limitations of PPPs.

As pointed out by Grimsey and Lewis (2004, p. 248), "PPPs are not, and probably never will be, the dominant method of infrastructure acquisition. They are too complex, and costly, for many small projects, and constitute 'using a sledgehammer to crack a nut'. In some cases, they may be beyond the capacity of the public sector agency to implement and manage. For other projects the tight specification of the outputs required may be difficult to detail for an extended period." Sustainable urban development in the 21st century is a challenging task and by no means the equivalent of 'cracking a nut'. The varied international experience of the past decade serves to demonstrate that the 'sledgehammer' of PPPs has become an important instrument in urban development policy. The transaction costs, however, can be high with long term success dependent on an array of factors spanning political, economic and institutional. Sustainability requires governments to remain central actors, PPPs be appropriately designed and regulated, and that citizens must ultimately benefit.[15]

REFERENCES

Annez, PC (2007). Urban infrastructure finance from private operators: What have we learned from recent experience? In Chapter 11 of Peterson, GE and PC Annez (eds.), *Financing Cities*, The World Bank, Washington, D.C. and Sage Publication India Pvt Ltd.

Aoust, JM, TC Bennett and R Fiszelson (2000). Risk analysis and sharing: The key to a Successful Public-Private Partnership. In Perrot, JY and G Chatelus (eds.), *Financing of Major Infrastructure and Public Service Projects: Public Private Partnership, Lessons from French Experience Throughout the World*, French Ministry of Public Works, Transport and Housing.

---

[13] Rodrik (2008) argues that the appropriate institutions for developing countries are 'second best' institutions which will often diverge greatly from best practice. He illustrates his argument using examples from four areas: contract enforcement, entrepreneurship, trade openness, and macroeconomic stability.

[14] Snowden and Boone (2007) advocate using the Cynefin Framework to determine the prevailing operative context in order to arrive at appropriate decisions. The framework sorts issues into five contexts: simple, complicated, complex, chaotic and disorder.

[15] Closing comments by Honolulu Mayor Jeremy Harris at the at the World Cities Summit Conference, 25 June 2008.

Barabasi, AL (2005). Taming complexity. *Nature Physics*, Vol. 1, Nov, 68–70.

Bittignies, JE and TW Ross (2004). The Economics of Public-Private Partnership. *Canadian Public Policy — Analyse de Politiques*, XXX(2), 135–154.

Crocker, K and S Masten (1996). Regulation and administered contracts revisited: Lessons from transaction cost economics for public utility regulation. *Journal of Regulatory Economics*, 9, 5–40.

Daniels, R and M Trebilcock (1996). Private provision of public infrastructure: An organizational analysis of the next privatization frontier. *University of Toronto Law Journal*, 46, 375–426.

Engel, E, R Fischer and A Galetovic (1997). Infrastructure franchising and government guarantees. In Chapter 4 of Irwin, T, M Klein, GE Perry and M Thobani (eds.), *Dealing with Public Risk in Private Infrastructure: Viewpoints*, World Bank Latin American and Caribbean Studies, Washington, D.C.

Estache, A, M Romero and J Strong (2000). In Chapter 6 of Estache, A and GD Rus (eds.), *Privatization and Regulation of Transport Infrastructure: Guidelines for Policymakers and Regulators*, The World Bank, Washington, D.C.

Gao, GF (2007). Urban infrastructure investment and financing in Shanghai. In Chapter 6 of Peterson, GE and PC Annez (eds.), *Financing Cities*, The World Bank, Washington, D.C. and Sage Publication India Pvt Ltd.

Gomez-Ibanez, JA and JR Meyer (1993). *Going Private: The International Experience with Transport Privatization*, Brookings Institution, Washington, D.C.

Gomez-Ibanez, JA (2003). *Regulating Infrastructure: Monopoly, Contracts, and Discretion*, Harvard University Press, Cambridge, MA.

Grimsey, D and MK Lewis (2004). *Public Private Partnerships: The Worldwide Revolution in Infrastructure Provision and Project Finance*, Edward Elgar, UK.

Halcrow Group Limited (2004). A Tale of Three Cities: Urban Rail Concessions in Bangkok, Kuala Lumpur and Manila. Report commissioned for the ADB-JBIC-World Bank East Asia and Pacific Infrastructure Flagship Study, Halcrow Group Limited, London.

Hammami, M, JF Ruhashyankiko and EB Yehoue (2006). Determinants of Public-Private Partnership in Infrastructure, IMF Working Paper WP/06/99, International Monetary Fund, Washington, D.C.

Hart, O (2003). Incomplete contracts and public ownership: Remarks and an application to public-private partnerships. *The Economic Journal*, 113, 486, C69–76.

Hodges, JT and G Dellacha (2007). Unsolicited infrastructure proposals: how some countries introduce competition and transparency. *Gridlines*, Note No. 19, March 2007. (Gridlines is a publication of the Public Private Infrastructure Advisory Facility at the World Bank).

Irwin, T, M Klein, GE Perry and M Thobani (eds.) (1997). *Dealing with Public Risk in Private Infrastructure: Viewpoints*. World Bank Latin American and Caribbean Studies. Washington, D.C.

Irwin, T (2007). *Government Guarantees: Allocating and Valuing Risk in Privately Financed Infrastructure Projects*. The World Bank, Washington D.C.

Kumar, S and CJ Prasad (2004). Public-private partnership in urban infrastructure. *Kerala Calling*, February 2004.

Lonsdale, C (2005). Post-contractual lock-in and the UK private finance initiative: The cases of national savings and investments and the Lord Chancellors Department. *Public Administration*, 83(1), 67–88.

Newsweek (May 26/June 2, 2008). 'Where Big is Best', 38–40.

Perez, BG (2004). *Achieving Public-Private Partnership in the Transport Sector*; iUniverse, Inc., New York.

Perrot, JY and G Chatelus (eds.) (2000). *Financing of Major Infrastructure and Public Service Projects: Public Private Partnership, Lessons from French Experience Throughout the World*, French Ministry of Public Works, Transport and Housing.

Peterson, GE (2007). Land Leasing and Land Sale as an Infrastructure Financing Option. In Chapter 10 of Peterson, GE and PC Annez (eds.), *Financing Cities*, The World Bank, Washington, D.C. and Sage Publication India Pvt Ltd.

Phang, SY (2007). Urban Rail Transit PPPs: Survey and risk assessment of recent strategies. *Transport Policy*, 14, 214–231.

Phang, SY (2005). Public Land Leasing for Urban Housing: Singapore's Experience. In Lee, J. (ed.) *A Review on Public Land Leasing System and its Feasibility in Korea*, Housing and Urban Research Institute, Korea.

Rodrik, D (2008). Second-Best Institutions. Working Paper 14050. National Bureau of Economic Research, Cambridge, MA.

Snowden, DJ and ME Boone (2007). A Leader's Framework for Decision Making. *Harvard Business Review*, Nov, 68–76.

Vercusi, WK, JM Vernon and JE Harrington, Jr. (2000). *Economics of Regulation and Antitrust*, 3rd Edition, The MIT Press, Cambridge, Massachusetts.

Vernon, R (1971). *Sovereignty at Bay: The Multinational Spread of U.S. Enterprises*. Basic Books, New York.

Wells, LT and ES Gleason (1995). Is Foreign Infrastructure Still Risky? *Harvard Business Review*, Sep–Oct, 44–55.

Yescombe, ER (2007). *Public-Private Partnerships: Principles of Policy and Finance*, Butterworth-Heinemann, Elsevier.

10 Sustainability in the Built Environment

CHYE KIANG HENG and JI ZHANG

INTRODUCTION

The year 2008 is a turning point as more than half of the world's population now live in cities. In this regard, the timing of the World Cities Summit 2008 is opportune, as it provides a landmark forum for leading researchers, practitioners, and policymakers to share their visions, ideas, and strategies on how we can make our cities a better place to live, work, and play in a sustainable way without compromising the ecological health of our planet. The four speakers during the "Sustainability in the Built Environment" session of the 2008 Summit, Kenneth Yeang, Kevin Hydes, John Keung and Poh Tay Kim, presented different critical aspects of the agenda for sustainability in the built environment, ranging from physical design and planning to regulatory frameworks, governance to participation in sustainable communities. The range of issues raised by the speakers and participants provided the opportunity to situate the discussions in the current wider discourse on sustainability.

The quest for sustainability echoes the pervading global concern. There are ever-increasing scientific evidence of global environmental degradation, resource depletion, and climate change that are caused by excessive and short-sighted human activities, as well as the long term impact that all these may have upon the planet on which we live.

However, the design profession, long dominated by inward aesthetic appreciation, has adopted the concept of sustainability at a rather slow pace (Buchanan, 2005). Given that building-related activities are major consumers of raw materials and energy and are responsible for a large proportion of greenhouse gas emissions (IPCC, 2001; Wilson and Yost, 2001), it is imperative to rethink and reorient the way we plan, construct, and maintain the built environment. In this sense, cities might hold the greatest hope for achieving a more sustainable future for our planet (Beatley, 2000). The Green-Building and Eco-Urbanism movements, which promote alternative starting points and objectives of design, represent a promising impetus that may expand the realm of the environmental design disciplines and encourage a benign development of cities.

THE CONCEPT OF SUSTAINABILITY AND ITS CHARACTERISTICS

Various interpretations have emerged from the debates and discussions regarding the concept of sustainable development since it was first stated officially in the Brundtland Report (World Commission on Environment and Development, 1987) and further outlined in Agenda 21 (United Nations, 1992) as "development that meets the needs of the present without compromising the ability of future generations to meet their own needs".

One interpretation emerging from the perspective of landscape and ecology regards sustainability as "a characteristic of a process or state that can be maintained indefinitely" (IUCN/UNEP/WWF, 1991), and stresses that it implies "a limitation on the degree and rate of human impact such that the natural carrying capacity of the earth's ecosystems can be perpetually maintained" (Thayer, 1994, p. 99). Building on this understanding, Thayer (1994, p. 100) defines sustainable landscape as "a place where human communities, resource uses, and the carrying capacities of surrounding ecosystems can all be perpetually maintained".

Campbell (1996), from the standpoint of planning, situates sustainable development at the centre of what he describes as the "planner's triangle" which consists of three Es, or three competing interests — those of economy, environment, and equity. He emphasises that sustainability can only be achieved by negotiating and balancing the dynamic conflicts inherent in the three Es. These conflicts are the property conflict between the pursuit for economic growth and the quest for social equity, the resource conflict between the request for economic growth and the need of resource conservation, as well as the development conflict between environmental protection and the interest in just distribution of available resources.

From a theoretical point of view, Neuman (2005) summarises the intellectual traditions from which the concept of sustainability draws as: 1) capacity, which emphasises the carrying capacity of a place to support certain amount of living beings, 2) fitness, which emphasises the mutual interaction and adaptation between species and environment, 3) resilience, which emphasises the flexibility to absorb both internal and external forces of change, 4) diversity, which emphasises both the variety of members in a community and the positive disposition of relations between them, and 5) balance, which emphasises equilibrium. Neuman argues that the common themes running through the five intellectual traditions are 1) the emphasis on long-term and dynamic process, 2) the quest for health for both the ecosystem and the human society, 3) the concern for place-specific conditions, or the context, and 4) the recognition of interrelationships and connections.

KEY CONCERNS REGARDING SUSTAINABILITY IN THE BUILT ENVIRONMENT

The challenge inherent in the pursuit of sustainability in the built environment lies in the broad spectrum of dimensions it needs to cover, ranging from technical, ecological, economic, political, social, cultural, to spiritual; the wide range of scope or scale it needs to dwell on, ranging from the indoor environment, building, community, city, region, to nation; the multivariate parties it needs to involve, ranging from professional, academia, industry, authority, and the public; the great number of issues and problems it needs to tackle; and the tremendous complexity that needs to be untangled and addressed.

Scale

Building

From a micro perspective, achieving sustainability may start from the immediate environment we live in, the buildings. From the early days of *The*

Autonomous House (Vale, 1975), environmentally progressive architecture has been accepted as one that uses renewable sources to generate energy, passive techniques for ventilation and illumination as well as incorporates, maintains, and recycles greenery, water, and waste. It should also use environmentally conscious construction techniques, and foster a livable and viable urbanism (Gissen, 2002).

For the contemporary architectural practice that has been dictated by form, fashion and theory in the last few decades, the sustainability agenda may represent a fresh stimulus and reinvigorate it with a meaningful purpose. In *Ten Shades of Green*, Buchannan (2005) argues that the impact of the green movement on building design is multifaceted. It not only influences the cross-section, the external envelope, the layout of buildings, but also affects the technological, ecological, economic, social, and even the cultural and spiritual aspects of building design. Accordingly, he proposes a series of 10 principles that regard sustainable architecture as 1) achieving low energy consumption and high performance; 2) harvesting replenishable sources; 3) eliminating waste and pollution through recycling; 4) reducing embodied energy; 5) encouraging long life and loose fit; 6) minimising total life cycle cost; 7) embedded in place; 8) facilitating accessibility with urban context; 9) enhancing health and happiness; and 10) contributing to community and connection. Of critical importance in these principles is the conviction that the architecture of the new long-term paradigm should transcend the modernists' objectivism and the post-modernists' relativism, and be built on an evolutionary and ecological perspective that cares for both the planet and people, and be grounded in the complex and sensual realities of place and lived experience.

City

Green architecture can only be effective when set in a city that is planned based on sustainable principles. Sustainable strategies need to be implemented on a larger scale, beyond that of individual buildings. As Kenneth Yeang puts it, ultimately, the fate of the battle for our environment depends on the success of the city-level practices, and hence his preoccupation on designing the eco-city. Yeang has written extensively on this subject.

The key component of an eco-city, according to Yeang, is what he calls the eco-infrastructure, which includes four strands of basic systems: the green infrastructure which refers to the linked greenways and habitats; the grey infrastructure, which refers to the eco-engineering infrastructure and sustainable engineering system; the blue infrastructure, which refers to the bio-drainage system; and the red, or human, infrastructure, which includes the communities of buildings and regulatory systems (Yeang, 2008a). What Yeang advocates is a city-level integration of the built and the natural environment, and the approach is to enhance the connectivity between them via nexus-like ecological bridges, eco-cells, and three-dimensional landscaping. Through his own design practices, Yeang demonstrates that eco-design is about design for bio-integration in a seamless and benign way, a crucial concept in ecology, which can only be achieved if the physical, systematic, and temporal aspects of such design are met (Yeang, 2007). Designers are required to reach out beyond the immediate boundary of the site of the project and to address the status quo, limitations, and potential impacts of the development on a scale larger than its footprint.

Yeang's recommendations could be situated in the wider context of the increasingly accepted European urban practices that advocate more ecologically responsible forms of living and settlement that strive to live within their ecological limits and fundamentally reduce their ecological footprints. While acknowledging their connections with and impacts on other physical environments of varying scales, these settlements should be planned to function in ways analogous to nature and strive to achieve, like nature itself, a circular rather than a linear metabolism (Beatley, 2000).

Besides city-level bio-integration, urban form, land use pattern, and public transportation system also play a crucial role in determining urban sustainability. Many European cities have demonstrated the advantages of dense and compact urban development. These include lower per capita energy use, lower carbon emission, air and water pollution, lower resource demands, and greater economic viability in the provision of amenities and facilities (Beatley, 2004; Jenks, Burton and Williams, 1996). Moreover, the vibrant historical core of many European cities suggests that relatively compact urban form and higher density need to work in conjunction with a flexible land use policy and an efficient public transport system in order to contribute fully to a sustainable urban living environment. On the one hand, mixed-use zones and diverse housing typologies may help to prevent the dense urban fabric from becoming homogenised and toneless patches in terms of function, activity, and physical form, and thus are essential to the vitality and quality of urban life. On the other hand, fast, comfortable, and reliable systems of public transport will form an integrated network that facilitates people's everyday commute in a seamless and convenient way.

However the jury is still out on compactness as a criterion of sustainable city. While the 20th century suburbanisation was in large part a reaction against the terribly unhealthy living environment of the crowded industrial revolution, the current compact city proposition is seen by some as a reaction to the contemporary excessive urban sprawl and suggests the need to re-appraise critically the benefits of relatively higher-density living (Wheeler, 2003). Although a sustainable city is usually characterised as one with compact urban form, sustainable transport, relatively higher density, mixed land uses, diversity in terms of function, activities, social configuration and building typology, passive solar design, and integration with nature (Jabareen, 2006), debate has been raised on whether the compact city is sustainable and the role of urban form in reaching the goals of sustainability.

To begin with, there is a lack of consensus on the definition of the compact city (Martine, 2008, p. 14). There is also the debate on the benefits of polycentric compact cities versus the monocentric variety (Newman and Kenworthy, 1992) although some go as far as to advocate the American model of disperse cities (Gordon and Richardson, 1989). By comparing compact city with the common themes running through the key intellectual traditions of the concept of sustainability, that is the emphases on dynamic process, overall health, place-specific conditions and interrelationships, Neuman (2005) concludes that compactness is neither a necessary nor sufficient criteria for a sustainable city, and using urban form strategies alone may be counterproductive. Instead, he argues that conceiving the city in terms of process which constantly shapes, and is shaped in turn by, urban form is more crucial and promising in pursuing urban sustainability. However, Neuman was criticised for being unclear about whether the process will take place in the form of a dialogue among social groups or in complete obedience to market forces (Martine, 2008, p. 15). Wheeler (2003, p. 491) also advocates a relatively simple, process-oriented definition of sustainable urban development as "development that improves the long-term social and ecological health of cities and towns" to avoid fruitless debates over ambiguous terms or sustainable end states. However, he still regards compact and efficient land use as one of the nine key features that characterise healthier human and natural communities, the other eight features being less automobile use and better accessibility; efficient resource use; less pollution and waste and restoration of natural systems; good housing and living environment; a healthy social ecology; a sustainable economy; community participation and involvement; and preservation of local culture and wisdom.

These complexities involved in the compact city debate have been addressed at length by Martine (2008), who pointed out that the potential of the compact city to meet its objectives may depend not only on its form as depicted on the drawing-board but also on political structures, societal values, and the general preparedness of the society (p. 14). Adopting a longer-term evolutionary (*laissez-faire*) approach as opposed to the "master designer" conception inherent in compact city development may have completely different implications for industrialised countries and developing ones due to their contextual differences regarding lifestyles and consumption patterns. For developing countries, he advocates solutions that are inclusive and open-ended, non-technocratic planning that incorporates the perspectives and aspirations of all participants and plans that reflect an environmental, rather than a formal approach to city growth (p. 16).

Region and Ecosystem

Yeang has pointed out that the built and natural environments are not mutually exclusive. Rather, they are integral parts of the ecosystem. Sustainability in the built environment cannot be achieved without setting it into a larger context of local and global ecosystem and addressing the mutual relationships between them.

Nature offers designers much food for thought. Beyond the law of gravity and the principles of aesthetics, architects can learn much from the laws and principles of the natural world and embrace economic, social, and ecological values that concern both human and natural communities. The approach to architecture, therefore, will be diversified and "form can become a celebration not simply of human intelligence but of our kinship with all of life" (McDonough, 2002, p. 9).

Pioneers in regional and ecological planning such as Ian McHarg (1992) and Richard Forman (1996) have reminded us that urban sustainability may depend to a large extent on the health of a much larger spatial context which is the product of natural forms and processes: "the solution will be at the landscape scale — working with the larger pattern, understanding how it works, and designing in harmony with the structure of the natural systems that sustains us all" (Dramstad *et al.*, 1996, p. 5). The coordination and integration of urban development with higher jurisdiction levels of planning and control, including regional and national government level, is also evident in some European cities such as Copenhagen which is characterised by large wedges of green space penetrating the urban fabric (Beatley, 2000).

Ecological concerns of green design have gradually evolved from focusing on environmental conservation to the concept of ecological footprint (Wackernagel and Rees, 1996) which is based on the understanding of the ecosystem's carrying capacity. Research indicated that our planet's resources are being abused at an unprecedented speed: humanity's ecological footprint, the area of biologically productive land and sea required to provide the resources we use and to absorb our waste, has exceeded the planet's ability to regenerate by about 25 per cent. This has more than tripled since 1961 (WWF, 2006). The tremendous impacts of urban living that go beyond the immediate boundary of urban settlement urge us to shift from open-ended resource consumption, in which nonrenewable resources are harvested, used, and discarded by human systems, toward closed-loop urban metabolism in which resources are reused and recycled (Beatley, 2000; Wheeler, 2003).

Cities like Den Haag and London are using their calculated ecological footprints as reference for their policy-making (Beatley, 2000), and the EcoDensity initiative as proposed by the city of Vancouver also represents such an attempt to reduce the city's ecological hinterland on a regional planning scale. The concept of EcoDensity is based on the understanding that high quality and strategically located density nodes can help to contain Vancouver's ecological footprint. Specific strategies focused on increasing density and diversifying design and land use patterns were suggested, aiming at creating a sustainable urban environment with lesser energy and resource consumption, greater efficiency of facility usage, deeper affordability, and better liveability.

Dimensions

Economic

A sustainable city is not all about environmental issues. What Buchanan (2003, p. 23) emphasised was that sustainability also requires economic viability and greater social equity since economic viability may strengthen the feasibility of environmental initiatives and social equity is crucial to social and political stability which are crucial to the long-term viability of sustainability endeavor. The discussion of the economic dimension of sustainable development is even more relevant to the cities of Asian countries as well as most developing countries where poverty reflected in inadequate housing remains a challenge to local governments in these regions.

The public housing programme in Singapore and its accumulated experiences over the years, as reviewed by Kim Poh Tay, CEO of Singapore Housing and Development Board (HDB), represents a good example of the important role of flexible and viable economic strategies in the process of building sustainable communities that goes beyond physical planning. Through generous government subsidy and considerate functional design of the public housing flat, the HDB was able to price the flats way below that of private housing so that they are within the reach of most Singaporeans. Therefore, affordable pricing, availability of cheap financing, and flexible payment scheme such as the Central Provident Fund (CPF) guarantee that 90 per cent of Singapore's households can afford at least a basic flat. The authority also ensures that the monthly installment of the mortgage loan of house buyers will not become an unbearable burden to them. Moreover, the diverse range of flat types offer a variety of choices for house buyers, thus further strengthening the housing affordability. The resulting high homeownership among Singaporeans contributes not only to a high quality of living but also to a strong sense of pride and belonging among the residents, the latter being a crucial step toward creating sustainable communities.

Social

Besides economic strategies, other non-technical aspects such as sociological, psychological, cultural, and spiritual are also crucial dimensions of sustainability. As pointed out by Buchanan (2005), sustainability needs to offer everybody a sense of meaning, deep satisfaction and opportunities to fulfil their individual potential and gain a sense of connectedness. It is exactly this kind of sense of attachment that transcends physical inconvenience or social undesirability that planners and designers are expected to inspire in the neighbourhood they design (Keller, 1968).

Singapore's public housing programme is manifested not only in its physical form but also in a whole package of long-term policies to guarantee that it is economically as well as socially viable and sustainable. The comprehensive infrastructure planning at the town level and diverse communal spaces and facilities provided at the neighbourhood and precinct level create an environment that encourages and facilitates community interaction and bonding. Active management prevents the estates from falling into the vicious cycle of continuous degradation. The estate upgrading programme and the selective en bloc redevelopment scheme not only improve the physical condition of the old estates and enhance the value of the flats, but are also mechanisms contributing to the adjustment of the population profile in a positive way. With these social concerns, communities benefit from stronger social ties and the nation benefits from the intensified land use. In this regard, the HDB public housing programme as a social project has laid down a firm foundation for achieving liveability of the built environment and the social solidarity of communities.

Political

The strong growth of the Dow Jones Sustainability Index versus the Dow Jones Industrial Average Index in recent years as cited by Kevin Hydes during his presentation indicates that the performance of the leading sustainability-driven companies worldwide is making steady progress.

It suggests that the industrial sector has gradually realised that applying environmental principles is beneficial to industrial processes, and that it can boost brands and help to situate them in a vantage position in the competition. Hydes illustrated that the voluntary involvement of more people in pursuing sustainability may require two forms of communication — educate how and convince why — so that those unengaged, either skeptical or uninformed, can be transformed to enthusiastic campaigners.

However, the success of sustainability may depend to a large extent on the intensity and scope of the support from related authorities in the form of policies and legislations. The EU and the north European countries in particular have adopted a top-down approach in promoting the green agenda. Their governmental structure, economic and planning framework promote and facilitate the pursuit of urban sustainability. Good progress has been made in reducing greenhouse gas emission, promoting a higher level of recycling and air-quality, reducing waste and energy consumption, and increasing renewable energy supplies at the policy level. Energy evaluation has even become mandatory for projects above certain scale in several European countries. The EU also funds pilot research by architects designing energy-efficient buildings and it is argued that the relatively more attractive fee structure has encouraged European engineers' involvement in design-related research and innovation (Buchanan, 2003).

Hydes suggests that incentives and regulations are like 'carrot and stick'. On the one hand, incentives are very important in the initial stage of promoting sustainability since they help to smooth the realisation of demonstration projects, which in turn may encourage more voluntary practices that will foster a wide range of discussion among the public. In Linz, Austria, subsidy is provided to cover up to 35 per cent of the cost of the installation of green roof and this has proven quite effective as reflected in the abundance of green roofs in the city. On the other hand, regulations screen out unsound practices and pricing policies help to promote greater energy conservation and efficiency improvements and encourage behavioural transformation of individuals. Both incentive and regulation can help to boost trial and experimentation and shift the building industry from one that is dominated by typical practices to one in which leading and innovative practices constitute the majority.

BENCHMARK

In response to the growing appeal of quantifying sustainability, examination of the effectiveness of the isolated attempts and spontaneous experiments on sustainable architecture are gradually operationalised in a coordinated way with the adoption of green building rating systems in many countries, such as LEED in North America, BREEAM in UK, Green Mark Scheme in Singapore, Green Globes from the Green Building Initiative (GBI), and SBTool from the International Initiative for a Sustainable Built Environment (IISBE), to name a few. Though their underlying concepts, structure, and emphases vary, these rating systems share a common aim to provide objective criteria for evaluating building performance against a broad spectrum of sustainability issues.

Singapore's Green Mark Scheme represents such a regional endeavor to promote environmental awareness in the construction and real estate sectors, to encourage green building design, construction and technology, and reduce the impact of buildings to the environment. The Green Mark Scheme, introduced by John Keung, CEO of Singapore's Building and Construction Authority (BCA), focuses on five key environmental areas. This has witnessed an exponential increase in the number of certified green buildings in Singapore since its inception. This demonstrates the keen interest of the local industry and public in pursuing sustainability. The vitality of the Green Mark Scheme lies in the broader vision of BCA's Green Building Masterplan which delineates the roadmap of Singapore's green building development by emphasising integration of incentive scheme, R&D and training framework, consumer and industry education, and regulations. Therefore, the implementation of the Green Mark Scheme is part of a package of policies and strategies to ensure that innovative and committed efforts are encouraged, that the professionals are fully equipped and the policies, adequately enforced, and that the decisive forces of the green building movement — the consumers and the market — are actively engaged.

However, most of the current green buildings rating systems seem to have overemphasised the quantifiable aspects of building performance and implementation of sustainability-oriented technologies, and exhibit a lack of concern on the qualitative impacts and the social and political implications of buildings (Guy and Moore, 2005). Even on the quantitative front, it is extremely problematic that the rating system assesses a building based on prediction of energy savings instead of energy actually saved by the buildings (Gifford, 2008). Another weakness of the current green benchmarks lies in its inability to address the bio-climatic and cultural specificities of a project and the low customisability which prevents consideration of different on-site situations. This raises the question of whether the implementation of a building rating system should be context-specific. Cities in temperate and tropical zones would differ in the way they respond to sunshine and harvest solar energy. Therefore, the application of the same solar-energy-related technology may have different weight in the rating system for buildings located in different climatic zones. Edwards (2001) also raised similar concerns by pointing out the lack of social considerations in the currently universally applied green building assessment techniques.

In a recent comparative study, the American Institute of Architects proposed a series of principles to assess three leading sustainable building rating systems. These range from review processes of submission, documentation required, crucial environmental considerations to be covered, to mechanisms that encourage innovation (AIA Sustainability Discussion Group, 2008). Among these principles, life cycle assessment, acknowledgment of national, regional, and bioclimatic differences, and the social and cultural aspects of green building have been endowed with equal significance as that for other technology-oriented criteria. The message is twofold: on the one hand, green building rating systems need to expand their vision and base their rationale on wider temporal framework; on the other hand, a flexible rating system needs to allow the particularities of the specific context of a development to be evaluated, whether bioclimatic, geographical or socio-cultural. In the process of assessment, such flexibility will be more adaptable and reasonable in terms of implementation.

THE CULTURAL CHALLENGE

Achieving sustainability is a cultural endeavour which demands a radical shift in the mindset of individuals and the society. This remains the most important and yet the most onerous task. The privileged and dominant culture of consumerist corporate capitalism as spread by globalisation is unsustainable — its insatiable appetite for natural resources and immensely wasteful production and distribution processes have imposed tremendous pressure on the earth beyond its replenishing capacity (Buchanan, 2003). According to the Living Planet Report (WWF, 2006), five more Earths might be needed to support the whole world if everybody follows the average American lifestyle which, unfortunately, is still a seductive model to emulate for many underdeveloped and developing countries. Research shows that rather than building and environmental standards, people's habits or their behaviours and lifestyle are actually the most crucial factors that will affect their mode of energy consumption (Bech-Danielsen, 2003; Weber and Perrels, 2000). Sustainability, Buchanan (2003, p. 27) asserts, "is not only about curbing environmental abuse; it is even more about enjoying a saner and more just way of life".

Wang (2003) calls the appeal of the seductive paradigm its "cultural footprint" and points out that the "cultural footprint" of a building which denotes the socio-cultural milieu fostering and supporting a specific value system of a lifestyle may far exceed its ecological footprint. The specific socio-cultural conditions that ensure the realisation of certain types of building as cultivated by the mass media hype and a finely tuned desire for spectacle are hard to change through rational argument. However, the reduction in a building's cultural footprint may be far more crucial than the reduction in its ecological footprint because the former represents the deeper motivations behind the building. Accordingly, Wang proposes four aesthetic principles, emphasising that an architecture in favour of the reduction in the cultural footprint of building is one that 1) aims at providing long-term inhabitation of space rather than serving the ever-hungry media; 2) presents itself as background to life rather than foreground spectacular; 3) has an aesthetic life expectancy consistent with that of its materials; and 4) follows the compositional principles of material abstraction. He further proposes five material principles that encourage less construction, longer life expectancy of built elements, maximal reuse and recycling of materials, prohibiting use of non-recyclable materials, and finally, retaining, sustaining, and maintaining the built elements.

Many of the principles proposed are congruent with those practiced in vernacular environments. Emanating from an era before the advent of cheap energy, vernacular architectures and settlements are invaluable sources for us to learn about environmentally responsive design strategies.

The wind-catcher and other natural ventilation devices widely used in some hot and arid areas, for instance, are examples of sensible and wise architectural design. They are resource-efficient, pollution-free, involving no high technologies, easy to manage, economically viable, and adaptive to local climate and ecology (Beazley, Harverson, and Roaf 1982). The aesthetic qualities, the climatic adaptability and the economic feasibility that have been achieved by these vernacular and traditional architecture through trial and error over the years are exactly what today's sensitive architects are searching for (Alp, 1990).

In Singapore, the incorporation of the monsoon window in the design of a high-rise housing project by local design firm WoHa is a good example. It is a manifestation of the implementation of environmentally friendly design strategy inspired by tradition and responding to the local climatic context. It does not compromise but rather contribute to the aesthetic quality, operational unpretentiousness, and architectural integrity of the resulting built form (Yeang, 2008b).

CONCLUSION

While it is widely accepted that the three components to sustainable development are economic growth, environmental protection, and social equity, the sustainability of the built environment depends on three pillars: design, technology and behaviour.

The importance of design cannot be overemphasised. From the building to the urban scale, vernacular traditions have shown that with ingenious design strategies developed and improved over long periods of time, climatically sensitive buildings can be built. With clever design and the little technology at their disposal, our forefathers have managed to build relatively comfortable structures using local materials. Wherever possible, building materials were recycled and reused. Even at the scale of settlements, the lack of cheaply available energy meant erecting compact settlements that took into account environmental conditions and challenges, convenience of use, social and religious practices as well as aesthetics.

Unfortunately, with the availability of abundant and cheap energy, many architects, engineers and planners have forgotten or abandoned the ingenious design strategies, depending instead on technology as a panacea. Glass-clad buildings, for instance, appear in all parts of the world regardless of climatic conditions, relying on high performance glass and air-conditioning to solve the problems of an inappropriate architecture. It is critical that the design of the built environment begins once again with environmentally sound design strategies, employing technology only to further enhance it.

The sustainability of our built environment also depends largely on the behaviour of everyone, from the government to the developers, from the consultants to the users. With incentives and regulations, or carrot and stick in their broadest definitions, behaviours (and desires) could be modified such that responsible environmental practices are adopted at all levels, and by everyone. Sustainability in the built environment is, above all, dependent on responsible behaviour in an environment based on ingenious design strategies and enhanced with the appropriate technology. Only then can the careful balance with the natural environment be maintained, without which, many a settlement and even civilisation have perished in the past.

REFERENCES

AIA Sustainability Discussion Group (2008). *Quantifying Sustainability: A Study of Three Sustainable Building Rating Systems and the AIA Position Statement.* American Institute of Architecture.

Alp, AV (1990). Vernacular climate control in desert architecture. *Energy and Buildings,* 15–16, 809–815.

Beatley, T (2000). *Green Urbanism: Learning from European Cities.* Washington, DC: Island Press.

Beatley, T (2004). Planning for sustainability in European cities: A review of practice in leading cities. In Wheeler SM and T Beatley (eds.), *The Sustainable Urban Development Reader.* London, New York: Routledge, 249–258.

Beazley, E, M Harverson and S Roaf (1982). *Living with the Desert: Working Buildings of the Iranian Plateau.* Warminster, Wilts, England: Aris & Phillips.

Bech-Danielsen, C (2003). Ecological reflections in unbounded architecture. *The Journal of Architecture,* 8, 321–336.

Buchanan, P (2003). Invitation to the dance: Sustainability and the expanded realm of design. *Harvard Design Magazine,* 18, 23–29.

Buchanan, P (2005). *Ten Shades of Green: Architecture and the Natural World* (1st ed.). New York, NY: Architectural League of New York.

Campbell, S (1996). Green cities, growing cities, just cities?: Urban planning and the Contradictions of Sustainable Development. *Journal of the American Planning Association,* 62(3), 296–312.

Dramstad, WE, JD Olson and RTT Forman (1996). *Landscape Ecology Principles in Landscape Architecture and Land-use Planning.* Harvard University Graduate School of Design; Island Press; American Society of Landscape Architects.

Edwards, B (2001). Design challenge of sustainability. *Architectural Design,* 71(4), 20–31.

Gauzin-Müller, D (2002). *Sustainable Architecture and Urbanism: Concepts, Technologies, Examples.* Basel: Birkhaüser.

Gifford, H (2008). A Better Way to Rate Green Buildings. http://www.energysavingscience. com/.

Gissen, D (2002). Introduction. Gissen, D (ed.), *Big and Green: Toward Sustainable Architecture in the 21st Century.* New York: Princeton Architectural Press, pp. 10–17.

Gordon, P and HW Richardson (1989). Gasoline Consumption and Cities: A Reply. *American Planning Association. Journal of the American Planning Association,* 55(3), 342–346.

Guy, S and SA Moore (2005). The paradoxes of sustainable architecture. Guy, S and SA Moore (eds.), *Sustainable Architectures: Cultures and Natures in Europe and North America* (First edition). New York: Spon, 1–12.

Hall, P (1988). *Cities of Tomorrow: An Intellectual History of Urban Planning and Design in the Twentieth Century.* UK: Oxford; New York, NY: Blackwell.

IPCC (2001). *Climate Change 2001: Summary for Policymakers.* Intergovernmental Panel on Climate Change.

IUCN/UNEP/WWF (1991). *Caring for the Earth: A Strategy for Sustainable Living.* Gland, Switzerland: The World Conservation Union (IUCN), Worldwide Fund for Nature (WWF), and United Nations Environment Programme (UNEP).

Jabareen, YR (2006). Sustainable urban forms: Their typologies, models, and concepts. *Journal of Planning Education and Research,* 26, 38–52.

Jenks, M, E Burton and K Williams (1996). Compact cities and sustainability: An introduction. M Jenks, E Burton and K Williams (eds.), *The Compact City: A Sustainable Urban Form?* London; New York: E & FN Spon, 3–8.

Keller, SI (1968). *The Urban Neighborhood: A Sociological Perspective.* New York: Random House.

Martine, G (2008). *Preparing for Sustainable Urban Growth in Developing Areas.* New York: Population Division, Department of Economic and Social Affairs, United Nations Secretariat.

McDonough, W (2002). Preface. Gissen, D (ed.), *Big and Green: Toward Sustainable Architecture in the 21st Century.* New York: Princeton Architectural Press, 8–9.

McHarg, IL (1992). *Design with Nature.* New York: J Wiley.

Moore, SA and R Brand (2003). The banks of Frankfurt and the sustainable city. *The Journal of Architecture,* 8(1), 3–24.

Neuman, M (2005). The Compact City Fallacy. *Journal of Planning Education and Research,* 25, 11–26.

Newman, PWG and JR Kenworthy (1989). Gasoline consumption and cities: A comparison of US cities with a global survey. *Journal of the American Planning Association,* 55(1), 24–37.

Newman, PWG and JR Kenworthy (1992). Is there a role for physical planners? *Journal of the American Planning Association,* 58(2), 353–362.

Thayer, RL (1994). *Gray World, Green Heart: Technology, Nature, and Sustainable Landscape.* New York: Wiley.

UNFPA (2007). *The State of World Population 2007: Unleashing the Potential of Urban Growth.* The United Nations Population Fund.

United Nations (1992). *Agenda 21*, from http://www.un.org/esa/sustdev/documents/agenda21/english/agenda21toc.htm.

Vale, B and RJD Vale (1975). *The Autonomous House: Design and Planning for Self Sufficiency*. London: Thames and Hudson.

Wackernagel, M and WE Rees (1996). *Our Ecological Footprint: Reducing Human Impact On The Earth*. Gabriola Island, BC: New Society Publishers.

Wang, W (2003). Sustainibility is a cultural problem. *Harvard Design Magazine*, Spring/Summer, 18, 1–3.

Weber, C and A Perrels (2000). Modelling lifestyle effects on energy demand and related emissions. *Energy Policy*, 28(8), 549–566.

Wheeler, S (2003). Planning sustainable and livable cities. LeGates, RT and F Stout (eds.), *The City Reader* (3rd ed.). New York: Routledge, 486–496.

Wheeler, SM (2000). Planning for metropolitan sustainability. *Journal of Planning Education and Research*, 20, 133–145.

Wilson, A and P Yost (2001). Buildings and the environment: The numbers. *Environmental Building News*, 10(5), 10–13.

World Commission on Environment and Development (1987). *Our Common Future*. New York: Oxford University Press.

WWF (2006). *Living Planet Report 2006*. Gland, Switzerland: WWF–World Wide Fund For Nature.

Yeang, K (2007). On green design (Part 1): Some basic premises for green design. *Architectural Design*, 77(5), 136–137.

Yeang, K (2008a). Ecomasterplanning. *Architectural Design*, 78(5), 128–131.

Yeang, K (2008b). On green design (Part 3): The basic premises for green design. *Architectural Design*, 78(1), 130–133.

Sustaining Cities with Climate Change: Is there a Future For Human Livelihoods?

VICTOR R SAVAGE

INTRODUCTION

Since the arrival of *Homo sapiens* in Africa some 80,000 to 100,000 years ago (see Oppenheimer, 2004), we have seen three major demographic changes of human settlement. Firstly, we have, for nearly 99 per cent of the history of *Homo sapiens*, the evolving human species as a transient and migrant species. During this early period, *Homo sapiens* undertook the greatest migration journeys across the globe. Secondly, 10,000 to 15,000 years ago, humankind's 'discovery' of agriculture created a new wave of human spatial behaviour. Human beings became a sedentary, settled species.

The third phase of human living and livelihood is the creation of cities and urbanisation as a way of living. Urbanisation refers to the process of growth in population living in towns, suburban areas, cities and mega-cities, as well as a new means of livelihood within the nucleated entities. It was only made possible by the agricultural revolution. The birth of cities developed in the Tigris and Euphrates River Valleys some 4,000 years ago. And now 6,000 years later, the urban revolution seems to be completing its course. *Homo sapiens* as an urban dweller is thus a new phenomenon that represents less than five per cent of human history. In 1,000 AD, the ten largest cities were in the Old World; by 1900, most of the largest cities were in industrial Western Europe; and by 2000, the tropical developing world had seven of the top 10 cities (Brown, 2001, pp. 189–190). In 1600, only 1.6 per cent of Europe's population lived in cities of 100,000 inhabitants and by 1800, it was still only 2.2 per cent (Wolf, 1982, p. 360). By 1900, it was Britain that became the first urbanised society in the world. While agriculture created a general centrifugal spatial dispersal of population towards arable lands, urbanisation has been propelled by centripetal forces towards nodes, centres and places.

In economic terms, urbanisation is a barometer of a country's per capita income: the correlation coefficient is around 0.75 and 0.80. Hence it is no wonder that the level of urbanisation is often seen as synonymous with economic development. The high urban levels in the developed world also correlate with high per capita incomes. Cities were often seen as the innovators of human creative endeavours or the point of contact of foreign cultural innovative ideas that were diffused to other parts of a kingdom. This is what Fernand Braudel (1973, p. 373) meant when he noted that towns are "electric transformers".

Against this global backdrop of rapidly changing economic, cultural and political scenario and paper inputs and discussions from the World Cities Summit Conference in Singapore (24–25 June 2008), this paper explores the impact of growing urbanisation, and its implications and ramifications on the environment, food and natural resource consumption and coping mechanisms for climate change. The issues at stake have less to do with academic debate and political negotiations but more with how the global community and its member states are able to demonstrate political will, develop enlightened policies, and implement pragmatic programmes in managing urban environments within a rapidly changing global climatic, economic and political landscape.

THE 21ST CENTURY: THREE CHALLENGES

The global community seems to be faced with three major intersecting crossroads which are challenging not only the future of human development but the very existence of humankind. Firstly, the 21st century will witness for the first time in human history, a world where cities and urban living will become the norm of livelihood. In August 2007, 50 per cent of the world population was classified as living in urban areas, which translated to some 3.2 billion people. We can finally be called the urban species of animals: *Homo urbanicus*. It took a little over a century for the world to move from the first urban state of Britain (1900) to a global urban community (2007).

The United Nations estimates that two-thirds of the world's population will live in cities by 2020. The human species now lives in 408 cities of over one million and 20 other mega-cities with over 10 million people. By 2030, four of the five global urban residents will be in what we refer to now as the 'developing' world. This huge urban population will be residing in 377 cities of between one to five million residents spread over Africa (59 cities), Latin America and the Caribbean (65 cities) and Asia (253 cities) (Flavin, 2007, p. xxiii).

Secondly, the new environmental challenge of the 21st century will certainly be global warming and climate change, environmental issues that human societies have little experience in coping and managing on a global scale. Yet, climate change in human history has been a plus point as much as it has been a negative factor in human development. Over the last 80,000 years of *Homo sapiens* history, the ice age made it possible for early human beings to cross over land bridges and explore, experiment and populate many areas around the world. Global warming has been taking place over the last 20,000 years and certainly over what scientists call the Holocene (10,000 BP) period. The global warming Holocene was a period of much human creative activity — agricultural origins, plant and animal domestication, genesis of cities, development of religions, technological developments, pottery and writing. Steven Mithen's (2004) book, *After the Ice* documents these creative human developments and argues that human history between 20,000 to 5,000 BP "reached a turning point during a period of global warming" and set the stage for the "origins of human civilisation" (Mithen, 2004, p. 504).

Ironically, for the first time in "glacial time" (Castells, 2004, p. 183), climate change is not a natural phenomena but a product of human-induced activities which scientists call the "Anthropocene" and "Anthropozoikum" to underscore the need for an Earth Science System which positions humankind as an "integrated part of the Earth System" (Ehlers and Krafft, 2006, p. 11). At the root of this Anthropocene-based Integrated Earth System are the rising urban agglomerations around the world. Humankind has changed urban environments radically or what Anne Spirn (1984) called the "granite garden" to underscore the human engineered built-up environment.

Thirdly, globalisation and its implications are seeing not only incredible economic, political and cultural transformations but also a changing global power system where Western political and economic supremacy are likely to have to accommodate ascendant Asian powers. As Samuel Huntington (1996, p. 308) argues, the emerging politics of culture of non-Western civilisations, and the "increasing cultural assertiveness of their societies" are widely recognised: China, India, Japan and the Middle East. Kishore Mahbubani (2008) in his book, *The New Asian Hemisphere,* has been less apologetic about this Asian assertiveness, which he succinctly summarised as the political and economic rise of Asia that the Western world needs to accommodate. Other commentators are less enthused by Kishore's analysis of China's rise given her ageing population (334 million over 60 years by 2050), her dependence on non-Chinese owned factories (60 per cent in 1980), and her dismal environmental record (50 per cent of population lack clean drinking water and 70 per cent of lakes and rivers are polluted).

The three processes taking place in the 21st century pose major urban sustainability challenges for the global community. If the international community does not come together to manage the deteriorating 'global commons', then one would see by the close of this century major urban problems, global environmental degradation abetted by conflict and competition for natural resources, food and water amongst different states, cities and communities. What will be the future of the city? Will the inhabitants of the city, with their arsenal of high educational status, infrastructural achievements and culture of innovation be able to manage the global problems of the world? Clearly, while the global community has reached its highest levels of development compared to any other time in human history, it also faces the most critical phase of its own history as a living species on earth. The mantras on global warming and climate change portend a dismal future for human beings this century. For once in the history of global physical systems, human actions and behaviour are now going to be a major shaper of climate change and activity. Will we be able to survive our own actions as a physical designer of nature, environment and the global ecosystem?

CLIMATE CHANGE AND GLOBAL WARMING: THE CURRENT ENVIRONMENTAL CHALLENGE

Despite the current challenges that confront urban governments about ensuring liveability and sustainable environments, the global community now has to contend with global warming and climate change. At the crux of the issue is that climate change involves three components: temperature increases, greenhouse gases and the emission levels. While scientists are busy measuring global temperature changes and levels of green house gases in the earth atmosphere, the global community is locked in a heated debate about who is responsible for these heat increases and gas emissions. It is at the level of identifying the culprits of heat and gas emissions and adapting to and mitigating these issues that requires more than a scientific response. While we need a reliable science to nail the magnitude, changes and varying levels of climate change we need a common political purpose and will to confront this global challenge more. Coming to grips with climate change cannot be left to scientists alone; it requires governments and politicians, bureaucrats and lawyers, planners and policy makers and a whole range of academic expertise from the arts and social sciences, medicine, business schools and religious theologians and practitioners to collectively address these global and far-ranging challenges.

At the international level, the challenge of global warming and climate change seem to be four-fold. Firstly, the scientific community and public need to be convinced that global warming and climate change are taking place and that the climatic process will continue unless we do something collectively to halt it. As early as November 2000, *The Economist* (2000, p. 19) in its feature editorial on global warming noted that climate modeling was in its infancy and that in the past "hot-headed attempts to link specific weather disasters to the greenhouse effect were scientific bunk". The consistent line, according to George Monbiot (2007, pp. 27–28), on climate change is that the "science is contradictory, the scientists are split, environmentalists are charlatans, liars or lunatics" and if governments took action they would be "endangering the global economy". The last few years, however, have changed scientific opinions about global warming. Secondly, we need to convince everyone, both academics and the public that human activities are a major cause in global warming and climate change. The heat waves, prolonged droughts, intense floods, snow storms, heavy rains, typhoons and hurricanes, melting mountain snow caps, sea level changes, the melting of Greenland and arctic ice caps over the last four decades are not a product of natural weather and climatic phenomena but issues that have been induced by and related to human activities. The main human cause has been the use of 2.7 trillion barrels of equivalent (BOE) oil, gas and coal that has been used to date (Stern, 2007, p. 212). This is the main reason why carbon dioxide concentrations in the global atmosphere have risen from 280 parts per million (ppm) pre-industrially to 380 ppm by 2005. The most recent figures show that CO_2 has reached dangerous levels of 385 ppm (Editors, 2008, p. 21). Think of what would happen to the impact on climate change if human beings used the remainder 40 trillion BOE that lies in the ground; seven trillion are said to be economically recoverable (Stern, 2007, p. 212). Thirdly, there is a general belief in many circles that mitigation issues on climate change are directly linked to the economy. In Spain, Tabara (2003) showed that climate change policies lagged behind because they were repeatedly portrayed as being a potential drag on economic growth. Certainly, the Bush administration's lukewarm response to the Kyoto Protocol boils down mainly to economic issues. Fourthly, arising from the above two scenarios, we need to ensure that the international political climate should respond more quickly and more pro-actively to climate change and global warming. Unfortunately, there is a lack of global leadership and political will to tackle this global issue.

There is sufficient climatic evidence to demonstrate that our Earth is in the throes of global warming and climate change (see Flannery, 2006; Linden, 2007; Stern, 2007; Walker and King, 2008). Between 1999 and 2006, the world has experienced some of the worst droughts of the century, the worst floods in 500 years, the strongest El Niño in 130,000 years and the worst tropical storms in recorded memory (Linden, 2007, p. 249). Despite the controversial book, *Skeptical Environmentalist* by Bjørn Lomborg (2001), the 935 peer-reviewed scientific papers on climate change between 1993 and 2003 all have accepted that "humans are changing climate" (Linden, 2007, p. 228).

The question is why has the international community shown such a blasé attitude to climate change, despite all the growing signs of the impact of climate change on human beings? Several reasons can account for such an international response. Firstly, the biggest culprits of climate change are the developed countries and major corporations and hence any mitigation issues would have to begin with them. Given that these climate change issues are so enmeshed with global capitalism, world trade and corporate profitability, no major country or corporation wants to take the lead in making changes. This is in a nutshell the message of Al Gore's "inconvenient truth". Secondly, the impact of climate has affected the international community in a rather sporadic and patchy regional manner. The impact of Katrina on New Orleans, or the recent typhoon Nargis in Myanmar has not been able to galvanise global support because of a host of political, strategic and economic issues. Thirdly, the disasters have affected the poorer places, regions and countries which obviously have less political clout to call for global attention to their plight — New Orleans is a relatively poor area in the US and Myanmar is one of the poorest states in the world. Finally, we have built a whole global economy lubricated with oil. The consequences of changing to alternative energy sources are really mind-boggling.

Apart from the inconveniences and deaths from occasional heat waves, droughts and floods, the pertinent question is how will climate change and global warming affect urban populations around the world? To date, deaths from heat waves are rising: Chicago (700 deaths in 1995), Andhra Pradesh, India (1,000 deaths in 2002), Europe (49,000 in 2003). In economic terms, the costs and risks of climate change according to Stern (2007, p. xv) translate to 5 per cent of the global GDP from "now and forever" and this might rise to 20 per cent if nothing is done. No one has the real answer to this question because the issue has little precedence in human-recorded history. Hence, many governments and even international agencies have shown very little interest in proposing mitigation programmes for a future catastrophe. However, despite the lack of specific historical correlations between climate change and human impacts, there are now growing historical examples that suggest that specific climatic factors have greatly impacted on civilisations throughout history. Eugene Linden's (2007) book, *The Winds of Change,* documents several sudden climatic events that have affected the demise of several civilisations. He argues that a sudden hot and dry climatic event could have led to the end of the Akkadian civilisation some 4,200 years ago which was recorded in "The Curse of Akkad" (Linden, 2007, pp. 50–53). Despite the over one hundred theories (e.g. deforestation; overpopulation) about the fall of the Mayan civilisation, Linden (2007, pp. 68–70) postulates that drought, water shortages, famine and disease saw the demise of this once powerful civilisation 1,100 years ago. Evidence shows increasingly that during the Little Ice Age (1343–1345), the Norse failed to survive and their culture died out.

CITIES UNDER CLIMATIC THREAT

In trying to understand the way past cultures and civilisations adjusted or adapted to sudden changes in climate, we can draw several conclusions that are pertinent to our global civilisation and its urban representations. Firstly, we have to accept that the more sedentary and fixated a civilisation is in place, the less its ability to respond and adapt to sudden climatic changes. Large populations residing in cities are less mobile. Hence, urban populations have to adapt to climate change and global warming *in situ* (meaning "in place") by ensuring that other forms of technological mitigation methods are optimised. Indeed, cities have adaptive mechanisms in place but they seem aimed more at handling military and security challenges, sociopolitical issues, and public health problems rather than handling climatic events and disasters. Few city governments have ever given much thought to dealing with climate change and its impacts. Given that cities are the biggest culprits of global warming, it is going to be a challenge to get city governments, officials, entrepreneurs and the urban population to change mind-sets, behaviour patterns and styles of living.

Secondly, mobile populations like hunters and gatherers or swidden cultivators will always have greater cultural flexibility to adapt to sudden climatic events because they are mobile, have small populations and carry a portable culture. Urban and sedentary rural populations lack this mobility because their investments are in material goods, irrigation networks, land tenure systems and property. One often forgets that moving to where the grass is greener is a major cultural adaptive mechanism that human beings have practised for centuries. Today, poor rural dwellers migrate (Chinese, Indonesians, Indians, Bangladeshis, Burmese, Thais, Filipinos, Malaysians) and form the major bulk of transnational labourers in many cities (Hong Kong, Tokyo, Singapore, Taipei, Kuala Lumpur, Bangkok) in Asia. People adapt by moving because "adaptation does not mean staying in one place regardless of what happens" (Linden, 2007, p. 155). Yet whole cities and civilisations cannot move easily and when natural disasters hit them, they perish and are wiped out. In our modern world, only the rich will have the ability and means to move when their lives are affected, such as when a sudden climatic event hits their habitat. The skilled and educated populations from the developing world are similarly moving to greener pastures in North America, Australasia and Europe. The poor of the world, who have less means for long distance mobility, probably will perish at the time of major climate disasters. We see the spectre of climatic-induced human fatalities already happening in Ethiopia and the Sahel when extreme drought conditions have led to hunger, famine, disease and starvation. An added dimension to human immobility is the question of large families and dense populations over limited resources. Such situations mean that all the stakeholders have little margin for survival and hence when a natural disaster hits, the effects are devastating on the human population.

Thirdly, of all the natural disasters and sudden climatic events, the most critical and fatal is prolonged drought and aridity. While sudden heat waves and floods might kill several thousand people in one place and time, it is prolonged drought that will have the most devastating impacts on human society and the ecosystem. Given that water is essential to life, a prolonged drought over decades will evoke slow and painful death for all inhabitants in an area. Without water, plants cannot grow, food is diminished, domestic animals perish and finally human beings have to succumb to water deficiency. In nearly all the correlations of environmental causes to the fall of civilisations, protracted drought, fall in precipitation and aridity are the nails in the coffin of civilisations. In the case of the Mayan civilisation, growing climatic evidence shows that the civilisation was exposed to several periods of aridity and droughts from 760 AD to 860 AD and 910 AD; a dry stretch that lasted about 200 years (Linden, 2007, pp. 168–169). Given that 70 per cent of the world water usage goes into agriculture, any major prolonged drought is going to affect food production severely and lead to starvation for its resident populations. The US intelligence agencies have forewarned that between 120 million and 1.2 billion people in Asia "will continue to experience some water stress" and that as many as 50 million could face hunger by 2020 (*The Straits Times*, 26 June 2008, p. 20).

Given the onslaught of global warming and climatic change for the rest of the 21st century and the likely outcomes of aridity, water shortages and decreasing precipitation, countries and cities should be mindful that they need to take steps to mitigate the anticipated long drought in the near future. In this area, a tripartite arrangement needs to be forged amongst city governments, companies (multi-national companies) and universities/research institutions to research and develop new technologies for increasing drinkable and clean water. Here is an area where environmental concerns can have positive economic outcomes. The International Water Week (23–25 June 2008) in Singapore, for example, attracted some 390 companies in the water-technology business. Many cities around the world could embark on a similar venture: using the urban environment as a test bed for many innovative water systems such as desalination, recycling and reclamation. No matter how affluent and economically buoyant a city is, if there is severe and prolonged water scarcity, its residents will migrate, the urban economy will fizzle out and the city will collapse.

Fourthly, cities are now the tinderbox for all sorts of political and economic conflagrations and global warming is the matchstick that is most likely to set cities on political fire. Given rising costs, inflation, growing poverty, and food insecurity in urban areas, the scenario of political chaos has shifted over the last 150 years. In the late 19th and early 20th centuries, the landscapes of discontent were the rural agricultural areas with farmers protesting and rebelling against the inroads of capitalism and colonialism (Scott, 1976; Popkin, 1979). Since World War II, the landscapes of discontent are now cities, industrial and office workers. Growing disparity in wealth is the underbelly for social discontent, riots, strikes and political chaos in cities. What we have seen in the closing decades of the 20th century is the rising tide of political dissent that dominates cities. Given its high concentration of large and generally poor populations utilising poor infrastructure, any major economic issue can set off strikes and riots quite easily in the cities of the developing world. In the first six months of 2008, a combination of high inflation rates, steep fuel price increases and rising food costs have led to a wave of discontent, riots and strikes in cities around the world. The persistence of such urban income disparities and economic inequalities does not augur well for the maintenance of public health and sustainable urban environments. More often than not, only 20 per cent of the urban wealthy population enjoys liveable environments, their housing areas and shopping malls stand out like an oasis in a dismal and deteriorating urban environment. Without active government intervention and subsidies, the urban poor will never be able to enjoy a basic quality of life that will maintain public hygiene and urban sustainability.

The issues of climate change and environmental problems clearly are straining political, economic and social relationships of communities and stakeholders within and between countries and cities. US agencies in their assessment of global warming report that climate change will weaken governments, foster internal conflicts and extend conditions for the war on terror (*The Straits Times*, 2008a, p. 20). Issues of national political instability arising from environmental stress already threaten national security in China. The *China Daily* reported that there were 50,000 environment-related riots, protests and disputes in China in 2005 (Roseland and Soots, 2007, p. 153).

We have seen how devastating droughts, floods, typhoons, hurricanes and natural hazards have disrupted food production and supplies and set food prices soaring around the world in 2008. Given the wide disparities of wealth and income globally, many poor communities have little access to food, clean water, energy and other resources. Certainly, the debate about whether globalisation increases or shrinks income inequality must be put to rest. The World Commission on the Social Dimension of Globalisation found that while the average person might be better off in absolute terms, in relative terms, however, people often are worse off. The World Commission found that 59 per cent of the population live in countries with widening inequality and only in 5 per cent of countries is disparity narrowing (Perry, 2008, p. 60). In South Africa, despite the end of apartheid, people living daily on less than US$1 increased from 1.9 million in 1996 to 4.2 million in 2005 (Perry, 2008, p. 60).

Fifthly, despite a regular pattern of El Niños over the last 5,000 years, scientists have only begun to be more aware of their patterns and destructive impact over the last 50 years. The impact of El Niño and La Niña is widespread, costly and global but manageable. As Linden (2007, p. 182) observes, in "the rogues' gallery of climate killers, El Niño may be a mere foot soldier". Yet, foot soldiers in the global scheme of climate change, El Niño and La Niña have wreaked havoc and massive deaths in many parts of the world. The 1888 El Niño produced the Great Ethiopian Famine that killed one-third of the population and 90 per cent of the country's livestock (Linden, 2007, p. 212). The impact of El Niño in 1982–83 once again produced a prolonged drought in Ethiopia that affected 7.5 million people and killed 300,000 (Linden, 2007, p. 213). In economic terms, however, the 1997–98 El Niño impact was disastrous for Indonesia: per capita incomes fell by 75 per cent from US$1,200 to US$300; unemployment went up to 40 per cent, in May 1998, food prices escalated by 4 per cent, and poverty levels increased from 22.5 million in 1997 (before El Niño and the currency crisis) to over 100 million in the spring of 1998 (Linden, 2007, pp. 209–210). The 1997–98 El Niño gave rise to forest fires that burnt some eight million hectares of land (Schweithelm and Glover, 2006, p. 1); the total economic damage of haze and fires cost US$4.5 billion (Schweithelm *et al.*, 2006, p. 3). The drought-causing El Niño is likely to have devastating impact (especially on food security and water supplies) on the urban populations in the future.

Finally, one of the ironic twists of global warming is how moving away from fossil fuels to other non-carbon emitting energy alternatives has led to other indirect problems for urban populations. Inflation and rising food costs, especially in staples, have been a direct outcome of food exporters switching to biofuel and biodiesel sales instead of maintaining the traditional food supply chain. In trying to reduce the environmental impact arising from petrol, the alternative use of biofuels and biodiesel has been causing inflation in food prices, shortages of food supplies with general malnutrition and hunger for many urban poor. No one knows for sure what the total impact of the change in agricultural output towards biofuels will have on the global economy of food outputs, inflation and food security. According to the aid agency Oxfam, biofuels are responsible for a 30 per cent increase in global food prices. Rich countries, according to the Oxfam report, spent US$15 billion in 2007 supporting biofuels which was damaging to global food security (*The Straits Times*, 2008b, p. 20).

Given that public behaviour is largely determined by price, fiscal incentives and household incomes (Anker-Nilssen, 2003; Minnesma, 2003), one can expect that high petrol prices and general urban inflation are likely to create the best public mitigation responses to global warming around the world. In some cities like Ho Chi Minh City, Jakarta or Manila, car or motorcycle dependence is a necessity because public transportation is not fully developed. If transport costs go up, then public mobility is likely to suffer and in turn urban development and the economic activities in the city are also likely to be affected. In other developed cities, people have responded to fuel price hikes by using public transport or modifying their travel habits. Clearly, urban governments can do more in making cities more compact, ensuring public transport is a viable alternative for mobility and generally reducing the dependence on fossil fuels for energy.

MITIGATING CLIMATE CHANGE
FOR URBAN SUSTAINABILITY

With the widening impact of global warming and climate change, are global thinkers, environmentalists, economists, technologists, social scientists and think tank scholars paying sufficient attention to how cities can become liveable environments and sustainable nodal entities for 75 per cent of the world's population?

In mitigating the effects of climate change on cities, governments and urban administrators need to view cities within two spheres. Firstly, there is the intra-urban environment and urban space. Essentially, intra-urban brown issues (energy, water, garbage, sewerage, transport) need to be managed effectively and this will in turn help to reduce global warming. These brown issues are tied with both population growth as well as urban affluence. Do we have the ability to develop an expanding and 'plastic' infrastructure that can accommodate an expanding resident and floating population (tourists, mobile labour) within the city? Population expansion is a worrying issue because growing urbanisation lies mainly with the growth of population in existing cities.

In a study of the 485 one million-person-cities from 1950 to 2010, researchers found that these cities would have grown 953 per cent in the 60-year period which means a non-compounded yearly growth rate of 15.9 per cent (Mulligan, 2006, p. 345). In short, the one million-person cities would have become 8.5 times more populous in 2010 than they were in 1950 (Mulligan, 2006, p. 345). This phenomenal population growth of existing cities poses the greatest environmental challenges for urban and national governments. Hence, unless city and national governments can plan, project and programme for a 'plastic' rather than static system, the intra-urban development of cities (essential infrastructure) would never be able to accommodate rapidly increasing urban populations. Essentially the World Cities Summit papers paid more attention to the intra-urban environmental issues — adequate housing, clean water, modern sewerage systems, garbage disposal, and efficient public transport networks.

Secondly, cities need to address their extra-urban issues. With massive populations concentrated in spatial nodes, the city becomes a major importer of many natural resources, food, water and other creature comforts to sustain its population. This becomes a major challenge because poverty reigns in many cities of the developing world, and a two-tier social system of the haves and have-nots becomes starkly evident. The question of supporting and sustaining urban populations is thus not an issue of the relationships to immediate hinterlands but whether urban populations can afford the imports of food, water, energy supplies and natural resources to sustain their living. Hence, if cities essentially are not economically sustainable entities, it would be difficult for resident populations within cities to lead sustainable livelihoods, much less cope with climate change impact. The conference papers at the World Cities Summit generally skirted this issue. It would seem that sustainable cities are only a product of maintaining an efficient and effective intra-urban environmental friendly infrastructure. But, the impact of urban population on surrounding and global hinterlands will have dire consequences, especially if all cities around the world want to maintain standards of living and quality livelihoods like those of the developed world.

The Intra-urban Infrastructural Challenge

The cities of the developing world in the last 60 years have gone through similar expansion as cities of the developed world in the 19th and early 20th centuries — with one major difference. While cities in the developed world grew in response to economic expansion within states and hinterlands, in the developing world, cities expanded in an artificial manner, responding to external impetus and economic stimuli from the colonial mother state. This was a product of what Andre Gunder Frank (1969) called the metropolitan-satellite relationship and Immanuel Wallerstein (1980) referred to as the core, semi-periphery and periphery relationship. Mitigating and managing the effects of climate change thus becomes an increasingly complex issue at a global level because cities form a network of economic exchange, trade flows, migratory labour circuits, financial relationships and natural resource movements. Rather than look at the traditional specific mitigating policies for climate change (see Stern, 2007), a more macro and holistic perspective is advocated of urban change and management, that will not only enhance a better quality of living standards, but reduce disparities of wealth and living standards, and invariably help governments better manage the challenges of climate change for their urban populations. From an intra-urban perspective, better housing, comprehensive infrastructure and transportation systems are needed in the adaptive mechanisms for climate change as well as innovative environmental systems for enhancing the quality of life. Adaptation is defined here as "any adjustment in natural or human systems in response to actual or expected climatic stimuli or their effects, which moderates harm or exploits beneficial opportunities" (Stern, 2007, p. 458). The investments in infrastructure are pertinent because poor cities and countries have less chance of adapting to climate change challenges. The statistics show that in the 1990s, 200 million people a year were affected by climate-related disasters compared to only one million in the developed countries (The World Bank, 2008, p. xviii). The World Bank's Global Monitoring Report for 2008, a half-way assessment of the Millennium Development Goals (MDGs) by 2015 noted that given the developing world's poverty, their lack of development and dependence on natural resources and agriculture, makes developing countries "less able to adapt" to the impact of climate change (The World Bank, 2008, p. xviii).

A. Housing

Globally, few cities in the developing world have been able to provide proper housing for their burgeoning populations. Of the estimated one billion people living in informal settlements worldwide (Chafe, 2007, p. 115), more than 900 million urban dwellers live in slums in low- and middle-income nations (Satterthwaite and McGranahan, 2007, p. 28). Slum populations worldwide are increasing annually by 25 million (Chafe, 2007, p. 115). The rural-urban migration that feeds into slum and squatter settlement growth in cities explains why cities in poor countries are expanding rapidly.

A city that cannot house its population in reasonably good housing can never solve its intra-urban environmental challenges or be able to tackle the problems of climate change. The brown issues within cities will not be wished away if public housing projects are not addressed for slum and squatter dwellers. If brown issues are not contained and moderated in cities, it will be difficult to see how governments can control intra-urban climate change challenges. The biggest problems confronting slums and squatter settlements are the environmental risk factors (lack of water, sanitation, poor public hygiene, indoor pollution, and poor waste disposal) which are the major causes of diseases (diarrhea, malaria, lower respiratory infections). In developing countries, 25 per cent of all deaths have been attributable to environmental risk factors (The World, Bank, 2008, p. 79). Furthermore,

94 per cent of all diarrheal cases worldwide are attributable to environmental factors (unsafe drinking water, poor sanitation) (The World Bank, 2008, p. 80). With climate change, there is danger of the rise in malaria and only improved environmental management can contain or control this rise. Since 2000, changes in climate have caused 150,000 deaths and a loss of over 5.5 million DALY's (disability-adjusted life year) annually (The World Bank, 2008, p. 85). The eradication and replacement of slums and squatters with proper housing is a major way of creating a clean and hygienic environments to maintain public health, and is also one of the best adaptive measures for the climate change challenge.

In Singapore, without the ambitious public housing programmes by the Housing Development Board (HDB) since 1960, which now houses 86 per cent of Singapore's 4.6 million population, the city-state's rapid and outstanding development over the last 40 years would never have been possible. The Republic's transformation from Third World to First World could not have taken place if 35 per cent of its urban population in the 1960s still remained in slum and squatter settlements today. Public housing has solved many problems which confront cities in the developing countries: adequate sewerage and modern sanitation, clean water, efficient garbage disposal, clean energy and healthy living environments. The quality of life and living for the majority of all urban residents is what makes cities the beacons of human civilisation and sustainable systems.

B. Brown Infrastructure

Much emphasis in the World Cities Summit Conference was paid to urban infrastructure development. The provision of basic infrastructural services is generally lacking in all the major cities in the developing world. Despite the fact that cities cover only 2 per cent of the world's surface area, they account for 78 per cent of carbon emissions, 60 per cent of residential water use and 76 per cent of wood used for industrial purposes (Brown, 2001, p. 188). Without effective urban management, cities become receptacles of pollution and environmental degradation. China's breakneck economic development has left the country with 16 of the 20 most polluted cities in the world (Roseland and Soots, 2007, p. 153). The lack of safe drinking water also kills. Every day in India, 1,000 Indian children die of diarrheal sicknesses (*The Economist*, 2008, p. 33). Cities in the developing world also cannot cope with their sewerage, refuse disposal and other urban pollution issues due to a host of reasons: power scarcity, lack of expertise, poor management systems, inadequate technical facilities, political indifference and corruption. In India, for example, only 13 per cent of the 33,200 litres of daily sewerage that cities produce are treated in sewerage plants (*The Economist,* 2008b, p. 33).

Growing urbanisation has a direct impact on electricity requirements. Cities, by nature of their affluent populations generally consume more energy to maintain their comfortable lifestyles and high mobility patterns as Anker-Nilssen (2003) demonstrated in Oslo, Norway. The general calculations are that a 1 per cent increase in people living in cities leads to a 1.8 per cent demand for installed capacity. Furthermore, a 1 per cent rise in income per head in cities leads to a 0.5 per cent increase in electricity demand. Put these figures together and it explains the 140 per cent surge in electricity capacity in China and the 80 per cent rise in India projected for the next decade (2008–2017) (*The Economist,* 2008a, p. 78). With the estimated 75 per cent rise in electricity demands in the emerging economies over the next decade (2008–2017) (*The Economist,* 2008a, p. 78), all of which are dependent on fossil fuels, the vision of air pollution and global warming in our near future look grim. Domestic energy consumption at home is also increasing because of the massive growth of electronic home appliances, gadgets and entertainment systems. In the United Kingdom, houses now consume 25 per cent of electricity (Monbiot, 2007, p. 73). In short, no matter how much green technology is invented, the multiplication of home gadgets is likely to undermine any targets set to reduce the carbon footprint. Given their high consumption patterns and wealth, it is thus not surprising that the more affluent communities and cities in the developed world (North America; Europe) are also the major emitters of carbon dioxide (see Table 1). The latest figures show that while each person in the world contributes to 4.6 tonnes of carbon dioxide emissions annually, the US citizen is responsible for 20.2 tonnes, the British 12 tonnes and the Chinese 4.6 tonnes a year (Sawday, 2008, p. 9).

Currently, the US and China are major urban emitters of greenhouse gases because they still use coal for the generation of electricity. The change to renewal energy sources is not an easy option. Wellington, with a population of 180,000, provides a model where, according to the Mayor, Ms. Kerry Prendergast, 65 per cent of the city's electricity comes from

Table 1   World Population Data Sheet (Mid-2008)

Country	Population mid-2008 (millions)	Percent urban	GNI PPP per capita (US$) 2007	Carbon dioxide emissions per capita (metric tons) 2002
World	6,705	49	9,600	4.0
More developed	1,227	74	31,200	11.7
Less developed	5,479	44	4,760	2.1
Less developed (Excl. China)	4,154	44	4,560	1.9
Africa	967	38	2,430	1.1
Northern America	338	79	44,790	19.6
Latin America/ Caribbean	577	77	9,080	2.5
Asia	4,052	42	5,650	2.6
Southeast Asia	586	45	4,440	1.7
Europe	736	71	24,320	8.4
Oceania	35	70	23,910	12.2

Source: Population Reference Bureau, 2008 World Population Data Sheet, Washington, D.C.

renewable sources: geothermal, hydropower and wind. By 2020, the city hopes to increase it to 90 per cent. In Britain, a study found that the country would have 170.5 terrawatt hours of energy by 2025 based on supplies of "practical" renewable resources (wind, wave, tidal, hydroelectric) which is less than even the current energy usage of 400 terrawatt hours of electricity (Monbiot, 2007, pp. 101–102). Many countries however, are trying to reduce their carbon imprints by using alternative energy sources: Brazil's biofuels from sugarcane and Iceland's renewable geothermal power.

The more radical alternative as seen in the current international political climate is for urban governments to adopt James Lovelock's (2007) prescription of nuclear energy. Lovelock (2007, p. 196) argues that "Nuclear energy is free of emissions and independent of imports from what will be a disturbed world. We would be right to cut back all emissions to a minimum, and this includes emissions of methane from leaking pipes and landfill sites. But most of all we need electricity to sustain our technologically based civilisation". There are currently 439 nuclear power stations in 31 countries (Huber, 2008, p. 78) and only France has embarked on nuclear energy in a major way increasing nuclear energy 40 fold between 1977 to 2003

(Stern, 2007, p. 231). But with rising oil prices and a booming economy, China plans to build another 100 nuclear plants in 20 years time (Huber, 2008, p. 78). Yet, the adoption of nuclear energy is not an easy option for many countries because it is contingent on heavy government financial involvement and management, how cities will be able to treat and store nuclear waste materials safely and effectively, and the vexing issue of security in a terrorist-phobic global environment. The tragedy, however, is many countries in North America, Europe and East Asia have returned to the "Coal Age", as George Monbiot (2007, p. 83) has noted because the world has one trillion tones of recoverable coal, enough for 200 years of supply at current levels.

C. Transportation and Communication

With the invention of the car, cities of the 20th century have become automobile cities. In 1970 there were 200 million cars globally, but by 2006, there were 850 million cars and it is estimated that by 2030 there will be 1.7 billion cars (Newman and Kenworthy; 2007, p. 67). Essentially, cities of the 21st century are going to be shaped more by their transportation systems.

Given that transport accounts for 14 per cent of global emissions of carbon dioxide, we need major changes in the transport sector to reduce one major source of global warming. Indeed, it is estimated that urban air pollution takes an estimated three million human lives annually (Brown, 2001, p. 200). Despite the fact that oil accounts for only seven percent of total energy usage globally, its impact is massive because this usage is almost totally concentrated in cities. In a study of 15 cities around the world in 1995, the most energy wasteful cities were Atlanta and New York — cities dependent on cars. The most energy efficient cities were Ho Chi Minh City and Shanghai. Based on gasoline usage, each citizen in these two American cities, Atlanta (2,962 litres per person annually) and New York (1,237 litres), were using 110 times and 45 times more gasoline respectively than the residents of the Vietnamese city of Ho Chi Minh (27 litres per person annually) (Newman and Kenworthy, 2007, p. 68).

The most important equation in energy efficient and environmental friendly urban environments boils down to the use of public transportation systems. Tokyo and Hong Kong are highly densely populated cities but they use 10 to 25 times less gasoline than residents in Atlanta because of a dense network of public mass transit and rail systems (Newman and Kenworthy, 2007, p. 68). Based on the various modes of urban transport, a study of 32 cities in 1990 shows clearly that cars have the lowest fuel efficiency and lowest occupancy rates amongst the four main modes of urban transportation (cars, bus, heavy rail on electric and diesel, and light rail) (see Table 2). The economic efficiency of urban transport system demonstrates that while freeway traffic carries 2,500 people per hour, buses carry 5,000–8,000 persons; light rails support 10,000–20,000 persons and heavy rails carry 50,000 persons per hour, 20 times more than the freeways (Newman and Kenworthy, 2007, p. 83). The economic savings of city residents is enormous in the choice between cars versus a transit system: transit-based urban systems spend about 5 to 8 per cent of GDP on transportation while car-based cities spend 12 to 15 per cent or in the case of Brisbane 18 per cent of GDP (Newman and Kenworthy, 2007, p. 82). In Singapore, despite the installation of the Mass Rapid Transit system in the 1980s, the system is not comprehensive. Moreover, the MRT system does not service the central areas where the richer Singaporeans live and work, and therefore encourage wealthy Singaporeans to continue to use their cars to get to work. This might be partly rectified by the 16.6 kilometre MRT line (Downtown Line Two: DTL2) which will be ready by 2016, which will service the central Bukit Timah area (Neo, 2008, p. 2) comprising all the landed property and condominium housing estates.

Table 2   Average Fuel Efficiency and Occupancy by Mode in 32 Cities, 1990

Mode	Average fuel efficiency (megajoules per passenger-kilometer)	Measured average vehicle occupancy (number of occupants)
Car	2.91	1.52
Bus	1.56	13.83
Heavy rail (electric)	0.44	30.96
Heavy rail (diesel)	1.44	27.97
Light rail/Tram	0.79	29.73

Note: Rail mode occupancies are given on the basis of the average loading per wagon, not per train. The average occupancy of cars is a 24-hour figure.

Source: Starke, L (ed.) (2007). *2007 State of the World: Our Urban Future*. New York and London: WW Norton & Co, p. 73.

In East Asia, South Asia and Southeast Asia, the growth of the *nouveau riche* has given rise to an explosion of car and motorcycle ownership. In China, India, Vietnam, Cambodia, Taiwan and Malaysia, there is a graduation of transportation from bicycles to motorcycles, and finally, the car of all brands and sizes. Hence, in the booming economies of China and India, car populations are likely to increase by 15 times and 13 times over the next 30 years (Schaefer-Preuss, 2008, p. 26). Bus systems are not well coordinated and to make them economically viable, bus routes generally cover long distances. Commuting within a city takes a long time. Mass rapid transit systems such as trains, on the other hand, are costly and have been slow to develop within large and congested megacities like Jakarta and Manila. In Thailand, South Korea, China, India and Malaysia, there are now national car industries that need to be protected above environmental concerns.

The Extra-urban Connections: Hinterlands and Footprints

In Southeast Asia, Elson (1997, p. 241) argues that over 200 years, colonialism had engulfed the rural landscape and the peasant world was "radically reconstituted". With inroads of national and international economics, the peasant in the last 200 years has been "transmogrified from peasant into farmer, worker and now citizen" (Elson, 1997, p. 238).

For environmentalists, however, this equation between urban consumption and hinterland exploitation is viewed as a product of economic clout and demand-supply variables. Environmentalists view all consumption patterns within the context of sustainability variables. Given the globalising impacts on cities, one sees a change from the urban geography of 'hinterlands' being translated into an environmental issue of defining city 'footprints'. While the concept of the hinterland was meant to demonstrate carrying capacities for city size and developments, the ecological footprint concept is a much more a social and political concept. As Michael Cahill (2002, p. 165) argues, the ecological footprint is meant "to demonstrate the practicalities of resource conservation, social justice for the world's poor countries today and equity for future generations".

Summing up urban sustainability in the light of climate change, city governments face two interrelated challenges. First and foremost, can they develop cities that are liveable for their inhabitants with the new impending climate change challenges? Do they have the skills, technical know-how and expertise to plan, design, develop and manage cities for their populations? This is a major infrastructural problem that has to address all the brown challenges (sewerage, clean water, garbage disposal, housing, electricity, non-polluting public transportation) which are major contributors to global warming.

There is an interrelated four-part solution to this intra-urban environmental challenge. The first deals with employing cleaner technologies, using mass transport systems and more efficient electrical and water systems to minimise waste. In Germany, houses to reduce energy use were built in the 1980s. The prototype is called *Passivhaus* or passive house. These technological innovations for the environment will certainly have a direct bearing on what Stern (2007, p. 421) sees as stabilising the 550 ppm level for carbon by 2050. The second part of the solution lies with the debates about costs and the negative impact on the economy. In Bjørn Lomborg's (2001, p. 310) calculations, this cost of keeping global warming down at 2.5 degrees above 1990 levels would run into US$8.5 trillion and at 1.5 degrees above 1990 levels it would be US$38 trillion; economic costs that he feels would burden the global community more than the benefits of global warming. George Monbiot (2007, p. 49) totally disagrees with Lomborg's economic conclusions both in terms of its "amoral means of comparison" and in his economic calculations, "the economic costs of letting climate change happen greatly outweigh the economic costs of tackling it". What is more disturbing is that a study for the International Panel on Climate Change stated that a life lost in the developing world could be priced at US$150,000 while for a person from the developed world it is assessed at US$1.5 million (Monbiot, 2007, p. 50).

The third relies on behavioural changes that the urban public needs to make. Changes in civic behaviour and public hygiene, and responsible lifestyle changes will help tremendously to ensure that dense urban populations can coexist as a community. All urban citizens must embrace their city as a common-pool commodity that needs to be cared for and used in a civic conscious manner. The city cannot have free-rider citizens who only want to use and benefit from common-pool commodities but are not interested in maintaining and prudently safeguarding their long-term sustainable use. This is not impossible when you look at how civic minded the denizens of Tokyo are in observing eco-friendly behaviour.

Finally, the fourth part lies with governance and management issues of urban authorities. Without leadership, foresight and expertise in urban government, cities will never be able to manage, much less minimise their urban problems in the light of growing climate change developments. Leadership and governance are critical factors in whether cities can provide amenities and facilities for their citizens in a sustainable manner or whether the city languishes in poverty, pollution, political chaos and economic deprivation and disparity. At the World Cities Summit Conference, we have seen that urban leadership can make the difference in the management and governance of cities. We have seen the effectiveness of city mayors from Melbourne (John Soh), Honolulu (Jeremy Harris), Yokohama (Hiroshi Nakada), Wellington (Kerry Prendergast) and Quezon City (Feliciano Belmonte, Jr) in managing their cities as places of economic dynamism, liveability and comfort, and environmental sustainability. Effective governance also means good and farsighted urban planning. It also requires "honest bookkeeping" and a "pro-active" mandate in dealing with urban problems as Mayor Jeremy Harris notes. Singapore is a good example of effective urban planning. Given its limited land area, planning becomes a major issue for government authorities because it needs perpetually to consider the future land use demands, population projections and changing demographics.

Secondly, a point which the World Cities Summit Conference paid less attention to was the issue of the nexus between the city and its hinterland. This is a more difficult problem for city mayors and governments to address because the relationship of the city and its hinterland lies outside of the direct administrative, environmental and financial jurisdiction of the city government. All cities and their inhabitants leave an ecological footprint in their surrounding areas. The size and nature of the ecological footprint is a product of the size of the city population (Tokyo's over 20 million population compared to Kuala Lumpur's one million population) and the level of affluence of its urban residents or what James Martin (2007, p. 15) calls "eco-affluence" (compare Singapore's S$31,000 per capita GNP with that of Yangon or Vientiane with less than S$6,000 per capita GNP). London has an ecological footprint of 120 times its city size (Wackernagel and Rees,

1996, p. 91). This means that while the average global footprint for each person is 1.8 hectares, in Shanghai, it is seven and in an American city, it is 9.7 (Schaefer-Preuss, 2008, p. 26). In general, cities have much larger footprints than countries because of their affluence, high consumption patterns and high tendency to import all produce. Hence, while London needs 120 times its size to sustain its population, Holland 'consumes' only 15 times more land than its size for its residents to survive (Wackernagel and Rees, 1996, p. 96). As cities proliferate and expand, it is inevitable that large parts of the global productive ecosystems will become part of the ecological footprint of cities.

With their varied economic prowess, cities can be ranked in a hierarchical nesting order: global cities like New York, London, Tokyo, Paris, Sydney, Hong Kong are tapping into global hinterlands and their citizens are tasting, sampling and using products of varied ecosystems around the world. Based on hinterland dependence, cities can be classified as ecosystem and biosphere cities. A biosphere city is a global city which is dependent on a global hinterland for all its sustenance, natural resources and materials. Global cities house biosphere people because the world is their hinterland. The less economically important and affluent cities, which might be better viewed as regional cities such as Cebu, Medan, Perth, Otago, Chiangrai, Sibu, Bandung and Agra have less economic power to command goods at an international level. Such cities depend on their immediate hinterlands or ecosystems that are closely located to the city. An ecosystem city is a town or city that relies on three or four ecosystems which are located within close proximity to the town/city for their creature comforts. Citizens of such regional and lower-order cities might be referred to as ecosystem people because they are dependent on three or four ecosystems nearer the city. In short, depending on the consumption patterns of global or ecosystem urban populations, there is a direct impact on local and global hinterlands which invariably contribute to global warming and climate change.

The ecological footprint can provide a measure of the spatial reach of urban consumer demands, the use and demands of productive ecosystems and the negative or positive impacts of urban consumption on environments around the world. As the world becomes increasingly globalised and climate change intensifies, cities will compete for hinterlands and in the process demarcate the boundaries of their ecological footprint. Those cities that cannot compete in the open market global system for hinterlands and footprints are likely to shrink, and in turn, lose their economic and political importance. In short, whatever the short term economic benefits are derived by rich cities and countries in this competition for global ecosystem hinterlands, it will not change the long term implications and impacts of climate change which will be irreversible if carbon levels cross over the tipping point (550 ppm) as calculated by Stern (2007). The fact that 74 per cent of the world's commodities come from the developing countries (The World Bank, 2008, p. 34), demonstrates how vulnerable they are in the competition for hinterlands in the face of climate change impacts.

CONCLUDING THOUGHTS

"Our freedoms, our comforts, our prosperity are all the products of fossil carbon, whose combustion creates the gas carbon dioxide, which is primarily responsible for global warming. Ours are the most fortunate generations that have ever lived. Ours might also be the most fortunate generations that ever will. We inhabit the brief historical interlude between ecological constraint and ecological catastrophe" (Monbiot, 2007, p. xxi).

If one accepts Braudel's (1995, p. 7) view that civilisation is "the common heritage of humanity", then all cities and civilisations around the world should share a responsibility in sustaining not just their cities but also the global human civilisation which I call the Gaian civilisation. Hence the software of Gaian civilisation should include the way society relates to Nature in an ecologically responsible manner as well as in the prudent use and conservation of environmental resources. The silver lining in the dark clouds of climate change is that there is a growing grassroots revolution in taking on the challenges of climate change. Despite the US government's intransigent position on the Kyoto Protocol and Climate Change, 30 states and 600 cities in the US have adopted policies to cut carbon emissions.

To address climate change the global urban communities would need to manage and implement simultaneously a three prong action-plan: (a) focus and accelerate carbon reduction technologies and environmental innovations; (b) change peoples' attitudes and promote responsible behaviour; and (c) develop sustainable eco-cities that are holistically and ecologically compatible with their hinterlands. Specifically, governments and planners around the world have attempted to green the urban development agenda by building 'eco-cities'. China in particular seems to be partnering various governments and corporations to build its new green-friendly eco-cities (Tianjin, Guangming, Yangzhou, Changzhou, Gegu, Guiyang). The British government will build 10 eco-cities by 2020. These eco-cities might not be the panacea for arresting global warming. The eco-cities are long and progressive in maintaining intra-urban environmental standards but less able to deal with reducing the extra-urban ecological footprint challenges. To reduce the ecological footprint of cities requires not just technological inventions but the more difficult changes in our economic thinking, our capitalistic system of trading, our materialistic value systems, our consumer-based ethos, our endorsement of common-pool resources and our ethical relationships to nature and community. Even in his many economic and technological suggestions and policy proposals for mitigating and adapting to climate change, Stern (2007) strongly advocated changing human behaviour in underpinning political action for climate change. Specifically, he suggested how public policy could change attitudes in two ways: (a) by changing notions for responsible behaviour; and (b) by promoting the willingness to co-operate (Stern, 2007, p. 448). Furthermore he felt that governments should not use top-down methods of "persuasion" and telling people what is best for them, but to engage citizens in public debate, dialogue and discussions so that individuals have a stakeholder's interests in these issues (Stern, 2007, p. 449).

If, by the end of this century, dramatic environmental and climatic changes and transformations take place as forecasted scientifically by Tim Flannery (2006) and economically by Nicholas Stern (2007), it would not be our cities or civilisations that will be in question, it will be the *Homo sapiens* species at stake.

Indeed, two books seem to place the 21st century as the definitive critical century for human survival. In Lord Martin Rees' (2003) book, *Our Final Century*, the question is whether we will survive this century as a species and in James Martin's (2007, p. 26) *The Meaning of the 21st Century*, there is a sense of foreboding that this century could see the termination of *Homo sapiens* or "if *Homo sapiens* survives, civilisation may not". For James Martin (2007, p. 4) the 21st century is the "critical century" or what he calls the "make-or-break century" because it is not sustainability but "survivability" that now matters. Suddenly, global warming seems to loom larger than it has ever been before in our print and mass media. *Time* magazine's 28 April 2008 front page heading equated global warming as a "war" and the issue at stake was "How to win the war on global warming" (Walsh, 2008). The rhetoric of war on nature is once again sadly misplaced for two reasons. Firstly, the enemy is not climate change and global warming, the enemy lies within each of us. We are the creators of the global warming monster. Throughout history, communities around the world lived sustainably within their given ecosystems because they never fought wars with nature; they learnt to live and adapt to nature in a harmonious and relational manner as peaceful participants (Peterson, 2001) rather than as conquerors of nature and their hinterlands. Hopefully, the human race in our comfortable urban abodes will be able to find the peaceful answers to our predicament, the will to make the difficult decisions and the courage to ensure the sustainability of Gaia.

ACKNOWLEDGEMENTS

I like to thank Professor Kenneth Corey (University of Michigan) for his comments and editorial inputs on this paper and my friend Irene Khng for helping to edit this paper.

REFERENCES

Anker-Nilssen, P (2003). Household energy use and the environment — A conflicting issue. *Applied Energy*, 76, 189–196.

Braudel, F (1995). *A History of Civilizations*, New York, New York: Penguin Book.

Braudel, F (1973).*Capitalism and Material Life 1400–1800*. New York: Harper Colophon Books.

Brown, LR (2001). *Eco-Economy: Building an Economy for the Earth*. New York: WW Norton and Company.

Cahill, M (2002). *The Environment and Social Policy*. London: Routledge.

Castells, M (2004). *The Information Age, Volume II: The Power of Identity*. Oxford: Blackwell Publishing.

Chafe, Z (2007). Reducing natural disaster risk in cities. Linda S (ed.), *2007 State of the World: Our Urban Future*. New York: WW Norton and Company, 112–133.

Editors (2008). Climate fatigue. *Scientific American*, 298(6), 21.

Ehlers, E and T Krafft (2006). Managing global change: Earth system science in the anthropocene. Eckart E and T Krafft (eds.), *Earth System Science in the Anthropocene*. New York: Springer, 5–18.

Elson, RE (1997). *The End of the Peasantry in Southeast Asia*. London, MacMillan Press Ltd.

Flannery, T (2006). *The Weather Makers: How Man is Changing the Climate and What it Means for Life on Earth*. New York: Grove Press.

Flavin, C (2007). Preface in Linda Starke (ed.), *2007 State of the World: Our Urban Future,* New York: WW Norton and Company, xxiii–xxv.

Frank, AG (1969). *Latin America: Underdevelopment or Revolution.* New York: Monthly Review Press.

Glover, D and T Jessup (eds.) (2006). *Indonesia's Fires and Haze: The Cost of Catastrophe.* Singapore and Ottawa: Institute of Southeast Asian Studies and International Development Research Centre.

Huber, P (2008). The carbon curtain. *Forbes Asia,* 4(14), 78.

Huntington, S (1996). *The Clash of Civilizations and the Remaking of the World Order.* New York: Simon and Schuster.

Linden, E (2007). *The Winds of Change: Climate, Weather, and the Destruction of Civilizations,* New York: Simon and Schuster Paperbacks.

Lomborg, B (2001). *The Skeptical Environmentalist: Measuring the Real State of the World.* Cambridge: Cambridge University Press.

Lovelock, J (2007). *The Revenge of Gaia.* London: Penguin Books.

Mahbubani, K (2008). *The New Asian Hemisphere: The Irresistible Shift of Global Power to the East.* New York: Public Affairs.

Martin, J (2007). *The Meaning of the 21st Century: A Vital Blueprint for Ensuring our Future,* New York: Riverhead Books.

Minnesma, ME (2003). Dutch climate policy: A victim of economic growth? *Climate Policy,* 3, 45–56.

Mithen, S (2004). *After the Ice: A Global History, 20,000–5000 BC.* Cambridge, Massachusetts: Harvard University Press.

Monbiot, G (2007). *Heat: How We Can Stop the Planet Burning.* London: Penguin Books.

Mulligan, GF (2006). Logistical population growth in the world's largest cities. *Geographical Analysis,* 38, 344–370.

Neo, CC (2008). Heartland to hotspots in under one hour. *Today,* 16 July, p. 2.

Newman, P and J Kenworthy (2007). Greening urban transportation. L Starke (ed.) *2007 State of the World: Our Urban Future.* New York: WW Norton and Company, 66–89.

Oppenheimer, S (2004). *Out of Eden: The Peopling of the World.* London: Constable and Robinson Ltd.

Perry, A (2008). Poverty trap. *Time,* 171(23), 60.

Peterson, A (2001). *Being Human: Ethics Environment and Our Place in the World.* Berkeley and Los Angeles: University of California Press.

Popkin, SL (1979). *The Rational Peasant.* Berkeley: University of California Press.

Population Reference Bureau (2008). *2008 World Population Data Sheet,* Washington, D.C.

Rees, M (2003). *Our Final Century: Will the Human Race Survive the 21st Century?* London: Heineman.

Roseland, M and L Soots (2007). Strengthening local economies, in L Starke (ed.), *2007 State of the World: Our Urban Future.* New York: WW Norton and Company, 152–171.

Satterthwaite, D and G McGranahan (2007). Providing clean water and sanitation. L Starke (ed.), *2007 State of the World: Our Urban Future.* New York: WW Norton and Company, 26–47.

Sawday's Fragile Earth (2008). *What About China?* Bristol: Alastair Sawday Publishing Co. Ltd.

Schaefer-Preuss, U (2008). Cities can and must cut energy use. *The Straits Times*, 25 June, 26.

Schweithelm, J, T Jessup and D Glover (2006). Conclusions and policy recommendations, in D Glover and T Jessup (eds.), *Indonesia's Fires and Haze: The Cost of Catastrophe*. Singapore and Ottawa: Institute of Southeast Asian Studies and International Development Research Centre, 130–143.

Schweithelm, J and D Glover (2006). Causes and impacts of the fires. D Glover and T Jessup (eds.) *Indonesia's Fires and Haze: The Cost of Catastrophe*, Singapore and Ottawa: Institute of Southeast Asian Studies and International Development Research Centre, 1–13.

Scott, JC (1976). *The Moral Economy of the Peasant*. New Haven: Yale University Press.

Spirn, AW (1984). *The Granite Garden: Human Nature and Human Design*. New York: Basic Books, Inc, Publishers.

Starke, L (ed.) (2007). *2007 State of the World: Our Urban Future*. New York and London: WW Norton and Company.

Stern, N (2007). *The Economics of Climate Change: The Stern Review*. Cambridge: Cambridge University Press.

Tabara, JD (2003). Spain: Words that succeed and climate policies that fail. *Climate Policy*, 3, 19–30.

The Economist (2008a). Economic focus: Record spending on infrastructure will help sustain rapid growth in emerging economies. *The Economist*, 387(8583), 78.

The Economist (2008b). The new face of hunger. *The Economist*, 387(8576), 30–33.

The Economist (2000). What to do about global warming. *The Economist*, 357(8197), 19–20.

The Straits Times (2008a). Global warming 'will harm national security'. *The Straits Times*, 26 June, 20.

The Straits Times (2008b). 30% of food price rises 'due to biofuel demand'. *The Straits Times*, 26 June, 20.

The World Bank (2008). *Global Monitoring Report 2008: MDGs and the Environment*, Washington DC: The International Bank for Reconstruction and Development/The World Bank.

Wackernagel, M and W Rees (1996). *Our Ecological Footprint: Reducing Human Impact on the Earth*. Gabiola Island, BC: New Society Publishers.

Walker, G and D King (2008). *The Hot Topic: How to Tackle Global Warming and Still Keep the Lights On*. London: Bloomsbury Publishing.

Wallerstein, I (1980). *The Modern World-System. Mercantailism and the Consolidation of the European World-Economy, 1600–1750*, Vol. 2, New York: Academic Press.

Walsh, B (2008). Why green is the new red, white and blue. *Time*, 171(16), 31–42.

Wolf, ER (1982). *Europe and the People without History*. Berkeley: University of California Press.

12 Financing Environmental Infrastructure

URSULA SCHAEFER-PREUSS

The ability of cities to manage their water resources and waste and to address the challenges of climate change is critical to their environmental sustainability. However, many cities in developing countries face difficulties doing this because of their lack of financial resources, capabilities and supporting institutions. The aim of the session on *Financing Environmental Infrastructure* at the World Cities Summit is to explore new financial structuring mechanisms, approaches to capability development and coordinating structures. This chapter summarises the discussion during the session.

There are two parts to this chapter. The first part of this chapter on "Water Supply and Sanitation Infrastructure" is based on the presentations on "Leveraging Local and National Funds for Water and Sanitation: Water for Asian Cities Programme Experiences" by Mr Andre Dzikus, Chief of Water and Sanitation Section II at UN-Habitat, and "Sub-sovereign Finance for Local Governments in India" by Mr KE Seetharam, Principal Water and Urban Development Specialist at the Asian Development Bank, at the World Cities Summit Session on *Financing Environmental Infrastructure*.

The second part of this Chapter on *Climate Change Infrastructure* is based on the presentations on "Financing Infrastructure for Climate Change Adaptation and Mitigation" by Mr Michael Lindfield, Principal Urban Development Specialist at the Asian Development Bank, and "*Making the*

Money Work: Developing the Essential Pillar for Capacity" by Mr Douglas
Gardner, Deputy Director for the Bureau for Development Policy at the
United Nations Development Programme, at the World Cities Summit
Session on *Financing Environmental Infrastructure.*

PROGRESS IN WATER SUPPLY AND
SANITATION COVERAGE

Asia has made significant progress with the United Nations Millennium
Development Goals (MDG) Target 10 on water and sanitation coverage.[1]
Nevertheless, 80 per cent of the global population without access to
improved sanitation and two-thirds of the people without access to clean
water are in Asia. Investment in sanitation is very important because for
every US$1 invested, the benefits are estimated at US$8 to US$10 in terms
of reduced health burden and increased productivity. The discussion which
follows highlights the processes involved in the realisation of MDGs for
countries such as India.

India's Progress towards the MDGs

Although the figures show that India has successfully achieved the MDG
target for water supply coverage in 2001 (Figure 1), in reality many cities in
India still do not have access to clean, potable piped water supply, 24 hours
a day, seven days a week. India will also be unable to reach the MDG
target for sanitation coverage successfully by 2015 if current trends continue
(Figure 2). However, the targets for water supply and sanitation coverage
are still achievable by increasing and accelerating infrastructure investment.

Jawaharlal Nehru National Urban Renewal
Mission (JNNURM)

The Government of India has recognised the challenge. In 2005, it
established the ambitious and visionary Jawaharlal Nehru National Urban
Renewal Mission (JNNURM), under which the central government will

---

[1] The UN MDG Target 10 aims to "halve, by 2015, the proportion of the population without sustainable
access to safe drinking water and basic sanitation".

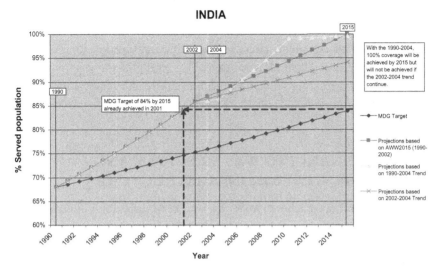

Fig. 1   Trends in total water supply coverage in India 1990–2015

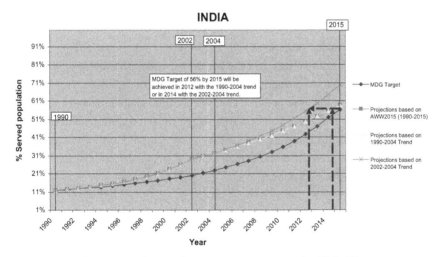

Fig. 2   Trends in total sanitation coverage in India 1990–2015

Source: Asian Development Bank, 2007. Staff estimates.

invest nearly $11 billion in urban renewal. As of March 2008, it has already committed $7 billion, of which about 80 per cent is in water supply, sewerage and solid waste management. These are basic infrastructure developments for improving living conditions. It is not advisable to postpone these investments because the infrastructure could cost more in future and renewal would be much more daunting.

FINANCING WATER SUPPLY AND SANITATION INFRASTRUCTURE

There are several approaches to financing water and sanitation infrastructure. These are (i) public-private partnerships, (ii) domestic capital markets, (iii) domestic tax revenues and (iv) international debt financing. Many local authorities and communities, e.g., in India, do not fully leverage the available resources and development schemes. The first thing to do is to map these schemes and resources so that additional resources can be mobilised.

In 2000, the public and domestic sectors were the dominant investors, contributing 85 per cent of total investment in water infrastructure. In contrast, total international private investment in water and sanitation infrastructure actually decreased. The Camdessus and Gurria Panels[2] on financing water infrastructure and the Sachs Report on the UN Millennium Project[3] agreed that investment in water and sanitation infrastructure had to roughly double in order to achieve the MDGs. The challenge is not only in infrastructure investment but also in financing improved water and sanitation services. This should be done not just by increasing aid and coverage, but also by leveraging required additional local resources and improving access and affordability for the poor.

---

[2] Formed in 2001, the World Panel on Financing Water Infrastructure also called the Camdessus Panel presented its final report *Financing Water for All* at the Third World Water Forum in Kyoto in March 2003. The Global Water Partnership, the Secretariat of the Fourth World Water Forum and the World Water Council convened in 2005 a Task Force led by Angel Gurria to continue the work initiated by the Camdessus Panel on financing water for all. http://www.financingwaterforall.org/.

[3] The UN Millennium Project was commissioned by the UN Secretary-General in 2002 to develop a concrete action plan for the world to achieve the MDGs. In 2005, the independent advisory body, headed by Professor Jeffrey Sachs, presented its final recommendations to the Secretary-General in a synthesised volume *Investing in Development: A Practical Plan to Achieve the Millennium Development Goals*. http://www.unmillenniumproject.org/.

Pro-Poor Investments

ADB and UN-Habitat emphasise the importance of pro-poor investments in water and sanitation. There is also a need to raise awareness and increase investment from the private sector to meet the needs of the poor. Sustainability of investment should be linked to improved (pro-poor and principled) governance, decentralised decision-making and implementation, and management at the level as close to the ground as possible.

Reasons for Leveraging Local Resources

It is particularly important to leverage local resources for infrastructure investment for several reasons. First, a country needs to spend two to three per cent of its GDP to achieve economically feasible levels of sector expenditure. This makes it important to tap every possible source of funds, including local resources. Second, there should be different levels of service, and public funds should focus on basic access and the needs of the poor and vulnerable. Third, local resources should enable rehabilitation and augmentation with existing projects, with a strong focus on operation and maintenance. Fourth, local resources could contribute to the development of the local financial sector through new business lines in water projects for micro-finance and domestic finance institutions.

The recognised options for leveraging local resources are (i) public-private partnerships, (ii) municipal bonds, (iii) pooled finance, and (iv) funds from other levels (central and provincial) of government. Other options include (i) convergence of funds from other governmental development schemes and sectors, (ii) strategic partnerships at different levels of government and private sector, and (iii) community partnerships and contributions towards water and sanitation investments.

Convergence of Funds

Sources of investment funds include the One UN Country Programme and Budget, country sector coordination groups in water and sanitation, regional developmental banks, budgets of the national, regional and local governments, and private sector investments. The Water for Asian Cities Programme, announced in March 2003, is a joint initiative of the ADB and the UN-Habitat. It has a strong focus on local urban water and sanitation governance. It has supported projects to improve water and sanitation in a number of countries such as India, China, Laos, Cambodia, Nepal, Indonesia and Pakistan.

Strategic Partnerships with Governments, Local Authorities and NGOs

It is also important to leverage counterpart contributions from government agencies, local authorities and NGOs for the funds committed by international development agencies. For example, counterpart contributions ranged from 43 per cent to 53 per cent in several countries that UN-Habitat was involved in. A specific example was a partnership between UN-Habitat, Water Aid (an international NGO working in India), and the government on a project with an investment of more than US$1 million to improve water and sanitation for 100,000 people. The capital cost per capita for the project was US$11.70, and the total investment was borne equally by each of the three parties. Notably, local architects and engineers did the design work for these projects instead of big international engineering firms, so that more people would benefit at a lower cost.

Community Partnerships

Community partnerships are also very important. Communities have a long tradition of managing water supply and sewerage schemes. In these schemes, the communities can provide the sweat equity (labour) or the counterpart contributions, or they can invest their resources through, for instance, creation of community-based revolving funds, credit and thrift societies and cooperatives. These community initiatives have to be linked to initiatives supported by local and national governments, NGOs and other community stakeholders such as the private sector.

Revolving Funds

Revolving funds have been helpful in overcoming the burden of financing. For instance, the main obstacle to water supply is the connection cost. Developing revolving funds at community and local authority levels have been very useful in increasing the coverage of water supply and sanitation in community-managed water supply and sanitation system (CMWSS) projects, which can be replicated and upscaled later. For example, UN-Habitat was involved in a CMWSS project in Madhya Pradesh, which cost US$68,000 and benefited 1,500 households. This was a reimbursable seeding operation by UN-Habitat and the payback time for this entire project was 32 months.

Corporate Bonds

Funds for infrastructure investment can also be raised through issuance of corporate bonds. For example, UN-Habitat has worked with Nanjing, China to issue corporate bonds for financing waste water systems.

Corporate Social Responsibility

Another way to leverage private sector resources is through corporate social responsibility. Examples include Coca Cola, BASF and Satyam Foundation in India, and an Australian mining company Oxiana Australia in Lao PDR. UN-Habitat also has a partnership with Google to place citizen report cards on water and sanitation coverage on Google Earth maps to increase awareness of UN-Habitat's efforts and stimulate investments to improve the situation.

ADB'S FINANCING MECHANISMS IN INDIA

Until recently, ADB had been engaging the provincial/state governments in India for its financing mechanisms; about 90 per cent of the financing was done through the government and public sector. ADB focuses on urban management, policy reforms, capacity development, poverty alleviation and infrastructure improvements. Much of its investment has been directed toward rehabilitation, building capacities and improving the quality of these services. ADB's ongoing pipeline of financing for India is US$1.6 billion and its planned pipeline until 2010 is about another US$760 million. However, a huge shortfall in financing remains due to policy constraints and lack of absorptive capacity at the local level to attract investments, including those from the private sector.

ADB has encouraged local leaders and governments to take a larger role in projects and come up with ways of sustainable financing for infrastructure. To sensitise and raise awareness among leaders and policymakers, for example, ADB brings them to best practice cities to see how these cities have succeeded, and to conferences such as the World Cities Summit to network and learn best practices that they can implement upon their return. ADB also conducts high-level Public-Private Partnership (PPP) workshops for them.

It is not sufficient, however, just to raise enthusiasm and awareness. In the last few months, ADB has reappraised the financing plans prepared by the Indian local governments with a view to developing them from mere financing of infrastructure into "bankable projects" with financing structures to recover expenses and sustain operations and maintenance over the long term.

Innovation and Efficiency Initiative

To support all these efforts, ADB launched an Innovation and Efficiency Initiative, which included a series of products to facilitate development. In the past, lenders would make loans to central sovereign governments, and the sovereign governments would pass the funds on as back-to-back loans or subsidised loans-cum-grants to the provincial governments. The local governments had no concept of cost recovery and did not have to repay the loans directly to the original lenders because the central governments were guaranteeing the loans. Now, through the Innovation and Efficiency Initiative, ADB will directly engage the local governments, and the loans will be backed up by the projects. To help meet the huge financing requirements, ADB can bring in other partners, such as commercial financiers, who would otherwise not have financed the municipal governments for those projects. To encourage private sector participation, ADB has established pilot credit enhancement facilities of about US$3 billion until September 2008. These facilities reduce the political and credit risks but not the commercial risks of private sector investors.

Financing Models

Both ADB and private sponsors can provide financing through a variety of financing models. The municipal governments can guarantee the financing, be responsible for repayment, and provide subsidies for the project. There are, however, various issues to resolve, including tariffs, policies and legal frameworks.

ADB envisions three specific models for infrastructure projects. Under the first model, the actual operation, maintenance and ownership of the project would remain with the municipal governments. ADB would bring a Special Purpose Vehicle to be the conduit for receiving the money and getting it back from the government. This is an easy-to-use model because not many institutional changes are required.

The second model separates supply and distribution of services. Independent producers supply the services, and the municipalities are in charge of distribution and repayment of the loans. This model is already used in the energy industry and can be replicated for water supply and sanitation.

Under the third model, a company would be formed to own and operate the new investments and the assets that are created. The company would be supervised and regulated by the local government, which can help the company operate in a sustainable manner. These three models are an ideal progression of steps for projects to become sustainable and bankable, and are currently under experimentation and introduction.

Shorter ADB Business Timelines

ADB can now process project proposals in six months instead of 24 months, as was the case in the past. This is important especially for private sector partners who want to complete projects quickly because time is money to them.

Outlook for India

Although the outlook for India is positive with enormous opportunities, the Indian municipal governments still need handholding. Early wins and success stories are needed to start a catalytic effect. ADB is keen to engage with the municipal governments and is committed to sub-sovereign financing.

CITIES IN DEVELOPING COUNTRIES
AND CLIMATE CHANGE

The developing world is urbanising rapidly, and more than half of humanity is living in cities. The proportion of people living in cities in Latin America is 75 per cent and is expected to reach 50 per cent in Asia and Africa by the year 2030. However, urbanisation is not without its problems. In Asian cities, there are over a billion people living in slums, high levels of unemployment, poverty and disease, and low levels of education. The problem is not urbanisation *per se* but the fact that urbanisation in many developing countries has not resulted in greater prosperity for all, or a more equitable distribution of resources. Efforts to improve the lives of the urban poor have not kept up with the rate of urbanisation.

Cities use about 85 per cent of the energy and generate about 75 per cent of the greenhouse gases worldwide but they contribute about 80 per cent of gross domestic product. CO_2 emissions in many developing cities are as high as in developed cities. Asia will contribute over half of the greenhouse gas emissions over the next 20 years and cities are responsible for the majority of that. Therefore, cities are best placed to generate the "nega-watt" or energy savings needed to deal with climate change from the demand side and avoid the problems that could occur.

The UNDP's Human Development Report,[4] launched at Bali in December 2007, showed the links between climate change and its real impact on people. It concluded that, beyond a total increase in temperature to a maximum of two degrees centigrade, there would be dangerous occurrences. To keep temperature increases within this limit, the quantity of emissions on an annual basis and atmospheric CO_2 concentrations must also be kept within a certain level. Very much depends on what is done now.

Asia's urban populations are growing rapidly at an average of three per cent per annum, and Asian cities are especially vulnerable to climate change. For example, Metro Manila, where ADB is based, has Laguna du Bay on one side and Manila Bay on the other, and the whole area is only a few meters above sea level on average. Many other Asian cities are similarly situated on the coast and are protected by natural levees. Rising sea levels and more frequent extreme weather events could put millions at risk, so there is an urgent need to take action.

---

[4]United Nations Development Programme (2007). *Human Development Report 2007/2008, Fighting Climate Change: Human Solidarity in a Divided World*. New York: United Nations Development Programme.

Environmental infrastructure not only addresses environmental issues but also provides much needed jobs and basic services. However, institutional and incentive structures applying to project developers and consumers in Asian cities do not really encourage investments to address the environmental issues.

Environmental Management Issues in Developing Countries

Public transport is one of the key environmental issues in cities. The Asian middle class is increasing rapidly, and buying more cars in the process. The issues are not about ownership of cars (because people in the West own cars too) but about the types of cars and their usage. One of the most important factors in terms of reducing global greenhouse gas emissions is to keep the Asian middle class out of their cars for their daily commute.

Pollution legislation exists but is not enforced in many places. Planning for city form exists in theory but not in practice, or is not enforced. There are very few local and global incentives for energy efficiency to assist cities in Asia to implement climate-friendly policies and investments.

Challenges of Climate Change in Developing Countries

Several key challenges stand in the way of effectively addressing climate change in developing countries. First, institutional capacity in developing countries is low, especially for coordination of investment and enforcement of standards. Second, there are the compelling and competing priorities of short-term poverty relief as against long-term global benefits. Governments will find it difficult to convince their political constituencies of the importance of spending money to mitigate climate change if large numbers still live in slums. Third, there is relatively low technical capacity in climate change-related finance and engineering in developing countries. Fourth, there are perverse incentives, with pricing of services often encouraging increased consumption. In some cases, because energy prices are not charged per unit of consumption, it would be cheaper to regulate the temperature by opening the window rather than installing a thermostat. Last, there is a need to engage in multiple sectors to produce results. For example, improving public transport may involve slum upgrading.

CAPACITY DEVELOPMENT

Capacity development is important to address the challenges set out above. Such capacity development not only produces good results in projects, but also provides a mechanism to engender national ownership of projects. UNDP is currently advocating a very basic capacity assessment method. It starts with basic mapping of the assets — identifying gaps, designing cost options and capacity development options, and then implementing those programs. Capacity development can vary from high levels for integrated climate change strategies, to individual national focal points for implementing programs. Hence, capacity development can be applied to individuals or institutions.

Capacity Development of Individuals

At the individual level, capacity development programmes need to focus on nurturing and supporting mature champions and leaders for environmental issues, such as those who are attending the World Cities Summit. These leaders will work within their own circles of influence to implement the initiatives they have brought back from such events. Public awareness campaigns can be established to find those leaders within, for example, educational institutions, NGOs, local governments and the media. These are the individuals who are "tuned in" and "turned on" and are critical for the success of environmental investments. Capacity development programmes involve much more than training, and oftentimes include focusing on systems and trying to instil integrity, particularly among those who are responsible for public resources.

Capacity Development of Institutions

Institutions are groups of individuals with organisational responsibilities. Capacity development of institutions is particularly critical for regulation — to ensure appropriate policies are in place and institutions are empowered to apply them. This is a matter of both capacity and governance. A graphic example of institutional failure followed the recent China earthquake when schools collapsed. Builders and regulators are being investigated for failing to apply standards. In contrast, an example of institutional success is the efficient operation of the road-pricing system in Singapore, where motorists are charged a fee to drive in certain areas at specific times of the day. These kinds of institutional capacities are critical for project success.

Adequate capacities are fundamental not just for the success of environmental infrastructure but for national ownership, which is essential for scaling up investments. Capacity development and investments go hand-in-hand; both are required for project success. Having the right capacities in place will lead to successful investments.

FINANCING INFRASTRUCTURE FOR CLIMATE CHANGE

Over the next 22 years, US$700 billion will be needed each year for energy supply infrastructure worldwide to meet growing energy needs. Of that amount, about half will be needed in the developing countries. Official development assistance (ODA) and international financial institutions (IFIs) provide about US$6–7 billion per year, or fifteen per cent of this required amount. From where can the gap be covered?

The private sector could provide most of the required funds. The availability of funds from the private sector and host governments will be critical for covering the energy investment gap. The double challenge is finding ways to attract enough investment to meet that growing demand while steering investments away from carbon intensive patterns and toward low emission technologies.

Shortcomings of International and Asian Capital Markets

There are several problems with financing environmental and climate change infrastructure using international capital markets and local Asian capital markets. These markets are highly liquid, but cannot supply the long-term financing needed. There are often no clear regulatory structures in the capital markets, leading to high transactional costs. Problems of inter-jurisdictional coordination also make project formulation and structuring difficult. There are high levels of savings in Asia, but the money is generally available only for short-term finance. Mechanisms to encourage institutions such as pension funds and life insurance companies, which hold long-term funds, to invest in infrastructure are limited in Asia. There is also a lack of mechanisms for public sector finance of environmental infrastructure and for enabling governments to engage in Special Purpose Vehicles with the private sector.

In spite of the limitations, there are many international and national schemes providing funds for environmental investments. For example, the ADB, UN-Habitat and Global Environment Fund (GEF) can provide official development assistance (ODA). There are also huge windows of opportunity from carbon finance and export credits, especially when purchasing hardware that many producing countries will be very interested in supplying. Other sources of "green" funds may finance environmental infrastructure.

UNDP has a three-step approach to leverage carbon finance. The first step is to remove the barriers to direct investments in climate-friendly technologies by, for example, tapping the GEF. Step two is to establish efficient host country procedures for review and approval of carbon saving projects. The third and final step is to provide project management services to individual project developers for the carbon finance windows. ADB has an Asia Pacific Carbon Fund and UNDP also has a MDG carbon finance window.

Clean Development Mechanism

The Clean Development Mechanism (CDM) is currently the key international support for climate change initiatives. The CDM is a prototype for what would be needed on a much larger scale post-Kyoto Protocol. It has been utilised largely in four countries — China, India, Brazil and South Korea — which together account for about 70 per cent of the projects and 80 per cent of the Certified Emission Reduction (CER) to 2012. It is surprising that Sub-Sahara Africa accounts for only two per cent of the registered projects. So there is tremendous growth possibility for CDM in other parts of the world, including the least developed countries. For example, the UNDP's arrangements to plug leaking pipelines in Uzbekistan helped to raise US$50 million.

Shortcomings of the CDM

However there are several key features of the CDM that make it user-unfriendly to developing countries, and particularly for cities in developing countries. First, high levels of technical competence are required. Second, there are high transaction costs in terms of time and expertise to get the methodologies approved and projects completed. Third, competent and specialised institutions are required for project implementation, monitoring and certification. Fourth, the CDM is unfriendly to 'multi-sector' projects. These features of the CDM are exactly the areas where developing cities face difficulty.

In addition, the CDM approach has several shortcomings. It is supply-driven, technically-focused and lacks:

(i) a clear concept to address demand-side mitigation issues on a systemic basis;
(ii) any effective structures to address adaptation;
(iii) a clear concept of how social and economic issues and costs need to be programmed into projects;
(iv) analytical tools and methodologies for trading off among, and prioritising, sectoral options; and
(v) mechanisms to link initiatives to local and international capital markets.

Furthermore, current carbon credit pricing does not provide significant incentives for the adoption of environmental investments in developing countries.

Needed Reforms to the CDM

Several reforms to the CDM would be needed post-Kyoto. One is a different approach to approved methodologies, which are currently not easily applicable to cities, multi-sector unfriendly and technology driven. Another is to reduce transaction costs of CDM mechanisms. Yet, another is to find ways of bridging current levels of carbon credits and investment costs for climate friendly infrastructure.

In one particular city, the total investment cost for a LNG clean busway, which could possibly reduce car usage, was $140 million, compared to US$100 million for a typical busway. The carbon credits available for that project at the current price were only about US$1 million and would not be enough to change the investment profile in the agencies responsible for the project. A better way of financing this sustainability gap (the US$40 million between the climate-friendly busway and the typical busway) is needed. It could be in the form of grants or soft loans. ADB has the Asia Pacific Carbon Fund, which can finance half of the carbon credits upfront rather than the normal way of requiring countries to earn them. There is a need to move beyond this practice in the post-Kyoto agenda to have a mechanism for effective intervention. This need to finance the sustainability gap applies at the individual consumption level when consumers in cities decide between lower-priced goods and services and higher-priced but more sustainable options.

Lastly, there is a need to think about how to help cities and governments enhance and upscale their capacities to formulate the types of projects that will be needed over the next 20 years. The ADB, along with the German, Swedish, and Spanish governments, has formed the Cities Development Initiative for Asia. It is specifically tasked with helping cities formulate and structure projects in environmental infrastructure, and the Initiative will be ramping up over the next few years.

Energy-Efficient Housing in Mongolia

There are many different types of environmentally friendly projects, including energy management in government buildings, solid waste management, and sustainable and energy efficient housing. All of these require clear financing schemes to make the projects viable, and this is a challenge for Asian governments and ADB over the next 20 years. An example of an environmentally friendly project being considered by ADB and KfW is a refurbishment of multi-storey housing in Mongolia. The-Entwicklungsbank savings from that project are potentially so significant that it would be possible to close one of the three power plants in Ulan Bator.

ADB'S VISION: LIVEABLE AND SUSTAINABLE CITIES FOR ASIA

Under ADB's Strategy 2020, cities constitute a key focus, specifically the promotion of liveable, competitive and environmentally attractive cities. Cities are also at the forefront of ADB's core strategic directions in terms of addressing climate change and the region's huge infrastructure deficit.

The technology, money, and skills necessary for tackling the challenge of urbanisation are available. But the urban institutional structures needed for coordination, financing, and capacity building are inadequate. A new approach for urban management is required to build the institutional and physical infrastructure to address these issues.

To implement such an approach, it will be necessary to achieve:

- Effective coordination through layered special coordination companies focused on identifying and implementing a priority set of strategic investments;
- Structuring of appropriate financing for such companies within the context of promoting strong local government finances and local capital markets; and
- Capacity building for the above tasks.

These activities are discussed in detail in the ADB's Managing Asian Cities study.[5] ADB aims to move forward with the innovative initiatives pursuing strategic partnerships with key development partners, as well as the private sector and civil society, that will help create an enabling environment to boost investments in the urban sector.

REFERENCES

Asian Development Bank (2008). *Managing Asian Cities: Sustainable and Inclusive Urban Solutions*. Metro Manila: Asian Development Bank.

Task Force on Financing Water for All (2006). *Report 1: Enhancing Access to Finance for Local Governments. Financing Water for Agriculture*. World Water Council.

United Nations Development Programme (2007). *Human Development Report 2007/2008, Fighting Climate Change: Human Solidarity in a Divided World*. New York: United Nations Development Programme.

United Nations Millennium Project (2005). *Investing in Development: A Practical Plan to Achieve the Millennium Development Goals*. London: United Nations Development Programme.

World Panel on Financing Water Infrastructure (2003). *Report of the World Panel on Financing Water Infrastructure: Financing Water for All*, March.

---

[5] Asian Development Bank (2008). *Managing Asian Cities: Sustainable and Inclusive Urban Solutions*. Metro Manila: Asian Development Bank.

13

Achieving Inclusive and Sustainable Growth: The Role of Cities and Urbanisation

EMIEL A WEGELIN and MICHAEL LINDFIELD

This chapter focuses on economic growth as a means to eradicate poverty. The discussion centres on how economic agglomeration offered by cities could construct vital networks that enable the whole stream of productive activities. Following this introduction, the chapter presents the key findings of the Commission on Growth and Development.

At the World Cities Summit, the Vice Chair of the Growth Commission, Mr Danny Leipziger, was invited to review a portion of the Commission's report that have a bearing on cities and to debate this with Prof Paul Romer and Mr Hiroto Arakawa under the topic, "Achieving Inclusive and Sustainable Growth: The Role of Cities and Urbanisation".

Their debate revolved around the issue of "growth" as the Commission was convinced that "growth" had fallen off the radar screen of many development practitioners and not many countries had meaningful poverty reduction strategies that would lead to high and sustained levels of economic growth. The Commission highlighted the core characteristics of high-growth economies and distilled the core lessons for other developing countries seeking growth as well as integration with the global economy. The "future orientation" of governments and the building of cohesive societies are considered essential for growth. It is often asserted that free markets are the key to prosperity. Now economists are starting to underscore the importance of the relationships that encompass all social and economic activities. In this age of rapid social and economic changes, it is important to minimise social inequality to foster social cohesion and bridge generational, gender, ethnic or even income divides. This chapter also discusses the role of government and institutions in creating growth and inclusiveness. The challenges of growth, urbanisation and globalisation and the importance of institutions (like governance and rules) in establishing the framework for a market economy to work are also discussed, as well as a case study of the Japanese growth and urbanisation experience.

· GROWTH COMMISSION — UNDERSTANDING ECONOMIC GROWTH

The debate session focused on the conclusions of the Growth Commission which has over the past two years and discussed a range of issues related to growth and development. The objective was to bring together the thoughts and views of academics, policy makers and businessmen which were very different but significant. The commissioned academic papers revolved around real-life cases which were discussed in workshops. In short, the key agenda of the Growth Commission was to find out what factors contribute to sustained growth.

The importance of growth and development in reducing poverty and improving standards of living are fairly non-controversial. However, the path to sustained growth is by no means easy. Erecting a framework to examine the diverse experiences of successful high-growth countries and stagnating less-developed economies is an equally complicated exercise.

Cities enable economic agglomeration and provide useful networks that make the whole stream of productive activities possible. Indeed, no country has ever caught up with advanced economies through agriculture alone. Hence, industrialisation is a major structural shift that economies must undergo as they grow and progress, and this has to take place in or around cities (Figure 1). The Growth Report also showed that although no country has industrialised without urbanisng, the process has never been entirely smooth. For instance, the influx of workers into industrialising cities could unleash a massive economic force for growth. However, the urban infrastructure would have to cope with the challenge of accommodating these workers.

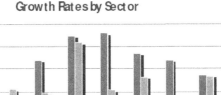

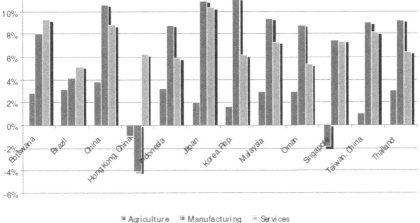

Fig. 1 Urban-based sectors drive growth

Source: Danny Leipziger's presentation slides at World Cities Summit 2008, Singapore, p. 26.

GROWTH — MEANS TO OVERCOME POVERTY AND ATTAIN PROSPERITY

The focus of the Commission was to look at the factors that have propelled the growth of 13 economies (including Singapore) that have grown at an average annual rate of 7 per cent or more for 25 years or longer (Figure 2). At this pace of expansion, an economy almost doubles in size every decade.

The Commission focused on growth because it is a means of reducing poverty and enabling the majority of the population to enjoy prosperity over time. The Growth Report identifies some of the *distinctive characteristics of high-growth economies* and queries how other developing countries could emulate them. These characteristics of high growth economies can be categorised into five areas:

(1) High growth countries tend to be open and integrated with the world economy.
(2) They have strong economic management.

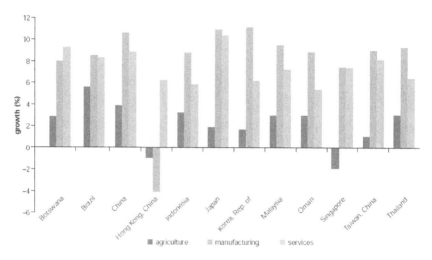

Fig. 2   Growth of economies

Note: The calculations apply for different periods indicated in parentheses because of different degrees of consistent data availability: Botswana (1965–2006); Brazil (1955–73); China (2000–06); Indonesia (1960–2005); Japan (1955–73); Korea Rep. of (1970–2006); Malaysia (1970–2006); Oman (1988–2004); Singapore (1975–2006); Taiwan China (1965–2006); and Thailand (1960–2006).

Source: World Bank World Development Indicators 2007; for Brazil; World Bank calculation using data from World Table 1976 World Bank and Institute of Applied Economic Research (IAER), Brazil (http://www.ipeadata.gov.tr); for Japan: World Bank calculation using data from World Tables 1976, World Bank and Maddison, Angus 2001; *The World Economy: A Millennial Perspective*. Paris: OECD.

(3) They are run by governments with a vision for the future.

(4) They are market-oriented and have developed their private sector well.

(5) They possess effective leadership and governments.

The governments of high-growth economies also have a strong commitment to ensure that the benefits of growth are distributed as widely as possible without distorting market incentives, so as to ensure that the above five characteristics can be sustained.

ENGAGING THE GLOBAL ECONOMY

No country has really achieved great progress in economic development without engaging the global economy. This is due to the fact that demand

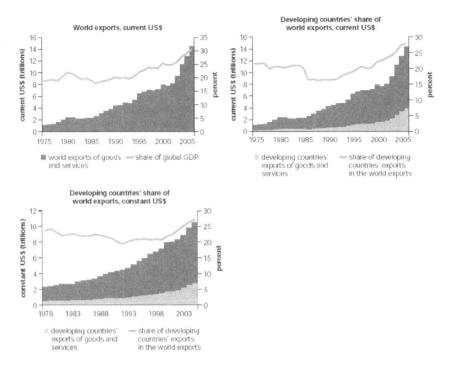

Fig. 3   Evolution of world exports and the share of developing countries, 1975–2003

Source: World Bank, World Development Indicators 2007.

from the global system far exceeds that from the domestic economy. Therefore, *the global economy offers these countries a deep, elastic market for their exports* (Figure 3). "Openness" also permits these countries to *import ideas, technologies and knowhow from the rest of the world*. In a globalised economy, supply chains span many countries, with components coming from different parts of the world. Therefore the importance of international trade to an economy could no longer be determined simply in terms of whether it runs a surplus or deficit. One needs to consider the productivity gains that come with industrial specialisation, which is an apparent feature of economic globalisation.

The Growth Report considered macro-economic stability to be necessary, but not enough. So *the old adage that all a country needs to do is to stabilise, liberalise and privatise is generally not sufficient.*

ROLE OF THE GOVERNMENT
IN GENERATING GROWTH

An area for concern is the *"future orientation"* of governments. Governments would need to convince the public that saving and investing are vital so that the next generation will be better off. Indeed, the pace of growth at the initial stage of development is limited primarily by *investment*, which, in turn, is affected by the availability of savings.

An area in which the report is most different from what one might have read 15 or 20 years ago is in its assessment of government. Governments have to be *pragmatic and willing to experiment*. However, they also need to be *consistent in the policies that they pursue*. The Commission found that the common characteristic of a number of successful economies was the presence of *effective government with a long policy horizon*.

Economies need to undergo significant structural transformations in order to be successful. For instance, the top five exports of Korea in the 1960s, 70s, 80s, 90s and the present are very different. In other words, *economies need to be dynamic and be able to shift resources from one sector or industry to another*. This kind of dynamism requires *collective effort* and thus development must be *inclusive in nature*. A country cannot have successful growth strategies over long periods of time if the benefits of growth are captured only by the elite, as the elite will resist structural transformation.

COHESIVE SOCIETIES ARE NECESSARY
FOR DEVELOPMENT

The prosperity of a family is ultimately determined by its ability to accumulate assets. These include physical assets like housing, human assets such as education and good health, social capital such as supportive community networks, and financial assets. The opportunity to accumulate these assets varies among households by income group, location, ethnicity, and other factors. When these disparities become wide, social tensions build and development is threatened. Thus, poverty, a shorthand for unacceptable levels of disparity, is central to the discussion on urban management, both at national and local levels. Urban management should focus on social improvements apart from the attainment of economic objectives. It should encompass the provision of housing and infrastructure as well as urban amenities like public spaces to improve the quality of life. However, the key challenge is often the lack of strong local governments to exercise effective urban management. At least as much or perhaps more importance should be given to resolving disparity in opportunities for building assets or achieving progress to allow social mobility. Sound urban management which rides on the positive effects of globalisation will be essential for improving the lives of people.

Thus, the poor suffer from disparity, even in rich societies such as the United States (Figure 4), where inequality could be reduced, but where it is perceived that there is equality of opportunity. The alienation that results from lack of opportunity, and from a lack of social context, grows and can threaten stability as well as well social cohesion. Managing such issues requires a multifaceted approach that helps low-income groups acquire assets such as housing, education, and access to health care, but does not neglect the social support and cultural context that provide a bulwark against alienation, and hence foster innovation.

CHALLENGES OF GROWTH, URBANISATION AND GLOBALISATION

Urbanisation is a global phenomenon and it is posing a challenge to governments because much of the infrastructure needed is going to be in urban areas, including the provision of housing and transport. The key areas of challenge are the environment and employment. The Growth Report deals with the issue of growth and the environment and it advocates that the strategy of "growing now and dealing with environment later" is a bad strategy. The report addresses the issue of high energy prices. Under the current scenario, untargeted or broadly targeted energy subsidies will not curb excessive consumption, and will only impose mounting fiscal burden and inhibits the participation of developing countries in global efforts to cut greenhouse gases.

The report makes some reasonable recommendations about how to deal with *global warming*. These include giving more generous subsidies for the development of energy-efficient technologies, the setting up of an international institution to monitor emissions cuts, and other mitigation measures.

The map below provides a more thorough picture of Gini coefficients and highlights that equity has regional dimensions. Inequality is high in many South American countries: Brazil is not unique. Tanzania, with a Gini coefficient closer to Asia's values, is an exception in a continent where income inequality is extremely high.

Gini Coefficients from the UN Human Development Report, 2007-2008

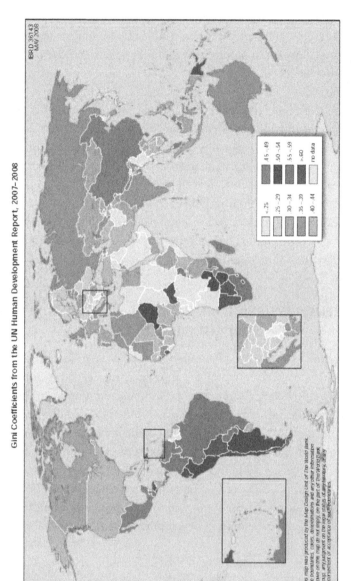

Fig. 4   Gini coefficients around the world

Structurally, globalisation undoubtedly has net welfare benefits for most countries. However, globalisation obviously does not affect everyone equally in any society: everywhere there are gainers and losers from this phenomenon of structural change. Therefore, a major remaining concern is how to deal with those parts of society that lose out. Additionally, recent events have demonstrated that globalisation also increases the exposure of nations to global short-term economic shocks. Both these issues need to be addressed through concerted national and international co-operation to reduce such vulnerability, for the potential full benefits of globalisation to be realised. Another key issue associated with long-term growth prospects is the apprehension that India and China might gobble up all additional demand out there and that other countries will not be able to follow in the footsteps of China and India. However, the issue is not one of crowding out new entrants but really one of creating opportunity for new entrants because as China and India move up the economic ladder, they are going to allow the entry of many other countries into the economic system provided that the system remains open. Another global trend that affects strategies for growth has to do with *demographics and ageing*. One could predict demographic trends (Figure 5) very well and know which regions would be net producers of workers and which would be net demanders for the workers. But the problem is *how to move labour around in response*?

THE IMPORTANCE OF NATIONAL INSTITUTIONS

Rules are needed prevent over-use of resources, to pollution and establish a framework for a market economy to work. However, one of the biggest factors holding back many countries in the world, according to the Growth Commission Report, is that many countries lack governments that can establish good rules and enforce them. Urbanisation is a critical illustration of the importance of good governance and rules in the growth process and a metaphor for ways to deal with the other global problems that concern mankind, especially the problem of global warming, which is looming ever larger in current thinking about the future.

The Growth Commission Report emphasises governance and rules that guide us. "Ideas" and "rules" enable people to surpass any constraints imposed upon them by scarce natural resources. For instance, in dealing

Since WWII, most of the growth in the world's population has taken place in developing countries.

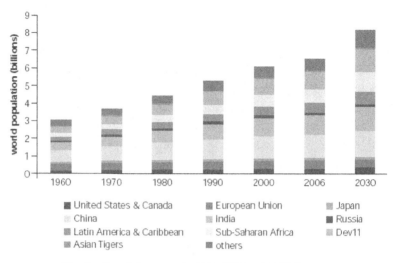

Fig. 5   Population growth, 1960–2006 and 2030 forecast

Source: World Bank, World Development Indicators 2007; forecast for 2030 from Maddison, 2001.

with climate change, we need more than market mechanisms like a cap-and-trade system and a carbon tax to reduce carbon emissions. Countries also need to consider the use of regulatory mechanisms like the imposition of emissions regulations to set specific limits to the amount of pollutants that can be released into the environment. Emission standards can be established not only for automobiles but also for emissions from factories, power plants and other motorised equipment. These standards are mandated by the state and do not involve market forces.

The institutions of sustainable society meet the needs of all citizens and do not leave the vulnerable and disadvantaged behind. The aim is to create cities where people want to live. It includes the promotion of prosperity for all, high-quality service delivery and giving people the ability to shape the places they live in and change what matters to them. For local improvements such as clean streets, local schools, health clinics or parks, people identify more with their street or block or neighbourhood. For others such as work or transport, people think about a wider area.

Poverty in cities is generally falling as a share of the population though, unsurprisingly, aggregate numbers are rising. Poverty is closely tied to unemployment, as demonstrated by the Asian financial crisis. Income disparities within cities and regional variations in income inequality within and between cities are increasing. These trends raise important political, governance, and social issues. There are no simple policy prescriptions and city governments do not have the full capacity to deal with all these issues. Therefore, the cities' role in broader equity and social welfare policy needs to take this reality into consideration.

At the local level, cities must plan strategically for inclusive development including access and equity issues, and involve communities in deciding economic and environmental investments. This can be accomplished by involving communities in the planning, design, implementation, and even financing of local infrastructure projects, and introducing participatory budgeting, where communities are involved in spending decisions and priorities of city governments.

City governments also need to help the poor by ensuring access and equity in asset distribution. This can be achieved in two ways. First, cities can design and implement systems for local communities to make decisions on facilities, especially in health and education. Second, housing and urban renewal strategies can be prepared and implemented to deliver basic needs and shelter provision in an affordable way. This includes slum upgrading and the rigorous enforcement of laws against illegal construction and land occupation, with the help of concerned communities.

Central government can play a positive role via the provision of resources although slum upgrading is often considered a local responsibility. Resources must be allocated on both the supply side to improve infrastructure and the demand side to enable people to purchase, develop and improve their houses. Slum upgrading programmes must be designed on the basic premise of what is affordable, that change can be accommodated, and the program is understood and supported by the poor. At the same time, the programme should be sustainable and not leave debt obligations to future generations.

Most low- and middle-income housing markets in Asian cities are characterised by households who self-finance and provide their own housing in an incremental manner. It is not uncommon for households to secure short-term consumption credit or small-business microfinance and use the proceeds for house improvement. Access to housing finance is limited for the majority due to the substantial down-payment required. Thus, slum upgrading programmes involve increasing the supply of long-term mortgage finance for house or land purchase through the banking system.

Perhaps the national government needs to ensure that appropriate incentives exist to increase the availability of long-term mortgage finance. This requires:

- A legal system that recognises and enforces property rights and security of tenure;
- A financial system that not only recognises that the poor are bankable by providing them with greater access to credit but also can provide support to local government in developing infrastructure;
- A framework within which the poor can fully participate in conceiving, designing, developing, financing, upgrading, and maintaining infrastructure and services.

For social development to occur at the local level, there must be plans for inclusive development, including greater community participation. Local communities need to be more involved in decision-making, especially on local matters. Nonetheless, national governments have vital roles to perform in ensuring the success of housing and urban renewal efforts. These encompass:

- Ensuring the effective operation of land administration and management systems: tenure rights, valuation and taxation and transferable development rights, especially in city regions;
- Providing incentives to encourage banks and other financial institutions to supply long-term mortgage finance for house purchase by low-income groups in urban areas, including guarantees;
- Fostering appropriate livelihood development schemes, such as small and medium enterprise development, through appropriate enabling frameworks for example, by amending usury laws to enable micro-credit;
- Promoting the securitisation of assets including mortgages and infrastructure revenues, to increase finance availability for city regions;
- Setting levels for social safety nets in city regions and considering sustainable subsidies for local governments who cannot provide services to these levels.

GROWTH AND URBANISATION —
THE JAPANESE EXPERIENCE

The challenges of urbanisation are a global problem today, encompassing both the developed and developing countries. Nevertheless, the nature and structure of the problem could differ as developing countries confront more complex and difficult issues in housing, healthcare, social security, employment and transportation. It is pertinent to note that the prescribed solutions to resolve these issues cannot be similar for every country. The development of modern industry has led to the development of new cities. As the second largest economy in the world, Japan is in a position to share with other Asian countries its experience in managing growth and urbanisation. The Japanese experience also demonstrates that industrialisation and modernisation will inevitably result in urbanisation which reinforces the conditions for further industrialisation and modernisation. The country experienced sustained high growth from the mid-1950s to early 1970s. During that period, industrial production was increasingly concentrated in the core areas, such as Yokohama and Osaka Kobe.

However, Japan witnessed *income disparities* between the industrial areas and the rural areas. Other challenges facing the country during that period included *overpopulation, heavy traffic congestion and pollution in the core industrial areas*. The central government offered *strong leadership* to create a shared vision to respond to these problems, but the corresponding policies evolved over time.

The integrated special development plans of 1962 addressed issues of "concentration" and "special disparity". The government then announced the development of the Pacific Ocean belt which was followed by massive infrastructure development to alleviate congestion problems. At the same time, it laid the foundation for the development of new regional clusters in an effort to build industries in areas other than the Pacific belt. However, promoting industry far away from the economic agglomeration along the Pacific belt proved to be very difficult. The second development plan of 1969 placed greater emphasis on "convergence", i.e. narrowing the gap in living standards between the urban and the rural areas.

The experiences of Japan support the conclusions of the Commission. First, a strong and versatile central government addressed the problems of concentration and land conversion. However, the development of the private financial sector in later years led to criticism of the central government. The core issue was how to optimise the role of central government and local government in confronting urbanisation challenges and capacity constraints. Second, the agglomeration of industries had promoted the rapid economic growth of Japan. Nevertheless, the construction of new industrial clusters in areas far away from the Pacific belt was a major challenge. The challenge here was how to benefit from economies of other nations while managing urbanisation as well income disparity. Third, how could the government find fiscal space to cope with massive urbanisation? Two possible solutions include raising public revenue and the employment of public-private partnerships (PPPs).

In the future, climate change may endanger sustainable growth and life in cities. This urban vulnerability would require governments to incorporate policies to mitigate the problems related to climate change in urban planning using a long-term perspective. The World Bank, Asian Development Bank and Japan Bank for International Cooperation (JBIC) are currently conducting a study called "Global Climate Change Impact and Adaptation in Asian Coastal Mega-Cities". The aim of this study is to quantitatively assess the socioeconomic vulnerability to floods caused by climate change in selective Asian mega-cities.

In the process of promoting economic growth, Japan experienced a period of serious pollution which resulted in health problems and even loss of lives in the post-war years. Japan has long recognised the need to preserve the environment by ensuring urban growth is environmentally appropriate (Figure 6). The idea of sustainable development is increasingly prominent in the international arena. Notwithstanding the popularity of the concept, it

USA	0.46
EU	0.29
Japan	0.19
China	1.67
India	1.30

Fig. 6   Gigatons of CO_2 emissions per trillion dollars of GDP

Source: Danny Leipziger's Presentation Slides at World Cities Summit 2008, Singapore, p. 41.

remains a complex and multi-dimensional concept that attracts a significant amount of political rhetoric. There are underscored risks to sustained growth in Asian coastal cities. It is necessary to achieve a balance between economic growth and response to climate change. What are the measures to undertake in order to address vulnerabilities? Vulnerabilities are within urban areas, such as impacts on industry, and cultural and urban poor zones. A balance has to be struck between urban and rural areas.

CONCLUSION

The Growth Report provides a useful framework for governments in the developing world to design their own unique growth strategies bearing in mind that economic success also depends very much on the circumstances and context of a particular country. It attempts to analyse the drivers of economic growth needed to attain a higher standard of living for people, and factors that could hinder economic progress. These key drivers include engagement with the global economy, as well as having effective leadership and governments who have a vision for the future, are market-oriented and have strong economic management. The Commission did not provide a blueprint but a framework for thinking about growth. In other words, there is no silver bullet or one recipe that would fit all countries. One cannot examine a policy in isolation but should look instead at the interaction between policies and how they affect development. Cities need to focus on the key elements of inclusive growth and coordinate their interventions across these elements in a coherent sustainable growth strategy. National governments should support cities in these efforts.

Economic success needs to be sustainable for cities to become more competitive in regional and world markets. To be sustainable, policies for economic development must ensure:

- Control of inflation at both national and local levels;
- Improving productivity and competitiveness through the development of human capital and infrastructure;
- Encouraging innovation, including sustainable technology, new products and processes; enterprise development including new starts and the growth of existing small business; and competitiveness, through a more

business-friendly environment that minimises regulation and taxation and encourages innovation and efficiency;

- In support of such innovation, the local financial sector needs to be encouraged to expand services to the range of entrepreneur groups and of consumers in the city-region economy. Incentives, for example, could be provided for expansion of bank branches or banking services through the extension of telecommunications to fringe areas;
- Effective protection of and investment in the environment, including the introduction of appropriate economic-based pricing policies for communal and municipal services;
- Providing greater opportunities for micro-enterprises and support for the informal sector;
- Modernisation of public administration so that it is transparent, efficient, and effective.

Such a multi-pronged approach is illustrated in the structure of the Regional Planning Advisory Committee for the Cairns Region in Australia (Figure 7).

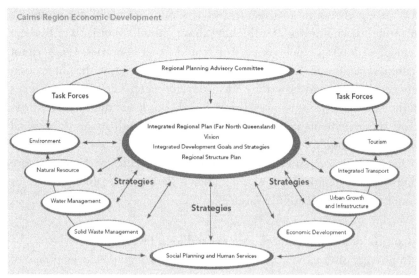

Fig. 7 Structure of the Regional Planning Advisory Committee for the Cairns Region in Australia

Source: Regional Planning Advisory Committee, 1996. Far North Queensland Regional Growth Management Framework Report.

A city must assess its advantages in terms of productivity and identify the key industry clusters that can drive its economy and growth. Based on this assessment, it should develop strategies which create an enabling environment for investment in clusters. These will integrate economic development with spatial planning and focus on matching people's skills to available jobs. They will ensure that efficient infrastructure supports these clusters and protects the environment. Given that 50 to 80 per cent of Asian economies are city-based, successful urban economic policies should be a core national economic priority.

REFERENCES

Asian Development Bank (2008). Managing Asian Cities: Sustainable and Inclusive Urban Solutions. Philippines: Asian Development Bank. www.adb.org/Documents/Studies/Managing-Asian-Cities/default.asp. Accessed 21 October 2008.

Leipziger, D (2008). Rethinking growth: learning from experience and adapting to new challenges. *Presentation at World Cities Summit 2008, Singapore* http://www.worldcities.com.sg/pdfs/Danny_Leipziger.pdf. Accessed 21 October 2008.

The Commission on Growth and Development (2008). The Growth Report: Strategies for Sustained Growth and Inclusive Development. The International Bank for Reconstruction and Development /The World Bank. http://cgd.s3.amazonaws.com/GrowthReportComplete.pdf. Accessed 21 October 2008.

The World Bank (2008). *World Development Indicators.* Washington, USA. April. International Bank for Reconstruction and Development.

14 Cities and Happiness in Environmental Goods

EUSTON QUAH* and QIYAN ONG

INTRODUCTION

A city is usually characterised by a population with higher purchasing power, better sanitation system, well-connected infrastructure and a more vibrant economy relative to the rural regions. With higher income and higher consumption, one would naturally expect that the cities are filled with the world's happiest people. However, this is not always true. Economic development did not only bring about improvements in living conditions but also environmental degradation as well as a host of social problems and ills. In particular, many major cities around the world suffer the effects of environmental degradation. Los Angeles, for example, is shrouded in smog and particulate pollution on most days; Pittsburg has recently replaced Los Angeles as the US city most polluted by short-term particle pollution (American Lung Association, 2008). Milan has more smog than any other city in Europe and the continent's second-highest level of ozone (Day, 2008). A natural pollution trap, Mexico City experiences exceedingly high ozone levels as car exhaust and soot gets trapped in a cloud over the city (Blacksmith Institute, 2006). In China, residents in Linfen (China's coal production hub) suffer from choking clouds of coal dust as well as drinking water polluted with arsenic (Blacksmith Institute, 2006) while its capital, Beijing, is perpetually blanketed with a fog all year round. In Southeast Asia, Bangkok faces massive traffic

*Corresponding author. E-mail: ecsquahe@ntu.edu.sg

congestion and consequently air and noise pollution. These cities serve to illustrate the phenomenon that while policymakers invest heavily in public amenities and generating high economic growth, they often neglect or underestimate the importance of the environment to the people's well-being.

Indeed, the resource allocation decision to provide environmental goods and other public goods is not an easy one. As many of these goods, especially environmental goods, are not traded in the markets and do not have prices to reflect their value, policymakers have great difficulty in determining which goods are more vital in the contribution to the people's welfare. To resolve this problem, economists have proposed two methods to derive the value of public and environmental goods — revealed preference approach and stated preference methods. Revealed preference approaches are indirect valuation methods which are based on the actual behaviours of individuals while stated preference approaches are valuation methods based on directly eliciting individuals' preferences. Of the revealed preference approaches, the hedonic pricing method is one of the most popular methods used to estimate the value of environmental goods whereas the contingent valuation method is the most commonly used stated preference method. Valuation of public and environmental goods allows policymakers to use cost-benefit analysis before the approval of any public project, leading to more efficient resource allocation. This in turn may translate to a greater happiness level for its people.

Recently, a further type of studies has emerged which combines the merits of both revealed and stated preference approaches. This new method in valuing public and environmental goods is known as the life satisfaction approach. Based on surveys in which individuals report their level of well-being (in terms of life satisfaction or happiness) as well as their socio-economic characteristics and where they are located, researchers are not only able to derive the value of public and environmental goods which they are exposed to but also compute the average level of happiness for an individual residing in a particular city. The latter result thus enables the comparison of the quality of life across different cities. Another method to directly determine which public and environmental goods are more important in increasing individuals' happiness is the paired comparison method. This novel method has been used to construct the damage schedule for environmental pollution. Unlike revealed preference and life satisfaction approaches where policies can only be rated after implementation, paired comparison approaches allow policymakers to derive policy implications before the implementation of the policies and thus enable them to allocate resources more efficiently. Relatively easy to implement, this method may therefore become a periodic exercise for policymakers to obtain feedback about people's happiness and the provision of public and environmental goods.

The purpose of this chapter is to review the available methods of valuing environmental goods and to present the findings of a study on happiness and the provision of environmental vis-à-vis other public goods in Singapore. In section two, we provide a literature review which will summarise the findings in both the revealed and stated preference literature as well as life satisfaction literature which together provide some insights on the value of public goods and environmental goods and their contribution to individuals' well-being. These values have been used in some studies to evaluate and compare the quality of life in different cities. We then introduce in section three the method of paired comparison, which allows individuals to rank different public and environmental goods. Findings from the Singapore study are presented in section four and some concluding remarks are made in section five.

LITERATURE REVIEW ON NON-MARKET GOODS VALUATION APPROACHES

Revealed Preference Approach

Hedonic pricing method is one of the prevalently used revealed preference approaches. This method involves the derivation of a price for a non-market good by examining the effect of its presence on the value of a relevant market good, such as housing and labour. The underlying foundation of the hedonic pricing method is that in equilibrium, individuals' utility is the same across locations since places with housing prices and/or wage rates will fully compensate for the differences in the public amenities available at different locations. However, this condition can only be achieved with strong assumptions of rationality, perfect information and perfect mobility of individuals across different locations. Transaction costs, menu costs, moving costs as well as imperfect knowledge are known causes which prevent residents from relocating even though the rent and wage differentials are higher than the economic value of the public good. Nevertheless, under the assumption of equilibrium, housing price and wage equations that include variables associated with the environment enable the implicit price of the relevant environmental goods to be obtained. This method allows policymakers to not only compare the importance of different public and environmental goods via the implicit prices obtained but also the magnitude of the difference in importance of the goods.

Numerous studies have been conducted to understand the importance of air quality and climate changes to individual welfare. Roback (1982) used the hedonic pricing method to analyse US cities and found that an average person is willing to pay US$69.55 per year for an additional clear day, US$78.25 per year to avoid an additional cloudy day, and US$5.55 per year to avoid an increase of 1 microgram per cubic metre in particulate matter. Kim et al. (2003) used a spatial-econometric hedonic housing price model to estimate the marginal value of improvements in sulphur dioxide (SO_2) and nitrogen oxide (NO_x) concentrations in Seoul. They found that marginal willingness to pay for a 4 per cent improvement in mean SO_2 concentrations is about US$2333 or 1.4 per cent of mean housing price. Rehdanz (2006) investigated the amenity value of climate change to UK households using a hedonic pricing method and found that UK households typically prefer high temperatures and lower precipitation in January. Thus, despite its other harmful effects, UK households are likely to benefit from temperature increase due to global warming.

Apart from air pollution, there have also been a number of studies determining the price of noise pollution. Day et al. (2007) applied a hedonic pricing method to the property prices in the city of Birmingham to estimate the cost of noise pollution. They found that the mean values for road noise range from £31.49[1] per annum for a 1 dB reduction from a 56 dB baseline to £91.15 per annum for the same change from an 81 dB baseline. The equivalent values for rail noise are higher, ranging from £83.61 to £139.65 per annum. Kim et al. (2007) investigated the impact of traffic noise on

---

[1] Estimated values are in 1997 prices.

property values in Seoul, Korea and found that a 1 per cent increase in noise pollution is associated with 1.3 per cent decline in land prices. The annual cost per kilometre due to traffic noise then amounts to about US$347,000.

In some studies, the implicit prices obtained from housing price and wage equations are also used to compute quality of life measures. Blomquist *et al.* (1988) computed the implicit prices of different public amenities such as climate, crime rate, teacher-student ratio, air pollution, storage and disposal sites for hazardous waste and total licensed waste for landfills in the county. These prices were then used to tabulate the quality of life indices for 253 US counties. For the entire bundle of public amenities, the authors found that the difference in compensation between the most desirable (Pueblo) and least desirable counties (St Louis City) is US$5,146. Berger *et al.* (2008) examined how changes in climate attributes, air and water quality, availability of utilities and crime affect the Russian housing and labour markets, from which they constructed quality of life indices for 953 cities in the Russian Federation. The range in quality of life is 229,000 rubles. The authors concluded that cities in southern and European region of Russia have a higher quality of life while lowest ranking city is Norilsk which is north of the Arctic Circle and is known for cold and severe pollution due to smelting and acid rain.

Stated Preference Approach

Stated preference approaches include contingent valuation, contingent behaviour and conjoint analyses. In particular, the contingent valuation method (CVM) had been widely used to assess the value of environmental amenities (Carson *et al.*, 1993, 2003; Seip and Strand, 1992). This approach requires the use of surveys to ask individuals hypothetical questions about non-market goods in order to derive the willingness to pay (WTP) or willingness to accept (WTA). In the case of environmental goods, individuals are asked how much they are willing to pay for improvements in the environment or how much they are willing to be compensated for the degradation in the environment. CVM is able to capture use value and non-use value separately by comparing the WTP or WTA of respondents who expect to consume the non-market good personally with those who do not. In this sense, CVM is superior to hedonic pricing method which does not capture non-use values since there is no behavioural trace. Willingness to pay estimates are akin to the implicit price of non-market goods and are often used in cost-benefit analysis of public policy before it is implemented.

However, there are known biases in individuals' valuation of non-market goods using this method. Individuals are highly susceptible to problems such as, embedding effect (Kahneman and Knetsch, 1992) as well as context and order effects (Carson *et al.*, 2001). In particular, this context dependence nature of WTP is "an unavoidable consequence of basic cognitive and evaluate processes that will not be eliminated by improved survey methods" (Kahneman *et al.*, 1999). Nevertheless, good survey designs will reduce some of these biases significantly.

Many studies have been conducted to estimate the willingness to pay for air quality improvement in recent years. Dziegielewska and Mendelsohn (2006) used a systems approach to value all damage components of air pollution (which include health, architecture and ecosystem damages) in Poland using contingent valuation method. Willingness to pay for 25 per cent pollution reduction is 0.77 per cent of GDP per capita and 0.96 per cent for 50 per cent reduction. Wang *et al.* (2006) used the open-ended contingent valuation method to estimate the residents' willingness to pay for air quality improvement in Beijing. Mean willingness to pay (WTP) for a 50 per cent reduction of harmful substances in the air was 143 Chinese Yuan (CNY) per household per year or 0.7 per cent of the household's annual income. Wang and Zhang (2008) adopted the same method to estimate the residents' willingness to pay for air quality improvement in Jinan, China. They found that residents are willing to pay 100 CNY per household per year or 0.7 per cent of the household's annual income for reduction of air pollution to meet residential area air quality standard.

Contingent valuation methods are also frequently applied to the estimation of willingness to pay for other environmental goods. Feitelson *et al.* (1996) used a contingent valuation method to elicit the value of airport noise pollution by estimating the effect of airport noise from airport expansion on the willingness to pay for residences near the airport. The authors found that the difference in willingness to pay between no-noise scenario and a frequent severe noise scenario ranges from 1.5 per cent and 2.4 per cent of house prices for home owners. In another study,

Amirnejad *et al.* (2006) estimated the mean of WTP for existence value of the northern forests of Iran to be US$2.51 household/month or annual value of US$30.12 for a household. Imandoust *et al.* (2007), on the other hand, investigated the willingness to pay to improve river water quality in Pune City, India. Mean willingness to pay was estimated at Rs. 17.6 (45 Indian Rupees = US$1) per family per month.

Life Satisfaction Approach

The life satisfaction approach is similar to CVM in that it also makes use of surveys. However, instead of eliciting individual's willingness to pay or willingness to accept directly, the life satisfaction approach[2] requires an individual's reported subjective well-being from which the value of non-market good is derived. Respondents are asked to evaluate their level of subjective well-being on a Likert scale.[3] An indirect utility function with income, other socio-economic factors and the availability of the public good of interest can then be estimated, where reported subjective well-being is the proxy for indirect utility. Typical questions on individual subjective well-being are *"Taking all things together, how would you say things are these days — would you say you're very happy, fairly happy, or not too happy these days?"* and *"On the whole, are you very satisfied, fairly satisfied, not very satisfied, or not at all satisfied with the life you lead?"*. Using the coefficient estimates of marginal utility of income and marginal utility of the public good, the marginal rate of substitution between income and the public good can be obtained. Willingness to pay or accept for a public good can then be estimated for different income groups and different base level of public good provision. It is therefore apparent that life satisfaction approach does not have the same problems as CVM as well as the hedonic pricing approach.

---

[2]The definition of subjective well-being can be vaguely described as a measure of three aspects: presence of positive affect, lack of negative affect (which added together provides the measure for net affect, usually proxied by happiness level) and life satisfaction (Diener *et al.*, 2003). The distinction between the two components is that happiness is a description of predominantly an emotional state while life satisfaction tends to address a more global cognitive evaluation of one's life (Compton, 2005). Despite their underlying differences, most studies on individual well-being, including this research, do not differentiate between happiness and life satisfaction. This study adopts the same view.

[3]Likert scales refer to levels which signify the level of intensity of the response. For instance, an individual may be asked from 1 to 10, how satisfied he/she is with her life, where 1 denotes very dissatisfied and 10 denotes very satisfied.

van Praag and Baarsma (2001) were among the first to use the life satisfaction approach to estimate the monetary value of noise damage in the case of Amsterdam Airport. They recognised that rent and wage differentials are able to capture some part if not all of the value of the public good. However, when equilibrium conditions do not hold, the part of the noise effect that is not captured in the rent and wage differential will be reflected in the residual shadow cost which is simply the change in income required to compensate the decrease in an individual's utility level due to the noise effect. In other words, the value of the noise damage is the sum of the rent and wage differential and the additional compensation that should be paid to an individual for enduring the noise. The authors found that the average monthly compensation per household concerned ranges from €17.13 to €56.63. Other studies which adopt this approach include Rehanz and Maddison (2003) which investigated the relationship between subjective well-being and climate and estimate the change in GDP per capita required to maintain the initial happiness level in the face of predicted climate change for 67 countries. The authors concluded that climate variables have significant effect on country-wide self-reported happiness. Countries in high latitudes would benefit from increase in temperature (climate change) while little precipitation reduces happiness, which they attribute to landscape effects.

Apart from estimating the implicit price of a specific environmental good, researchers also use the life satisfaction approach to evaluate the quality of life in different regions of a country. Morrision (2007) studied the relationship between subjective well-being and cities in New Zealand. The author found significant marked place effects even after controlling for individual socio-economic characteristics. For instance, 40 per cent of the residents in Rodney indicated they were "Very Happy" compared to the 27.2 per cent in Auckland. Although the cause behind this difference is not examined in this study, it suggests that characteristics of the cities may have an independent influence on well-being.

Moro et al. (2008) used subjective well-being data to study the difference in quality of life in 34 counties of Ireland. Instead of simply comparing the mean reported well-being across regions, the authors proposed two other measures for quality of life. The first method involves regressing reported well-being on individual's socio-economic characteristics as well as the availability of public amenities in the counties, after which the average well-being for a typical person with the country's average socio-economic characteristics is calculated for all relevant regions. Since different regions have different levels of public and environmental goods, the average well-being differs. Another method that is proposed is to weigh the environmental endowments in each location by the marginal rate of substitution between income and the amenity. The amenities discussed in this study include climate, the presence of coast or waste facilities, crime rate, population density and traffic congestion. The authors found that Galway county and Galway City are ranked first and second respectively in both measures while Dublin City and Dublin South are ranked the lowest. The authors concluded that counties in the west of Ireland all perform strongly while the major urban areas performed poorly. Bereton *et al.* (2008) conducted further analysis on the same topic by measuring amenities at the level of disaggregation at which individuals actually experience their surroundings using Geographical Information Systems (GIS). Therefore, apart from controlling for the availability or presence of environmental goods, this system allows the authors to measure the proximity to these goods, for instance, proximity to the airport, coast, landfills or hazardous waste facilities. The authors found that climate in terms of wind speed and temperature affects the happiness of individuals. Proximity to coast has significantly positive influence on happiness while the effect is reversed for proximity to landfills and waste facilities. In addition, the authors concluded that the inclusion of spatial variables improve the explanatory power of the happiness function substantially, signifying the importance of the environment to individual well-being.

Smyth *et al.* (2008) investigated the impact of atmospheric pollution, such as sulphur dioxide emissions, environmental disasters, traffic congestion, access to parkland on well-being of 30 cities in China in 2003. Using reported happiness and controlling for socio-economic characteristics as well as political issues which exist in the relevant cities, the authors found that environmental pollution and disaster as well as traffic congestion decrease individual well-being significantly. In contrast, in cities with greater access to parklands, individual-reported happiness is higher. Comparing the relative effect on individual happiness, the authors further concluded that reducing atmospheric pollution will improve the happiness of the Chinese the most compared to other environmental, political as well as economic variables.

In sum, studies which employ the life satisfaction approach to determine the impact of the environment on individual happiness provide strong evidence that (i) environmental amenities are important contributors to individual well-being; and (ii) more prosperous cities might experience lower happiness levels compared to those which are less prosperous due to less than desirable environmental experiences. Therefore, policymakers should be careful not to focus their attention on economic development at the expense of environmental degradation. Studies such as those by Smyth *et al.* (2008) on urban China and Moro *et al.* (2008) on Ireland serve as important reminders of the trade-off that city dwellers face in their pursuit of high economic growth and higher consumption.

PAIRED COMPARISON APPROACH

The paired comparison approach is similar to the stated preference approach in the sense that a survey is used to elicit individuals' preference for public and environmental goods. A set of elements are presented in pairs as discrete binary choices in a survey. The set of objects can include gains, losses, activities, environmental resources or whatever is being scaled. From each pair, respondents then choose one item to reflect which is more important, in the sense that larger compensation should be paid to it than the other (Rutherford *et al.*, 1998). The variance stable rank method is then used to derive the ranking. This method requires that the total number of times an element is selected by all respondents is divided by the maximum number of times it could have been selected. The result is then multiplied by 100 so that it lies on the scale of 0 to 100. Ordinal ranking is then derived based on the magnitude of the result. Unlike direct ranking, this method allows for some degree of indifference to occur since scores for different elements may be the same.

A similar approach to the paired comparison survey is known as the dichotomous choice contingent valuation study. The difference between the two approaches is that in the dichotomous choice CVM, respondents are presented with a public or environmental good and a monetary amount. Respondents are then required to choose between the good and the money.

In the event that a respondent chooses the money, the interviewer will repeat the choice with half of the previous monetary sum. The purpose of that approach is therefore to derive individual willingness to pay. In contrast, the paired comparison approach seeks only to derive ranking of a set of goods. When monetary amounts are included in the set, paired comparison of goods and money allows one to derive the monetary estimation of the good by bracketing the good between two dollar amounts in the individual preference profiles.

Peterson and Brown (1998) first demonstrated the ease and usefulness of this method to compare individual's preference for six public goods, four private goods and 11 monetary sums. Two of the public goods are pure public environmental goods that are non-rival and non-excludable. The other four public goods are made non-excludable by policy and non-rival as long as demand does not exceed capacity. The private goods are familiar market goods with suggested retail prices. The results demonstrated high reliability of individual preference order as substantial inconsistent choices were switched to consistent ones in repeated trials. The authors found that pure environmental public goods are ranked higher than other public goods and most of the private goods.

From a seller's point of view, willingness to accept is the minimum monetary sum that he is willing to accept in exchange of the loss of the good. On the other hand, willingness to pay is obtained from a buyer's point of view. It refers to the monetary sum that the buyer is willing to give up in exchange for the possession of the good. The disparity in the reference point is evidence for the significant difference in the estimates of willingness to accept versus willing to pay (Knetsch and Sinden, 1984). Paired comparison offers another reference point for consideration. Paired comparison questions are structured in a selector's reference point, that is, the selector possesses neither the good nor money. The selector is then asked to choose between alternative gains: the good or the monetary sum. As no real or perceived loss from a good occurs in this case, behavioural effects on willingness to accept measures such as loss aversion can be avoided (Kahneman *et al.*, 1999).

Studies that have made use of paired comparisons to rank environmental goods include those conducted by Rutherford *et al.* (1998), Chuenpagdee *et al.* (2001) and Chuenpagdee *et al.* (2006). Rutherford *et al.* (1998)

suggested that a damage schedule based on consistent judgments of environmental importance may be capable of providing more accurate indicators of community values if such judgments can be elicited directly from the public. There are significant cost and procedural advantages associated with using damage schedules in assessing environmental harms or resource losses, namely, it allows for the provision of pre-incident damage information so that environmental harm can be effectively deterred. Paired comparison can be used to obtain judgments of relative importance of environmental impacts, from which damage schedules can be drawn. Chuenpagdee et al. (2001) demonstrated how the damage schedule can be drawn up to aid in coastal zone management issues such as those in Thailand.

Chuenpagdee et al. (2006) proposed the construction of a public sentiment index. Surveying different stakeholder groups on their preference for nine ecosystem scenarios and their acceptability of policies, the preference scores from paired comparison were combined with the percentage of policy acceptance and normalised to yield a public sentiment index for the target coastal bay. Higher public sentiment index, due to high preference score and high level of acceptance thus suggests that there is potential for successful implementation of a particular policy.

Unlike hedonic pricing method and life satisfaction approaches, paired comparison offers the possibility of receiving feedback from the public regarding prospective public policies in a relatively controlled setting before the policies are implemented. This allows policymakers to implement policies and allocate resources in a more efficient manner. As individuals are presented pairs of environmental goods, they are also less likely to respond in a strategic manner, a problem that plagues contingent valuation methods.

PAIRED COMPARISON OF ENVIRONMENTAL GOODS IN SINGAPORE

Quah et al. (2006) was the first study to investigate the ranking of preferences for environmental goods in Singapore. A random sample of 100 respondents was chosen for the paired comparison study. The four most important environmental problems are identified through a pilot study. These are degradation of coastal and marine environment, polluted air,

Table 1   List of environmental options and their descriptions

1. *Severe food and water contamination* causing diseases such as cholera, typhoid etc. with some of them being contagious.
2. *Moderate food and water contamination* where hygiene is not at its highest level. It may cause slight food poisoning or feeling of nausea.
3. *Moderate level of damage to coastal and marine environment* where mangrove forests are only partially cleared and coral reefs are marginally threatened, implying that such losses are less irreversible.
4. *Severe damage to coastal and marine environment* where coral reefs are badly destroyed and mangrove forests are extensively cleared. Habitat loss thus occurs, in turn causing losses of various important marine and coastal species.
5. *Moderate level of air pollution*, PSI between 51 and 100, where the concentration of pollutants is such that adverse health effects are not observed. Unpleasant smells from landfills and slight haze prevail.
6. *Severe air pollution*, PSI between 200 and 299, where air quality is at a very unhealthy level. Respiratory health and vision is adversely affected.
7. *Severe ozone depletion* leading to a sharp rise in UV-B radiation (UV index above 7) where sunburn time is roughly 20 minutes or less, resulting in health problems like skin cancer, eye damage and premature aging as well as harmful effects like increased global warming and climate change.
8. *Moderate ozone depletion* where sunburn time is more than 30 minutes, implying minimal biological effects to living organisms. Adverse harmful effects such as skin cancer, eye damage may only result after constant prolonged UV exposure.

ozone depletion and unhygienic environment relating to food and water. Each of the four environmental problems was further varied at two different levels of provision of environmental quality namely, moderate and severe. This gives rise to eight options for comparison. Table 1 presents the set of elements or options for the paired comparison.

Paired comparison of the options is conducted in random order to avoid order bias. Since severe environmental problems of each type always matters more relative to the moderate level of the same type, such pairs are excluded in the paired comparison, leaving 24 possible pairs for comparison. Using the variance stable rank method, the proportion of times that each item is chosen relative to the maximum number of times it could be chosen by all respondents is calculated. This proportion indicates the collective judgment of the relative importance of different items being compared. The results of the paired comparison by 100 respondents are summarised in Figure 1.

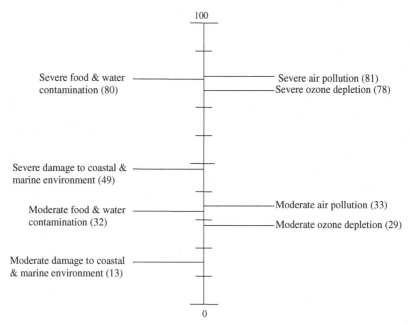

Fig. 1   Scale of relative importance of environmental problems based on the perceptions of Singaporeans

Figure 1 shows that Singaporeans are most concerned with severe air pollution followed by severe food and water contamination, and severe ozone depletion. The results are not surprising given the perennial haze that looms over the city-state, a result of Indonesia's forest fires. Food and water contamination on the other hand poses health risks to individuals and are therefore undesirable. The most interesting result is the perception of the importance of severe ozone depletion. Unlike the other two environmental problems, the negative effects of ozone depletion cannot be felt immediately. Its high score suggests that Singaporeans are aware and fearful of the global environmental problem of climate change. Severe damage to coastal and marine environment obtains the lowest score of all the several environmental problems probably because there is very little occurrence of water pollution in Singapore in general. Another observation from the ranking is that all severe environmental problems are deemed more serious than moderate problems of other types. In other words, there is no strict preference of a particular environmental problem over another type.

What is more important appears to be the severity of the environmental problem.

Are there any policy implications from such a study? Suppose that the ranking does not only reflect the importance of each environmental problem but also the severity of the impact of each environmental problem on individual happiness, policymakers should devote relatively more resources to those problems that strongly affect individual happiness. For instance, ensuring that the air quality in Singapore does not deteriorate should be prioritised over preventing damage to coastal and marine environment, if the severity of the two problems is deemed to be the same.

Ong *et al.* (2008) extended the paired comparison approach to compare not only environmental goods but also other forms of public expenditure in the areas of education and transportation. The motivation of this study is to propose how paired comparison can aid policymakers in (i) allocating budget for each category to different goods in the category; and (ii) allocating yearly budget to different categories of goods. In other words, two separate paired comparison studies are conducted. In the first study, respondents paired and compared four items within each category, two of which are framed as improvements in the amenities (or gains) while the others are framed as reduction in losses. Such distinction is to detect any behavioural asymmetries in the sense that individuals may be more adverse to losses than they are delighted with gains, even though the magnitude of the losses and the gains are equivalent. The items for each of the three categories of amenities (education, transportation and environment) are listed in Table 2. The amenities highlighted are those that reflect reduction in losses while the rest refers to gains.

Since the objective of the survey is to find out which public amenities improve individual well-being more than others, government budget appears as a fixed given amount in the question. 100 respondents are randomly selected for this survey. For each pair of public expenditure items, respondents are asked "suppose that the government has one hundred million dollars that will now be spent on improving public amenities, which public amenity in each pair contributes more to their life satisfaction".

The results of the paired comparison are shown in Figures 2–4 with the categories of education, transportation and environment respectively. In the category of education, it appears that reductions in losses are more

Table 2   List of education, transportation and environmental items

---

Education

1. Increase the number of teachers.
2. Increase the variety of subjects, courses or academic programmes available to students.
3. Lower dropout rates through increasing remedial lessons for academically weaker students and improving monitoring system to help teachers track development of students.
4. Lower student's depression and suicide rates through providing more help to students with behavioural and emotional difficulties and implementing more programmes to help students cope with stress.

Transportation

1. Provide public buses with more direct routes to central business district.
2. Expand the MRT network to more housing estates.
3. Reduce waiting time for buses by implementing more efficient central planning of bus network.
4. Reduce accident rates by improving road designs and erecting more signage and signals for road users.

Environment

1. Increasing the number of parks and/or green open spaces (grass fields).
2. Increase the amount of waste recycled by having more and bigger recycling bins, recycling more electronic waste and researching on more efficient recycling techniques.
3. Reduce carbon emissions in the air by investing in alternative energies such as solar power.
4. Reduce noise pollution by building noise barriers near housing estates and strengthening the enforcement of noise-curbing activities.

---

important contributors to well-being than gains. Decreasing dropout rate attains the highest score and is thus ranked as the most important contributor to well-being. This is then followed by decreasing students' depression and suicide rates. Increasing subject variety in school's curriculum is deemed more important than increasing the number of teachers and are ranked third and fourth respectively.

Figure 3 shows the scale of relative contribution of different types of expenditure on transportation goods on the welfare of individuals. Unlike in the case of education, the highest ranked and the lowest ranked items are reductions in losses. Decreasing waiting time for public buses is a major concern to Singaporeans and has a strong influence on Singaporeans' life satisfaction while reducing accident rates have less influence on life satisfaction. Another observation worth mentioning is how bus rides appear to affect Singaporeans' well-being more than the other mode of

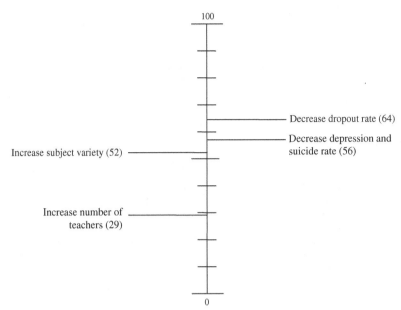

Fig. 2   Scale of relative contribution of different education expenditure to individuals' life satisfaction based on the perceptions of Singaporeans

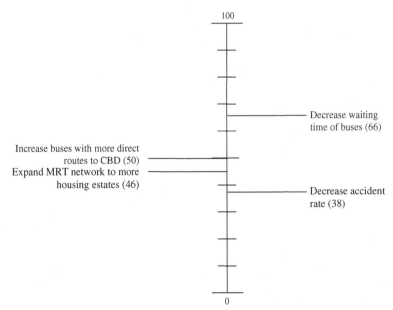

Fig. 3   Scale of relative contribution of transportation expenditure to individuals' life satisfaction based on the perceptions of Singaporeans

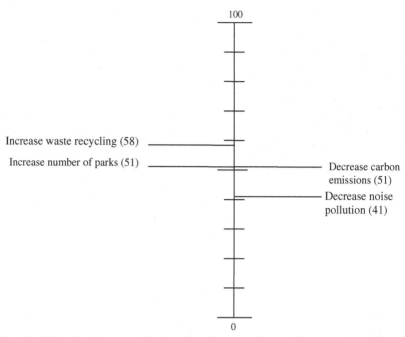

Fig. 4   Scale of relative contribution of environmental expenditure to individuals' life satisfaction based on the perceptions of Singaporeans

transportation, the Mass Rapid Transit (MRT), despite the huge investment in MRT network expansion. Decreasing bus waiting time and increasing bus rides with more direct routes to the central business district (CBD) are ranked first and second respectively as compared to expansion of MRT network in rank number three.

Figure 4 shows the ranking of the four types of environmental expenditure. Gains appear to be slightly more important factors influencing individual happiness than reduction of losses in this category. Improving recycling technologies and efficiency in recycling waste attains the highest rank while a tie occurs in the second place between increase in parks and decrease in carbon emissions. Noise pollution is less important compared to the other environmental expenditures in this survey. Compared to education and transportation expenditures, the ranking of environmental expenditures are much closer. This suggests that either Singaporeans have differing views on which environmental expenditure matters more or simply that the choice between environmental expenditures is itself a difficult decision.

The value of such an exercise is apparent. The results from within-category paired comparison reveals which items within the category improve individual well-being compared to others. Therefore, given a budget for a category of public expenditure, policymakers may want to prioritise those expenditures which have greater influence on individual happiness according to the ranks of the items within that category. A cross-category paired comparison study on the other hand, will allow policymakers to understand the relative importance of items from different categories of public expenditure which will provide a further guide to efficient resource allocation.

CONCLUSION

Any resource allocation decision is no easy task. There exist multiple facets in decision consideration and to make matters worse, some of these facets, in terms of environmental management, are more elusive than others. The chapter started with this question in mind: if economic development is a means to achieve greater happiness, why are residents in many cities more unhappy than those who do not live in the cities? At least part of the missing link can be explained by the city environment. In most cases, economic development has taken place at the expense of environmental degradation. This is especially severe in cities of developing countries. Therefore, it is imperative that methods are devised to value environmental goods such that sufficient resources can be channeled to maintain or improve the city environment.

This chapter provides a review of the existing methodologies used to study economic valuation of non-market goods, in particular, the environment. Research using hedonic pricing, contingent valuation and more recently, life satisfaction methods show that there is a value to environmental goods. Furthermore, most life satisfaction studies found that environment and public amenities are likely to be important determinants of individual's well-being.

Establishing the importance of public amenities, however, is not sufficient. One limitation of hedonic pricing and life satisfaction studies is that it is often impossible to include all the relevant public amenities in the regressions. Therefore, while there is general consensus that the provision of public amenities influences citizen's happiness, it is uncertain what should be included in the basket of public amenities. It is then useful to seek an alternative approach which allows the policymaker to understand the public's preferences of the different categories of public amenities. This study proposes the use of the paired comparison method to achieve this aim and demonstrated how public preferences in Singapore can be derived easily from using this method. In the ongoing study, instead of comparing public expenditure within each category of public good, citizens are asked to compare public expenditures across different categories of public goods. Such preference rankings will certainly enable policymakers to allocate limited resources across different categories of public amenities more efficiently, and this is, after all, based on what the citizens want.

REFERENCES

American Lung Association (2008). State of the Air Report, http://www.lungusa.org/site/c.dvLUK9O0E/b.4178621/(accessed September 4th, 2008).

Amirnejad, H, S Khalilian, MH Assareh and M Ahmadian (2006). Estimating the existence value of North forests of Iran by using a contingent valuation method. *Ecological Economics*, 58, 665–675.

Berger, M, GC Blomquist and P Sabirianova (2008). Compensating differentials in emerging labour and housing markets: Estimates of quality of life in Russian cities. *Journal of Urban Economics*, 63(1), 23–55.

Brereton, F, JP Clinch and S Ferreira (2008). Happiness, geography and the environment. *Ecological Economics*, 386–396.

Blomquist, GC, MC Berger and JP Hoehn (1988). New estimates of quality of life in urban areas. *American Economic Review*, 78(1), 89–107.

Carson, RT and RC Mitchell (1993). The value of clean water: The public's willingness to pay for boatable, fishable, and swimmable quality water. *Water Resources Research*, 29, 2445–2454.

Carson, RT, NE Flores and NF Meade (2001). Contingent valuation: Controversies and evidence. *Environmental and Resource Economics*, 19(2), 173–210.

Carson, RT, RC Mitchell, WM Hanemann, RJ Kopp, S Pressers and PA Ruud (2003). Contingent valuation and lost passive use: damages from the Exxon Valdez oil spill. *Environmental and Resource Economics*, 25(3), 257–286.

Chuenpagdee, R, J Knetsch and T Brown (2001). Coastal management using public judgments, importance scales, and predetermined schedules. *Coastal Management*, 29, 253–270.

Chuenpagdee, R, L Liguori, D Preikshot and D Pauly (2006). A public sentiment index for ecosystem management. *Ecosystems*, 9, 463–473.

Compton, WC (2005). *An Introduction to Positive Psychology*. Belmont, CA: Thomson Wadsworth.

Day, B, I Bretman and I Lake (2007). Beyond implicit prices: Recovering theoretically consistent and transferable values for noise avoidance from a hedonic property price model. *Environmental and Resource Economics*, 37(1), 211–232.

Day, M (2008). Milan 'is pollution capital in Europe', http://www.telegraph.co.uk/earth/main.jhtml?xml=/earth/2008/03/07/eamilan107.xml (accessed September 4th, 2008).

Diener, E, S Oishi and R Lucas (2003). Personality, culture and subjective well-being: emotional and cognitive evaluations of life. *Annual Review of Psychology*, 54, 403–425.

Doziegielewska, DAP and R Mendelsohn (2005). Valuing air quality in Poland. *Environmental & Resource Economics*, 30, 131–163.

Feitelson, E, R Hurd and R Mudge, (1996). The impact of airport noise on willingness to pay for residences. *Transportation Research Part D: Transport and Environment*, 1–14.

Imandoust, SB and SN Gadam (2007). Are people willing to pay for river water quality, contingent valuation. *International Journal of Environmental Science and Technology*, 4(3), 401–408.

Kahneman, D and J Knetsch (1992). Valuing public goods: the purchase of moral satisfaction. *Journal of Environmental Economics and Management*, 22, 57–70.

Kahneman, D, I Ritov and D Schkade (1999). Economic preferences or attitude expressions?: an analysis of dollar responses to public issues. *Journal of Risk and Uncertainty*, 19, 1–3, 203–235.

Kim, CW, TT Phipps and L Anselin (2003). Measuring the benefits of air quality improvement: A spatial hedonic approach. *Journal of Environmental Economics and Management*, 45(1), 24–39.

Kim, SK, SJ Park and YJ Kweon (2007). Highway traffic noise effects on land price in an urban area. *Transport Research Part D: Transport and Environment*, 12(4), 275–280.

Knetsch, J and J Sinden (1984). Willingness to pay and compensation demanded: experimental evidence of an unexpected disparity in measures of value. *The Quarterly Journal of Economics*, 99, 507–521.

Morrison, PS (2007). Subjective well-being and the city, social policy. *Journal of New Zealand*, 31, 74–103.

Moro, M, F Brereton, S Ferreira and JP Clinch (2008). Ranking quality of life using subjective well-being data. *Ecological Economics*, 448–460.

Ong Q, E Quah, KC Tan, KW Ho and J Knetsch (2008). Happiness and cross category paired comparison of public amenities, Working Paper.

Peterson, G and T Brown (1998). Economic valuation by the method of paired comparison, with emphasis on evaluation of the transitivity axiom. *Land Economics*, 74(2), 240–261.

Quah, E, E Choa and KC Tan (2006). Use of damage schedules in environmental valuation: the case of urban Singapore. *Applied Economics*, 38, 1501–1512.

Rehdanz, K and D Maddison (2003). Climate and happiness. *Research Unit Sustainability and Global Change, Working Paper No. FNU-20*, Centre for Marine and Climate Research, Hamburg University.

Rehdanz, K (2006). Hedonic pricing of climate change impacts to households in Great Britain. *Climate Change*, 74(4), 413–434.

Roback, J (1982). Wages, rents, and the quality of life. *Journal of Political Economy*, 90, 1257–1278.

Rutherford, M, J Knetsch and T Brown (1998), Assessing environmental losses: judgments of importance and damage schedules. *Harvard Environmental Law Review*, 20, 51–101.

Seip, K and J Strand (1992). Willingness to pay for environmental goods in Norway: A CV study with real payment. *Environmental and Resource Economics*, 2, 91–106.

Smyth, R, V Mishra and X Qian (2008). The environment and well-being in urban China. *Ecological Economics*, Article in Press.

The Blacksmith Institute (2006). *The World's Most Polluted Places: The Top Ten*, http://www. blacksmithinstitute.org/wwpp2007/finalReport2007.pdf (accessed September 4th, 2008).

van Praag, B and E Baarsma (2005). Using happiness surveys to value intangibles: the case of airport noise. *The Economic Journal*, 115, 224–246.

Wang, XJ, W Zhang, Y Li, Kz Yang and M Bai (2006). Air quality improvement estimation and assessment using contingent valuation method, a case study in Beijing. *Environmental Monitoring and Assessment*, 120, 153–168.

Wang, Y and YS Zhang (2008). Air quality assessment by contingent valuation in Ji'nan, China. *Journal of Environmental Management*, Article in Press.

Chapter
15
Conclusion: World Cities — Towards a Liveable, Sustainable and Vibrant Future?

GIOK LING OOI and BELINDA YUEN

World cities are 'basing points' in the global economy (Friedmann, 1995) or global cities that are command and control centres in the world economy (Sassen, 2001). While world cities were originally defined in terms of the number of multinational headquarters or producer services found in cities, later studies have found inter-linkages among the cities based on branch office networks (Beaverstock, Smith and Taylor, 2000; Alderson and Beckfield, 2004; Taylor, 2004) or air travel (Shin and Timberlake, 2000; Smith and Timberlake, 2002). These major cities are increasingly connected by flows of capital, trade, trans-national multi-city businesses, information and knowledge, labour, tourism, and media as well as cultural exchange. The papers in this book further highlight that world cities are also similar in many ways such as the social and environmental challenges that they face.

Being world cities suggest that they are subject to global forces that are often beyond their control of these cities, particularly in terms of their rate of growth and expansion. These cities, therefore, appear to be propelled by "... the interaction of extraordinary technological innovation combined with the world-wide reach driven by global capitalism that give today's change its particular complexion. It has now a speed, inevitability and force that it has not had before" (Hutton and Giddens, 2000, p. vii; Hutton, 2002; Friedman, 2005). Urban scholars, however, have shown that with cities competing to become strategic nodes for investment and production in the space of global economy flows (Castells, 1996; Sassen, 2002), new centres as well as margins are created, that is, globalisation's winners and losers. In other words, the cities that succeed in plugging into the global economy in strategic ways are privileged in their bid at drawing international talent, investments, resources and power. World cities are, therefore, as much the actors in determining their own development agendas as international and national actors like multinational corporations and federal states (Savitch and Kantor, 2002). Indeed, cities in today's global world appear to have enhanced status and economic clout, which sometimes overshadow that of the nation-states of which they are a part (Denters and Rose, 2005).

If global pressures faced by world cities are the same, the response of the city governments certainly vary considerably. This is underscored in the discussions presented in this book. Important to note, too, are the gaps in economic vibrancy and opportunity within world cities (Smith, 2001). The statistics on urbanisation trends and related concerns such as urban housing as well as environmental quality, highlight that in the largest cities in countries of the South, millions are living in squalor, poverty and increasingly polluted environments often without security of housing or land tenure (Neuwirth, 2005; Davis, 2006; Ooi and Phua, 2007; Ooi, 2007). These are the issues, among others that have been the foci of the discussions in this book on world, cities. At heart is their urban liveability, sustainability and vibrancy. The essays in this book examine these issues from several perspectives, in terms of the tangible urban development areas as well as the less tangible, subjective concerns of well-being, happiness and health, and also the policy and practice of governance, financing and partnership that challenge implementation.

THE POLITICS AND ECONOMICS OF URBAN LIVEABILITY AND SUSTAINABILTY

In the discussion on the more tangible areas of urban development with which world cities are concerned — land transportation, climate change, biodiversity protection, solid waste management and the financing of environmental infrastructure — the authors pinpoint the political as well as economic constraints in implementing the optimal solutions or putting sound strategies to work. The discussion also underscores the differences between cities particularly those that are more affluent compared to those poorer cities that struggle just to provide basic services, such as waste removal. Yet, these same cities also face urban traffic congestion from the rise in private car ownership and its use.

Urban policies have created the transit cities dependent on rail and mass rapid transit networks just as in many cities particularly in North America and now a large number of developing countries, the auto-based cities (see chapter by Vuchic in this book). The chapter on urban land transportation highlights that it is equally possible for city governments to develop walkable cities, that is, cities that are walkable and one might add, cyclable. Public transport, it is emphasised in the discussion during the Summit, contributes a key role in liveability as well as sustainability. Policy incentives encourage walking and bicycling as well as the use of public transport and use disincentives to reduce use of the car.

Global success stories and urban best practices revolve around governments which have decided on public transport as the mode of transport for their city. Bogota as its mayor explained at the Summit, built 400 km of bicycle paths used today by 350,000 bicyclists. Creation of bus lanes, however, needed strict police enforcement which can be a challenge in cities in India, according to the Director of Urban Transportation in the Ministry of Development. In New Delhi and Mumbai as well as other cities, busways for buses only face opposition. The importance of policy implementation and enforcement has been underscored by the experience of cities such as Singapore. Here, the decision to make public transport the main mode of urban land transport has been successfully implemented through disincentives to reduce or contain car ownership as well as use of the car. At the same time, a comprehensive bus and mass rapid transit system was developed which enabled urban commuters to switch or rely solely on the use of public transport.

Urban management decisions concerning solid waste management face similar political and economic constraints (see chapter by Scheinberg in this book). In proposing integration for solid waste management, differences are highlighted between more affluent and poorer cities. As Scheinberg wrote, " ... there are literally thousands of others living from, working with, and affected by waste management". Usually unrecognised stakeholders include (female) street sweepers, (male) workers on collection trucks, dumpsite scavengers or 'waste pickers' — some of whom may actually live on or at the edge of the dumpsite — and family-based businesses that live from recycling of solid waste.

A solid waste management system for cities which aims to be sustainable in terms of its operational, financial, social, political, institutional, legal and environmental aspects needs to consider not only disposal but also storage, recycling, composting, recovery as well as cost containment and event effort at reducing waste generation. Each aspect in the management of solid waste has to be weighed in relation to economic conditions such as costs and viability (Marcotuillo and Nishida, 2000). Solid waste management, however, competes for budgets with other urban services such as water, sanitation, health, housing and transport. In many poorer cities, solid waste management usually ends up at the bottom of most priority lists among city governments.

Financing urban infrastructure and, particularly environmental infrastructure such as clean water supplies and sanitation can be a challenge for city governments in the global South. There has, however, been relatively creative ways that have been found to provide financing for services such as water supply and sanitation with partnerships between international agencies, NGOs and the state sector. One such project benefited 100,000 households in India (Schaefer-Preuss in this book). The Nanjing city government in China has worked with UN-Habitat on bond issuance to finance wastewater treatment systems.

Agencies like the Asian Development Bank have a slew of financial models to help cities finance environmental infrastructure. In areas of work needed to address pollution, the lack of enforcement and capacity for this is noted. In addition, this lack of capacity and other priorities including the issue of slum development is also a factor standing in the way of measures that have to be taken to address climate change. Often, the steps being proposed to improve urban transportation can conflict with interest of slum populations who usually face eviction to make way for highways or such development.

In a similar vein, spaces such as parks, nature reserves and wildlife centres are, and have been considered as useful social, recreational and educational amenities for cities that tend to be built-up and can be cement jungles. Yet, it is clear that in dense city centres, biodiversity remains a remote and unrealistic option as it stands in the way of city development, occupies expensive real estate and for economic considerations, certainly dispensable. Hence, "Dr Ahmed Djoghlaf, Executive Secretary of the Convention of Biological Diversity, reminded the World Cities Summit 2008 that large populations living in megacities consume massive amounts of energy, thus contributing to climate change, which has been identified as one of the most important driving force today in the loss of biodiversity. Planning is essential to arrest this loss and ensure an acceptable living environment" (Chou in this book), and one might add, particularly for cities that are growing rapidly.

While the trend appears to be a growing awareness among city governments that protection of biodiversity can deliver a range of goods and services, the biodiversity that is brought back to cities tends to be fragmented, scattered and restricted. Nevertheless, cities are seeing the cleaning up of polluted waterways as well as the restoration of rivers which was previously covered to make way for highways. The Curitiba Declaration on Cities and Biodiversity of 2007 as well as the 2008 Mayors' Conference on Local Action for Biodiversity point towards the consciousness that cities can contribute to the reversal in the destruction of biodiversity as well as benefit from the efforts.

Concerns about how climate change policies affect economic growth ensure that these policies lag behind (Savage in this book). Strong political will and leadership are needed to drive effective responses to address the impact of climatic change at the global and regional levels. Cities will first have to realise that the impact of climate change will be especially disastrous based on the experiences that we have seen in recent years — New Orleans, Yangon, Szechuan towns and villages. With their concentrations of population, infrastructure and economic activities as well as their locations in coastal zones so vulnerable to sea level changes, city governments have to negotiate political and economic barriers to better address the issues arising from climate change including use of alternative sources of energy as well as introduction of carbon-neutral development initiatives.

While adaptation might be the option involving moving to less vulnerable locations, this is likely to be available only to the rich. It is difficult to imagine the poor in the slum settlements of world cities being able to relocate to safer or alternative urban sites other than those in which they are living. So, as Savage argues in this book, to "… address climate change the global urban communities would need to manage and implement simultaneously a three-prong action-plan: (a) focus and accelerate carbon reduction technologies and environmental innovations; (b) change peoples' attitudes and promote responsible behaviour; and (c) develop sustainable eco-cities that are holistically and ecologically compatible with their hinterlands".

An overarching concern that all world cities share would be good governance with an emphasis on sustainable urban development and change. Indeed, the principles of good governance have been mapped out in cities such as Melbourne, which as Tan summarised in this book, is considered among the most liveable cities in the world. Leaders who are funding scientific research and providing financing as well as those having oversight of supplies of water and energy agreed that cities can only be liveable and vibrant if the basic needs such as water supply and energy among others, are met. Cities also need to ensure efficiency in the delivery of urban services through technological systems with effort at securing financing. Apart from the development of new infrastructure, the leaders spoke about maintaining and managing urban systems like those that provide water in order to reduce leakage and wastage. Other crucial elements in defining good governance concern the inclusion of stakeholders like women in policy decision-making as well as prudent investment in new technologies together with the sharing of city experiences with such technologies as wastewater recovery.

Political will is emphasised, particularly in financially strapped cities, which appear to be a larger proportion of cities in developing countries. Good governance calls for professionalisation, accountability and institutional processes that emphasise participation by citizens.

WELL-BEING, HAPPINESS AND SUSTAINABILITY OF THE BUILT ENVIRONMENT — OUTCOME OR DRIVERS OF CHANGE?

Cities that are well-governed should see dividends not only in terms of competitiveness but also in the emotional well-being of people living in them. Increasingly, research has been focusing on the intersections between emotions and places such as, cities, in the effort to understand feelings and attachments across a range of spatial and social contexts, environments and landscapes (Smith *et al.*, 2009).

In their discussion of the link between well-being, happiness, sustainability of the built environment and cities, the authors in this book have focused on how important these are in assessing the liveability and vibrancy of cities. The conditions — well-being and happiness — could serve as goals that can drive city governments towards the changes and improvements in urban living that are needed.

Gallup has defined subjective well-being as the presence of thriving, inspiration and feeling independent. Such well-being is important to citizens' ability to innovate, seek improvements and also be inventive (Liu in this book). It is a condition that requires engaged citizens, that is, people who are willing and also have the opportunity to contribute towards public life and interests in cities. They are citizens who work to build linkages among different individuals or groups of these within their communities in order to work at goals that serve the interests of these communities. In doing this, citizens help to build trust and cooperation within the community which in turn will help boost productivity and economic interests. Engaged citizenry can provide the urban conditions that have reportedly proven welcoming to people serving therefore to attract talented people to work and live in that community. This will boost the competitive edge of cities.

Generally, individuals have a high level of subjective well-being when they think and feel that their lives are going well. Individuals who have a high level of such well-being will have positive emotions, such as calmness, contentment, enjoyment, gratitude and love. These individuals will also see their life as worthwhile, and evaluate all aspects of living and their relationships with others in their community positively.

There are many definitions of happiness and one links it to positive well-being. In comparing Detroit, a city on the decline, with Myrtle Beach, South Carolina, happy cities such as Myrtle Beach tend to be characterised by safety, job opportunities, short commuting times, good schools and a high degree of multi-cultural integration. To quote Richard Florida and his views on creative capital, economic and mental vibrancy will depend not just on technological innovation and economic entrepreneurship, but also on artistic and cultural creativity. After all, a city, at its most basic, is the spatial organisation of people and places. Key to the spatial organisation is good governance, which is required to create the physical environment and provide the foundation for a well-functioning city (Liu; Quah and Ong in this book).

Researchers have surveyed individuals about their level of well-being in terms of life satisfaction or happiness as well as their socio-economic characteristics and where they are located in order to derive the value of public and environmental goods which they are exposed to and also compute the average level of happiness for an individual residing in a particular city (Quah and Ong in this book). Such research enables the comparison of the quality of life across different cities. Research using pricing has shown people and households are willing to pay for an extra clear day as well as less pollution. Even climate change has an impact on country-wide self-reported level of happiness according to research discussed by Quah and Ong in this book.

Sustainability of the built environment considers scale as an important factor with architect Kenneth Yeang arguing for city-level practices and the design of the eco-city (Heng and Zhang in this book). In considering how cities and the built form can be more sustainable, the debate continues about whether compactness is a contributory factor or the need for monocentricity or polycentricity. Singapore's choice of high-rise and high-density public housing implies a small territorial footprint for urban housing. A further argument suggests that urban processes shaping cities might be a more fruitful starting point to consider sustainability of the built environment. There are also cities such as, London and Den Haag, which are using their ecological footprints as the reference point in policy decision-making. The authors further highlight the need for economic vibrancy as much as environmental sustainability among cities because world cities can only thrive with both in terms of attracting and retaining economic activities as well as people.

FROM THE ABSTRACT TO PRACTICE

The authors of the papers have not only brought up issues that world cities must face and address but also broached strategies and solutions that have been successfully tried and tested in various cities. Public-private partnerships (PPP) are proposed in the bid to solve financial constraints that face city governments. As Phang pointed out in this book, these partnerships have covered areas of development such as transport, technology, water, operation of prisons, health care delivery, welfare provision and urban regeneration projects. In noting the risks that the public sector undertake with PPPs, the recommendation is that there be an effective regulatory framework in place together with flexibility that will allow renegotiations and contract extensions in the event of non-performance or problems such as cost overruns and programme interruptions, among others.

Creativity and innovations are the buzzwords in dynamic world cities seeking to position themselves as being ahead of the learning curve (Hall in this book). In contrasting the artistically creative cities from the technologically innovative, Hall in this book noted that the former relied on craft guilds and being the most important places in their time while the latter were upstart places in the periphery relying on "strong local networks, supplying specialised skilled labour and services, and creating a climate of innovation among small firms, even individuals, who shared knowledge while they competed with each other". Also considered is a hybrid — the creative innovative city — which combines art and technology for competitiveness in the cultural industries.

City typologies aside, there are authors who argue that above all, there is a need for cities to be inclusive and framing growth with reference to sustainability would be the emphasis that experienced professionals and practitioners see as crucial to the future of world cities (Wegelin and Lindfield in this book). This emphasis has been underscored in the discussions that have been shared in this book — engaging civic groups, citizens, operators of transportation, private and public sectors — are crucial to the successes among city governments in implementing policies aimed at liveability and sustainability in transport and other areas of urban development and management. Leaving stakeholders like women out of processes to improve urban services such as water provision would be tantamount to not engaging with the issues involved (see Ooi's chapter on good governance). Indeed, as Hall wrote in this book, the American model of bottom-up innovations with laissez-faire has been highlighted as the more enduring form of urban creativity seen to date among cities.

The Growth Commission, as Wegelin and Lindfield highlighted in this book, has emphasised that high growth economies have the following characteristics — openness and integration with the world economy, strong economic management, governments with visions for the future, market-oriented with well-developed private sectors, effective leadership and government. These economies are inclusive because growth is defined as overcoming poverty and distributing the benefits as widely as possible. The institutions of sustainability in society would meet the needs of all citizens and not leave the vulnerable and disadvantaged behind (Wegelin and Lindfield in this book). The suggestion while simple is not without its challenge. The essays in this book offer some consideration on how this and other issues of urban liveability, sustainability and vibrancy may be addressed in world cities.

REFERENCES

Alderson, AS and J Beckfield (2004). Power and position in the world city system. *AJS*, 109, 811–851.

Beaverstock, JV, RG Smith and PJ Taylor (2000). World-city network: a new metageography. *Annals, Association of American Geographers,* 90, 123–134.

Castells, M (1996). *The Rise of the Network Society*. Oxford: Blackwell.

Davis, M (2006). *Planet of Slums*. London: Verso.

Denters, B and LE Rose (eds.) (2005). *Comparing Local Governance. Trends and Developments*. Basingstoke: Palgrave.

Friedmann, J (1995). Where we stand: a decade of world city research. In Knox, PL and PJ Taylor (eds.), *World Cities in a World-system*. Cambridge: Cambridge University Press.

Friedman, T (2005). *The World is Flat. A Brief History of the Twenty-first Century*. New York: Farrar, Straus and Giroux.

Hutton, W (2002). *The World We're In*. London: Little Brown.

Hutton, W and A Giddens (eds.) (2000). *On the Edge. Living with Global Capitalism*. London: Jonathan Cape.

Marcotuillo, P and Y Nishida (2000). Converging global functions/diverging local Responses: a comparison of solid waste management policies in New York and Tokyo. In Ooi, GL (ed.), *Model Cities — Urban Best Practices*. Singapore: Urban Redevelopment Authority and Institute of Policy Studies, pp. 246–257.

Neuwirth, R (2005). *Shadow Cities. A Billion Squatters, A New Urban World*. London: Routledge.

Ooi, GL and KH Phua (2007). Urbanisation and slum formation. *Journal of Urban Health,* 84 Supplement, May, 27–34.

Ooi, GL (2007). Globalisation and Asian mega-cities. *Georgetown Journal of International Affairs*, 8(2), 39–45.

Sassen, S (2001). *The Global City: New York, London, Tokyo*. Princeton, NJ: Princeton University Press.

Sassen, S (ed.) (2002). *Global Networks. Linked Cities*. New York: Routledge.

Savitch, HV and P Kantor (2002). *Cities in the International Marketplace: the Political Economy of Urban Development in North America and Western Europe.* Princeton, NJ: Princeton University Press.

Shin, K-H and M Timberlake (2000). World cities in Asia: cliques, centrality and connectedness. *Urban Studies*, 37, 2257–2285.

Smith, DA and M Timberlake (2002). Hierarchies of dominance among world cities: a network approach. In Sassen, S (ed.), *Global Networks, Linked Cities.* New York: Routledge, pp. 117–141.

Smith, MP (2001). *Transnational Urbanism: Locating Globalisation.* Malden, Mass.: Blackwell.

Smith, M, J Davidson, L Cameron and L Bondi (2009). *Emotion, Place and Culture.* Farnham, Surrey, England: Ashgate.

Taylor, PJ (2004). *World City Network: A Global Urban Analysis.* London; New York, NY: Routledge.

About the Contributors

Loke Ming CHOU is Professor at the Department of Biological Sciences, National University of Singapore.

Sir **Peter HALL** is Professor of Planning and Regeneration at the Bartlett School of Architecture and Planning, University College London. He is also the Senior Research Fellow at the Young Foundation, United Kingdom.

Chye Kiang HENG is the Dean of the School of Design and Environment at the National University of Singapore. He is also a member of the Centre for Liveable Cities Advisory Board and the Urban Redevelopment Authority Board in Singapore.

Michael LINDFIELD is the Principal Urban Development Specialist in the Regional and Sustainable Development Department of the Asian Development Bank (ADB) and Programme Manager of the Cities Development Initiative for Asia (CDIA) on behalf of ADB.

Thai Ker LIU is the Chairman of the Centre for Liveable Cities Advisory Board and the Director of RSP Architects, Planners and Engineers Pte Ltd in Singapore. He was the former Chief Architect and Chief Executive Officer of the Housing Development Board, and Chief Planner and Chief Executive Officer of the Urban Redevelopment Authority, Singapore.

Qiyan ONG is completing her PhD Degree in Economics at the Nanyang Technological University of Singapore.

Giok Ling OOI is Professor at the Humanities and Social Studies Education Department, Singapore National Institute of Education, Nanyang Technological University of Singapore. She is also the Adjunct Professorial Fellow at the Institute of Policy Studies, Singapore.

Sock-Yong PHANG is Professor of Economics at the School of Economics, Singapore Management University. She is also a member of the Advisory Board for the Centre for Liveable Cities, Singapore.

Euston QUAH is the Acting Chair of the School of Humanities and Social Sciences and Head of Economics Division at the Nanyang Technological University of Singapore. He is also Adjunct Senior Research Fellow at the Institute of Policy Studies, Singapore.

Victor R SAVAGE is Associate Professor at the Department of Geography, National University of Singapore.

Ursula SCHAEFER-PREUSS is Vice-President of the Asian Development Bank (ADB) for Knowledge Management and Sustainable Development.

Anne SCHEINBERG, MPA, MSc. is Senior Adviser, and Solid Waste Division Coordinator, at WASTE, Advisers on Urban Environment and Development, Gouda, the Netherlands.

Andrew TAN is the Director of the Centre for Liveable Cities, jointly established by the Ministry of National Development and the Ministry of Environment and Water Resources, Singapore. He is concurrently the Chief Executive Officer of the Singapore National Environment Agency.

Vukan R VUCHIC is the UPS Foundation Professor of Transportation in the Department of Electrical and Systems Engineering and the Professor of City and Regional Planning at the University of Pennsylvania in Philadelphia.

Emiel A WEGELIN is the Cities Development Initiative for Asia (CDIA) Program Coordinator on behalf of GTZ, an international cooperation enterprise for sustainable development with worldwide operations.

Belinda YUEN is Associate Professor at the Department of Real Estate, School of Design and Environment, National University of Singapore.

Ji ZHANG is a Research Assistant at the Department of Architecture, School of Design and Environment at the National University of Singapore.

About Civil Service College

Civil Service College (CSC) Singapore is a statutory board under the Public Service Division, Prime Minister's Office. Its mission is to develop people for a first class public service.

CSC brings together public service officers from diverse backgrounds and provides them opportunities to plug into a service-wide network to exchange views, build shared ethos and perspectives, creating a rich environment for dialogue, knowledge sharing and learning.

CSC programmes and services are practitioner-focused. With access to public sector thought leadership and line management, much of the training is facilitated by highly experienced practitioners who speak with authority and offer first-hand knowledge and experience.

Through its programmes and services, CSC aims to build commitment and strategic capacity in governance, leadership, public administration and management for a networked government for the Singapore Public Service.

About Institute of Policy Studies

The Institute of Policy Studies (IPS) was established in 1988 as a think-tank dedicated to fostering good governance in Singapore through strategic policy research and discussion. An autonomous research centre in the Lee Kuan Yew School of Public Policy at the National University of Singapore, IPS focuses on domestic developments in Singapore and on external relations. It employs a multi-disciplinary approach in its analysis with an emphasis on long-term strategic thinking.

Index